MW00646979

History of
ASIAN
AMERICANS

History of
ASIAN
AMERICANS

Exploring Diverse Roots

Jonathan H. X. Lee

 GREENWOOD

AN IMPRINT OF ABC-CLIO, LLC
Santa Barbara, California • Denver, Colorado • Oxford, England

Library of Congress Cataloging-in-Publication Data

Lee, Jonathan H. X.
  History of Asian Americans : exploring diverse roots / Jonathan H. X. Lee.
    pages cm
  Includes bibliographical references and index.
    ISBN 978–0–313–38458–5 (cloth : alk. paper) — ISBN 978–0–313–38459–2
(ebook) 1. Asian Americans—History. I. Title.
  E184.A75L445   2015
  973′.0495—dc23   2014032354

ISBN: 978–0–313–38458–5
EISBN: 978–0–313–38459–2

19 18 17 16 15   1 2 3 4 5

This book is also available on the World Wide Web as an eBook.
Visit www.abc-clio.com for details.

Greenwood
An Imprint of ABC-CLIO, LLC

ABC-CLIO, LLC
130 Cremona Drive, P.O. Box 1911
Santa Barbara, California 93116-1911

This book is printed on acid-free paper ∞

Manufactured in the United States of America

For my son, Owen Edward Jinfa Quady-Lee

Contents

Preface

History of Asian Americans: Exploring Diverse Roots documents the historical experiences of Asian Americans since the early 1850s. It provides detail coverage of pre-1965 Chinese, Japan, Korean, South Asian, and Filipino American historical experiences, as well as post-1965 waves of Asian migration to the United States that include the post-1975 Vietnam War experiences of refugees and immigrants from Cambodia, Laos, and Vietnam. Moreover, it begins the work of documenting newer Asian Americans who arrived since the 1990s, such as Burmese, Indonesian, Thai, Mongolian, Tibetan, Nepali, and Pakistani Americans. It also uses 2010 U.S. Census data to illustrate the demographic and geographic diversity of the Asian American contributions to America's diverse mosaic.

It is important that I acknowledge Kim Kennedy-White, who invited and encouraged me to take on *History of Asian Americans: Exploring Diverse Roots*. I wish to also thank my students at San Francisco State University who informed much of the structure, coverage, and content of this volume. Funding from the College of Ethnic Studies at San Francisco State University, made it possible for me to work on and complete this volume. Thank you, John McClure of the Virginia Historical Society, for assisting me in fact-checking; thank you, Laurie Reemsnyder, photographer, for generously giving permission to publish photos that document Cambodian, Laotian, and Vietnamese refugees' resettlement; and thank you to my research assistant, Sidney C. Li, for assisting me in data collection and archival and library research. I also wish to acknowledge support from Mark S. Quady, Yaccaira de la Torre, Dominic Cabrera, Joel Cabrera, Earlita Chenault, and Johnetta G. Richards. Additionally, I wish to acknowledge my colleagues whose advice, conversations, and expertise assisted me in many ways. However, any error is solely my responsibility.

Introduction

The majority of scholarship on the history of Asians in the United States, or Asian American history, documents the experiences of older and larger Asian American communities, in particular the historical experiences of Chinese, Japanese, Korean, South Asian (from present-day India), Filipinos, and post–Vietnam War refugees from Cambodia, Laos, and Vietnam. The content and coverage is imbalanced in favor of the pre–Vietnam War Asians in America. In *History of Asian Americans: Exploring Diverse Roots*, I have endeavored to provide some correction to the imbalance in presentation and coverage; however, much more work remains. The structure and coverage is informed by limitation in length of the book, as well as by the target audience, namely undergraduate students. I have taught the History of Asians in the United States course at San Francisco State University since 2009 and have oscillated between assigning Ronald Takaki's *Strangers from a Different Shore* (1989) and Sucheng Chan's *Asian Americans: An Interpretive History* (1991). Chronologically, *History of Asian Americans: Exploring Diverse Roots* extends coverage beyond post-1975 Vietnam War refugee resettlements and is inclusive of more ethnic-racial communities.

The narrative of this book continues the earlier works in documenting and sharing the stories of Asian immigrants-cum-Americans who struggle for the right to be legally, socially, culturally, and economically *fully American*. It is informed by Michael Omi and Howard Winant's *longue durée* approach to the study of race, race politics, and racial formation in the United States (2015). A cursory glance at American history reveals that far from being colorblind, the United States has been an extremely "color-conscious" society. Color-conscious race politics informed public policies, flamed and fueled by social forces and ideological structures of white and

Christian supremacies that limited Asian Americans and their right to be *fully American*. Asian American citizenship and race, their being and belonging, is contested throughout American history and society in both collective actions and personal practices. In Chapters 1 through 5, one narrative that is highlighted is the manner in which white supremacy, as an ideology and practice, is able to produce a racial hierarchy that restricts Asians in America and Asian Americans from being *fully American*. It reflects Adrian Cruz's definition of white supremacy as "a social force that distributes resources—political, economic, and social—in such a way that the lived experiences and material outcomes are differentiated for each group" (2010, 30).

The goal of *History of Asian Americans: Exploring Diverse Roots* is to provide readers with a balanced narrative of the Asian American experience that puts Asian Americans squarely in historical discourse that is influenced by transnational and global historical forces, and not as sidenotes in American history. It presents narratives of how immigrants come to the United States to make new homes, transplant roots, create new ways of life and communities, and contribute to an ever-shifting American landscape. This book focuses on people, and the political, social, economic, and cultural variables that shape and inform their lives. It is grounded on the idea of *one* America, with many different varieties of Americans whose length of time in the United States and degrees of acculturation varies. Furthermore, *History of Asian Americans: Exploring Diverse Roots* continues the work of Asian American studies, which was born on March 20, 1969, when a settlement was signed at San Francisco State College (now University) to establish the country's first and still only School of Ethnic Studies (now the College of Ethnic Studies). This was one of the results of the Third World Liberation Front strike that began on November 6, 1968. This legacy informs Asian American studies' raison d'être—its pedagogy and research—inside and outside of the classroom. Asian American studies is founded on the dual principles of self-determination and social justice. Asian American self-determination is expressed—individually and collectively—from the demand of Asian American subjectivity: knowing Asian Americans through history, art, literature, social sciences, and education, but also as subjects of research.

History of Asian Americans: Exploring Diverse Roots is chronologically divided into the pre- and post-1965 Asian immigration waves. Chapters 1 through 5 individually examine Chinese, Japanese, Korean, South Asian, and Filipino American experiences, respectively. The foci of these chapters are factors of migration, resettlement, exclusion, and encounters with white supremacist constructions of "Asian" as a "racial category" that spans the early nineteenth century to the end of World War II. Chapters 6 and 7 cover post–Vietnam War migrations of Cambodian, Laotian, and Vietnamese refugees. In these chapters, attention is given to the diversity of refugees as well as to the differences in historical experiences that is anchored in larger social, political, and economic circumstances of the late 1960s–1990s. Chapter 8 begins the work of expanding the Asian American historical experience to include "newer," more "recent" migrants from Asia, who follow earlier groups in their pursuit of the "American Dream" or as refugees who flee their homelands as a necessity for survival. Although not inclusive of the diversity of Asian American ethnic and cultural communities, it enjoins students and others to continue the work of documenting the narratives of Asian Americans who continue to come to the United States and make it their home.

REFERENCES

Chan, Sucheng. *Asian Americans: An Interpretive History*. New York: Twayne, 1991.

Cruz, Adrian. "There Will Be No 'One Big Union': The Struggle for Interracial Labor Unionism in California Agriculture, 1933–1939." *Cultural Dynamics* 22:1 (2010): 29–48.

Omi, Michael, and Howard Winant. *Racial Formation in the United States*. 3rd ed. London: Routledge, 2015.

Takaki, Ronald T. *Strangers from a Different Shore: A History of Asian Americans*. Rev. ed. Boston: Little, Brown, 1989.

Chronology of Key Dates in Asian American History

October 18, 1587	Filipinos arrive at Morro Bay, San Luis Obispo, California, on board the ship *Nuestra Senora de Esperanza* skippered by Spanish captain Pedro de Unamuno. This site is now a Filipino American Landmark at Coleman Park at Morro Bay.
November 6, 1595	More than 70 Filipinos on board the Spanish galleon, the *San Agustin* skippered by Captain Sebastian Rodriguez Cermeno, while headed to Acapulco, were shipwrecked off the shores of Point Reyes, Marin County, some 30 miles from San Francisco.
July 2, 1635	An unconfirmed "East Indian" is listed in Jamestown, Virginia. He is listed as "Tony a Turk" and "Tony East Indian."[1]
1763	Saint Malo, a small fishing village at St. Bernard Parish, Louisiana, on the shore of Lake Borgne, is the first recorded settlement of Filipinos, referred to in English as "Manilamen" or Spanish as "Tagalas" in America. Saint Malo was established by Filipinos who escaped the Spanish galleon ships during the Manila-Acapulco galleon trade. Saint Malo was destroyed by the New Orleans Hurricane of 1915. An illustration of Saint Malo was first published in *Harper's Weekly*, March 31, 1883.
January 18, 1778	Chinese sailors arrive in Hawai'i with English explorer Captain James Cook.

August 9, 1785   The first recorded instance of the Chinese in the
                       continental United States are three Chinese seamen
                       named Ashing, Achun, and Aceun, who were left
                       stranded along with 32 "East Indians" lascars by
                       Captain John O'Donnell who left on the *Pallas*
                       after unloading his cargo at Baltimore.

March 26, 1790   The first U.S. Naturalization Act allows only "free
                       White persons" to become U.S. citizens.

April 1796   Andreas Everardus Van Braam Houckgeest, a
                       Dutchman who was formerly Canton Agent for
                       the Dutch East India Company, comes to the
                       United States from China with cargo of Chinese
                       arts and five Chinese servants. He settled in Phila-
                       delphia, organized the first exhibit on Chinese art
                       in America and authored the first book on China,
                       published in the United States, in 1797–1798.

1818   Wong Arce, Ah Lan, Ah Lum, Chop Ah See, and
                       Lieaou Ah-See are the first Chinese students to receive
                       an education in the United States, when they enrolled
                       at the Foreign Mission School in Cornwall, Connecti-
                       cut. The school was established in 1817 with the
                       expressed goal to teach "heathen" youths from
                       around the world to become Christian missionaries
                       in their own cultures. Lieaou Ah-See would become
                       the first Chinese Protestant convert in America.

1829   The Siamese twins Chang and Eng are the first Thais
                       to arrive in the United States. For four decades, they
                       toured the United States and the world. They were
                       born in 1811 of Chinese parents. Before going to
                       the United States, the twins were successful entrepre-
                       neurs in Siam (now Thailand). Captain Abel Coffin
                       contracted to manage the twins' touring schedule.
                       They were granted U.S. citizenship in 1839.

1830   The first U.S. Census records three Chinese in
                       America.

1840   The second U.S. Census records eight Chinese in
                       America. By 1850, the U.S. Census records 758
                       Chinese in America.

June 1841   While commanding a whaling ship, the *John
                       Howland*, in the Pacific, Captain William Whitfield

rescues five shipwrecked Japanese sailors. On November 1841, four of the rescued Japanese sailors disembark at the port of Oahu. Manjiro Nakahama stays on board and goes with Whitfield to Fairhaven, Massachusetts. On May 6, 1843, the *John Howland* sails into New Bedford harbor. Manjiro Nakahama would attend school in New England and adopt the Western name John Manjiro. Later on, John Manjiro would serve as an interpreter for Commodore Matthew Perry, and he would indirectly influence the treaty negotiations between Japan and Commodore Perry, which ended 250 years of Japanese isolation from the world.

August 29, 1842   China is defeated by the British Empire in the first Opium War, resulting in the Treaty of Nanjing, the first "unequal treaty," whereby China is forced to cede the island of Hong Kong and open five ports to foreign commerce.

May 7, 1843   The first Japanese arrive in the United States.

July 3, 1844   Following Britain's lead, the United States imposes the Treaty of Wangxia (Wang-hsia) on China, which gave the United States most-favored-nation treatment in trade and extraterritoriality (exemption from Chinese laws) for American nationals in China, and the right to be tried by the U.S. consular court.

1846–1850   Southern China is hit with social and political chaos due to a combination of natural disasters that resulted in crop failures, which led to famine and poverty that caused an increase in banditry and peasant uprisings.

January 1848   James W. Marshall discovers gold at Sutter's Mill in Coloma. At the beginning of 1849, there were only 54 "Chinamen" in California. They arrived wanting to be miners, but many would become a source of cheap labor for railroads, mines, fisheries, farms, orchards, canneries, garment and cigar factories, and so on along the Pacific Coast. By 1876, there were 151,000 in the United States, and 116,000 in California.

1850
The Taiping Rebellion (1850–1864), a large-scale revolt under the leadership of Hong Xiuquan, begins. In 1847, Hong failed the imperial civil service examination for the third time and reportedly became delirious for 30 days. When he recovered, he believed that he had been selected by heaven to conquer China, destroy the Manchu rulers, and establish the Heavenly Kingdom of Great Harmony, or Taiping Tianguo.

April 13, 1850
The California State legislature passes a law that imposes a $20 per month tax on foreign miners. The tax was enforced mainly against Chinese miners, who were often forced to pay more than once.

February 1851
The American freighter *Auckland* rescues 17 survivors from the sea and transported them to San Francisco. Joseph Heco (1837–1897) is one of them.

1852
Hawaiian plantation owners import 195 Chinese contract laborers; over 20,000 Chinese migrants enter California; and a Buddhist-Daoist temple to the Empress of Heaven, Tien Hau, is founded in San Francisco.

November 6, 1853
Missionary William Speer opens a Presbyterian mission for Chinese in San Francisco, which is the oldest Asian American Christian congregation in North America.

March 31, 1854
The Treaty of Kanagawa is signed between the Japanese government and Commodore Matthew Perry, establishing formal relations between Japan and the United States; Perry is representing the United States on his second expedition to open up Japan to the outside world.

Yung Wing graduates from Yale College, becoming the first person of Chinese ancestry to graduate from a U.S. institution of higher education.

October 1, 1854
The California Supreme Court rules in *People v. Hall* that no Chinese person could testify against a white person in court. This ruling would stand until 1873. During this period, California has the highest concentration of Chinese migrants in the United

States. The ruling overturned the conviction and death sentence of George W. Hall, a white man, for killing Ling Sing, a Chinese man. During the first trial, three Chinese witnesses had testified to the murder. Over on Hawai'i, the Chinese founded a funeral society, their first community association on the islands.

1856

The *Chinese New Daily News* is launched in Sacramento, California, becoming the first Chinese-language daily newspaper in the world. It was published by Ze Too Yune (alias Hung Tai. Publ.) It lasted nearly two years, first as a daily, then tri-weekly, then irregularly—sometimes once per week, sometimes once per month.

1858

The California State legislature passes an exclusion law that prohibits Chinese or Mongolians to enter the state except when driven ashore by weather or unavoidable accident. The penalty for violation of this act was a fine of $400 to $600, or imprisonment from six months to a year, or both.

June 1858

Joseph Heco (1837–1897) is the first Japanese national to become a naturalized citizen, and the first to publish a Japanese-language newspaper. Heco was a fisherman from the province of Sanyodo, Japan, who was shipwrecked and brought to California in February 1851 along with 16 other survivors.

1859

San Francisco opens a Chinese School, America's first public school for Asian immigrants. As a result, Chinese students are excluded from San Francisco public schools.

1862

Six Chinese district associations in San Francisco form a loose federation, which would become the Chinese Consolidated Benevolent Association (CCBA).

January 10, 1862

In his inaugural address as the eighth governor of California, Leland Stanford promises to protect the state from "the dregs of Asia."

April 26, 1862

The California State legislature passes an "anti-coolie tax" or "police tax" of $2.50 a month on

	every Chinese and Mongolian. The goals of the act are to protect white labor from Chinese labor, and to discourage the immigration of Chinese labor into the state.
1863	The first Chinese railroad workers are hired by the Central Pacific Railroad Company to build the western section of the Transcontinental Railroad. They are paid around $28 per month to do the hazardous work of blasting and laying ties over the treacherous terrain of the high Sierras.
1865	Presbyterian missionary Augustus Ward Loomis and his wife Mary Ann arrive to serve the Chinese in San Francisco from 1865 to 1867.
June 1867	Roughly 2,000 Chinese railroad workers go on strike for a week, demanding more pay and work hours similar to their white counterparts.
1868	Chinese Christian evangelist Samuel P. Aheong (aka Siu Pheoung, S. P. Ahiona; 1835–1871) starts preaching in Hawai'i and becomes one of the most influential Christian missionaries on the island, encouraging the local Christian community to embrace newly arriving Chinese immigrants.
June 19, 1868	Japan-based American businessman Eugene M. Van Reed illegally ships 150 Japanese laborers to Hawai'i and another 40 laborers to Guam to work on sugar plantations. This unlawful recruitment of Japanese laborers, known as the *gannen-mono*, meaning "first year people," marked the beginning of the global Japanese labor migration overseas. However, for the next two decades, Japan's Meiji government bans Japanese labor migration due to the "slave-like" treatment that the first Japanese migrants encountered in Hawai'i and Guam.
July 28, 1868	The United States and China sign the Burlingame-Seward Treaty to facilitate trading and emigration between the two countries. It also guarantees a suitable supply of Chinese labor for the railroad. Although the treaty establishes friendly relations between the United States and China that encouraged Chinese labor migration to the United States, naturalization was prohibited.

May 10, 1869	The first transcontinental railroad is completed after Chinese laborers dug over a dozen tunnels through solid granite in the Sierras during cold winter and hot summer months, under hazardous working conditions. Ninety percent of the laborers who built the Central Pacific section from California to Utah are Chinese.
June 8, 1869	A group of 22 samurai and their families arrive in the Gold Hill region, 1,200 feet above the Sacramento Valley. There, with the help of a benefactor, John Henry Schnell, the Japanese purchase the land from Graner and established the Wakamatsu Tea and Silk Farm Colony.
1870	California passes a law against the importation of Chinese, Japanese, and "Mongolian" women for the purposes of prostitution. Over in Texas, Chinese railroad workers sue the railroad company for not paying them.
July 14, 1870	The Naturalization Act of 1870 is signed into law by President Ulysses S. Grant. The act limits immigration and naturalization to "aliens of African nativity and to persons of African descent" and "whites," thus excluding all Chinese from receiving citizenship. The act also bans the entry of laborers' wives. Economically, a nationwide recession fuels anti-Chinese sentiments on the West Coast as white labor scapegoat "Cheap Chinese labor" as their problem. Mobs of white labor attack and destroy Chinese communities in many areas of California and other states.
July 24, 1870	The first Filipino social club, called Sociedad de Beneficencia de los Hispano Filipinos, is founded by Spanish-speaking residents of St. Malo. The club provides relief and support for members, including purchasing burial places for their deceased.
October 24, 1871	Chinese residents at Los Angeles's Chinatown are attacked, robbed, and killed by a mob of white men, over 500 strong. The riots happened on Calle de los Negros (now part of Los Angeles Street).

	A total of 17 Chinese men and boys, including a popular doctor, are hanged.
1872	California's Civil Procedure Code drops the law barring Chinese court testimony.
May 1873	The San Francisco Board of Supervisors passes the "Queue" and "Laundry" ordinances. The Queue ordinance requires that all Chinese prisoners in jail would have his hair cut or clipped to a uniform length of an inch from the scalp. The Laundry ordinance stipulates that those laundries employing one vehicle with a horse pay a license of one dollar per quarter, those who employ two vehicles pay four dollars per quarter and those who employ more than two, 15 dollars per quarter; whose who employ no vehicle, 15 dollars per quarter.
February 22, 1874	The *Empress of China* (aka *Chinese Queen*) leaves New York with cargo of ginseng. On May 11, 1875, it returns to New York. The success of this voyage encouraged others to invest in additional trade with China.
1875	The Union Pacific sends 125 Chinese workers to mine in Rock Springs, Wyoming.
January 30, 1875	The United States and Hawai'i sign a reciprocity treaty. The treaty is a free-trade agreement between the United States and the kingdom of Hawai'i starting in September 1876. In return, the United States gains land in the area known as Pu'u Loa, that would later house the Pearl Harbor naval base. The treaty encourages increase investment by Americans in Hawai'i's sugar plantations. The treaty is ratified by the kingdom of Hawai'i on April 17, 1875, and by the United States on May 31, 1875. The treaty foreshadows the annexation of Hawai'i.
March 3, 1875	The Page Law is enacted, barring Asian women suspected of prostitution and attempting to regulate contract labor from China. It also bars entry of Chinese, Japanese, and "Mongolian" felons, and contract laborers.
March 24, 1877	Five Chinese workers are massacred in a wood chopper's camp two miles from Chico, California.

October 1877	Denis Kearney organizes anti-Chinese meetings in San Francisco and establishes the Workingmen's Party of California, charging Chinese workers with being willing to work for lower wages, poorer conditions, and longer hours, which displaces white workers. The slogan "The Chinese Must Go" is widely repeated and popular.
October 6, 1877	Several Japanese Christian students residing in San Francisco assemble and organize the Fukuinkai, or Gospel Society for Bible Study, which also encourages mutual support for one another. This is the first immigrant association formed by the Japanese.
April 29, 1878	The California Circuit Court ruling *In Re: Ah Yup* declares that Chinese were not white and therefore ineligible to apply for naturalization.
March 6, 1879	California's second constitution prevents municipalities, corporations, county governments, and the state government from employing Chinese.
1880	Section 69 of California's Civil Code prohibits issuing of licenses for marriages between whites and "Mongolians, Negroes, mulattoes and persons of mixed blood."
October 31, 1880	The Hop Alley Chinese Riot erupts in Denver, Colorado. Anti-Chinese hysteria fueled a fight that turned into a riot after two Chinese men and three or four white drunks at John Asmussen's saloon at 16th Street and Wazee got into a fight. Most of Chinatown was destroyed. During the rioting, a Chinese man named Sing Lee was beaten and kicked to death, but those indicted for his murder were later acquitted. The rioting continued from noon until midnight before the violence was finally suppressed when the militia was called out.
November 17, 1880	The United States and China sign a treaty giving the United States the right to limit but "not absolutely prohibit" Chinese immigration.
1881	King Kalakaua of Hawai'i takes a trip around the world. He meets with rulers, perhaps wanting to find more laborers for Hawai'i's plantations. He also wants to learn the ways of other rulers to

better protect his own people. He first travels to San Francisco, then Japan, China, Siam (now Thailand), Burma, India, Egypt, Italy, Belgium, Germany, Austria, France, Spain, Portugal, and England.

1882

The Chinese Consolidated Benevolent Association in San Francisco (CCBA-SF) is established. One of its objectives is to provide leadership in the Chinese community to fight against anti-Chinese legislation.

May 6, 1882

President Chester A. Arthur signs the Chinese Exclusion Act, banning immigration of laborers and their wives from China for 10 years, and banning Chinese immigrants from becoming naturalized citizens. As a result, there is an increase in Japanese immigration to replace Chinese laborers.

May 22, 1882

The United States and Korea sign the Treaty of Peace, Amity, Commerce and Navigation, establishing diplomatic relations between the two countries.

1883

Chinese in New York establish the Chinese Consolidated Benevolent Association.

1884

Yu Kil-chun (Yu Gil Jun) becomes the first Korean to study in the United States when he enrolls at the Governor Dummer Academy in Massachusetts.

1884

Joseph and Mary Tape successfully sue the San Francisco school board to enroll their Chinese daughter Mamie in a public school. On January 9, 1885, Superior Court justice McGuire announces the decision in favor of the Tapes. On appeal, the California Supreme Court would uphold the lower court decision on March 3, 1885. Shortly after the decision, the San Francisco school board lobbies for a separate school system for Chinese and other "Mongolian" children. A bill passed through the California state legislature gives the school board the authority to create an Oriental Public School in San Francisco.

1885

San Francisco builds a new segregated "Oriental School" in response to the Mamie Tape case.

September 1885

Led by the Knights of Labor, local government officials order the expulsion of Chinese from the Puget

	Sound region of Washington Territory. The episode lasts until March 1886, resulting in several Chinese deaths and injuries, and hundreds are driven out by violence or threat of violence.
September 2, 1885	Rock Springs Wyoming, experiences one of the worst instances of anti-Chinese violence. White miners attack Chinese miners in Rock Springs on September 2; 28 Chinese miners are murdered, 15 are wounded, 75 Chinese homes are burned, and hundreds are chased out of town.
October 1885	White protesters in Tacoma announce that all Chinese residing in the city must leave by November. In early November, a mob of white residents, led by Tacoma mayor Jacob Robert Weisbach and backed by the Tacoma police, enter Chinatown and demand that the Chinese residents leave the city immediately. The mob marched the Chinese to a railroad station and forced them to board a train headed toward Portland, Oregon. This would become known as "The Tacoma Method" and an example of how to remove the Chinese from cities and towns throughout the United States.
January 28, 1886	American Robert Walker Irwin reaches an agreement with the Japanese government to allow its subjects to go abroad. This is known as the Irwin Convention, which would remain in force until 1894. While in effect, a total of 28,691 (23,071 men, 5,487 women, 133 children) government-sponsored Japanese laborers went to work on sugar plantations on three-year contracts. After 10 years, the emigration business is turned over to private companies.
May 10, 1886	Chinese laundrymen win in the *Yick Wo v. Hopkins* case, which declares that a law with unequal impact on different groups is discriminatory. In *Yick Wo v. Hopkins*, the U.S. Supreme Court, in a unanimous opinion, invokes the equal protection clause of the Fourteenth Amendment to protect Chinese laundry owners against an ordinance that on its face is race-neutral, but applied in a prejudicial manner.

May 27, 1887	A gang of white horse thieves appear on a steep hillside in Hells Canyon in Oregon. They open fire with high-powered rifles, killing 10 unsuspecting Chinese miners. Then they rob the camp and brutally mutilate the miners' bodies and threw them into the river. Their killing spree continued the next day as eight additional Chinese miners who happened along the river were killed: then another 13 at a second Chinese camp. In total, 31 Chinese miners were slain over the course of two days. This is known as the Snake River Massacre.
October 1, 1888	The Scott Act is passed by the U.S. Congress and signed into law by President Grover Cleveland, prohibiting the return of Chinese laborers who temporarily returned to China. It was introduced by Representative William Lawrence Scott of Pennsylvania. At the time of its effective date, 20,000 Chinese laborers possessed reentry certificates; 600 of them were in transit back to the United States, and none were allowed reentry.
March 2, 1889	Jodo-Shinshu priest Soryu Kagai arrives in Honolulu, surveys the situation, and later establishes Buddhist groups among the Japanese laborers on the plantations.
May 13, 1889	The U.S. Supreme Court decides, in *Chae Chan Ping v. U.S.*, that despite the Burlingame Treaty of 1868, the United States could freely prevent Chinese from immigrating to America, thus upholding the constitutionality of Chinese exclusion law.
July 4, 1889	The U.S. Congress passes the Newlands Resolution, annexing Hawai'i. President William McKinley signs it on July 7, 1889. Under this act, further immigration of Chinese into the Hawaiian Islands is prohibited.
October 29, 1889	Katsu Goto is lynched in Hawai'i. A prominent merchant and interpreter, Goto was murdered for his advocacy work on behalf of Japanese plantation workers.
February 1890	Tsunetaro Jo and Tadoyoshi Sekine's shoemaking business is forced to close by the Boot and

Shoemakers' White Labor League. In response, 20 Japanese American shoemakers in San Francisco formed the Nihonjin Kutsuko Domeikai, the Japanese Shoemakers' League, the first Japanese trade association in the United States. They shift to shoe repair to avoid competing with white shoemakers.

January 1, 1892	Ellis Island is opened. It would become the gateway to America for European immigrants.
May 5, 1892	The Geary Act renews exclusion of Chinese laborers for another 10 years. Under this act, all Chinese in the United States are required to carry their registration certificates with them at all times. Any Chinese without a certificate would be subject to immediate deportation.
January 17, 1893	Queen Lili'uokalani, the last native ruler of an independent Hawai'i, is deposed in a bloodless coup d'état by five American nationals, one English national, and one German national. All were living and doing business in Hawai'i and opposed her efforts to establish a new Constitution. President Grover Cleveland refuses to annex Hawai'i because he felt the Americans in the sugar industry engineered the overthrow, and that the Hawaiian people did not want revolution.
May 15, 1893	*Fong Yue Ting v. U.S.* upholds the constitutionality of the Geary Act. In this ruling, the U.S. Supreme Court declares that Congress had the right to legislate expulsion through executive orders. Congress would amend the Geary Act to make it more difficult for Chinese businessmen to enter the country.
June 27, 1894	Shebata Saito, a Japanese man, applies for U.S. citizenship, but the U.S. circuit courts decided that he not be granted citizenship because he is neither "white" nor "black." This case predates the Takao Ozawa case (1922) by nearly three decades.
July 26, 1894	Japanese immigrant Namyo Bessho, a U.S. Navy veteran of the Spanish-American War and World War I, files for naturalized U.S. citizenship under the act of July 26, 1894, which granted citizenship to "any alien" over 21 years of age who served five consecutive years in the U.S. Navy or Marine

	Corps. Bessho finally becomes a U.S. citizen through a measure signed by President Franklin Roosevelt on June 24, 1935, granting Asian veterans citizenship rights.
November 24, 1894	Sun Yat-sen founds his first revolutionary organization, the Xingzhonghui in Honolulu, to "promote the interest and uphold the dignity of China."
1895	The Planters' Labor and Supply Company is reorganized under the name Hawaiian Sugar Planters' Association (HSPA). Its goal is the "advancement, improvement and protection of the sugar industry of Hawai'i, the support of an Experiment Station, the maintenance of a sufficient supply of labor for the sugar plantations of Hawai'i and the development of agriculture in general."
May 27, 1895	In *Lem Moon Sing v. U.S.* the U.S. Supreme Court rules that district courts can no longer review Chinese *habeas corpus* petitions for landing in the United States.
1896	Ulysses Shinsei Kaneko, a Japanese businessman and labor contractor in Riverside, California, becomes a naturalized citizen. He was the first Issei to buy land in Riverside in 1897.
May 6, 1896	The U.S. Supreme Court upholds the "separate but equal" concept in its decision on *Plessy v. Ferguson*. The decision legalizes "Jim Crow" laws for nearly 60 years.
March 28, 1898	The U.S. Supreme Court, in *Wong Kim Ark v. U.S.*, rules that Chinese born in the United States cannot be stripped of their citizenship under the Fourteenth Amendment.
May 1, 1898	U.S. Commodore George Dewey captures Manila Bay.
June 12, 1898	Emilio Aguinaldo proclaims Philippine independence.
July 7, 1898	With the support of President William McKinley, a joint resolution in Congress to annex the Hawaiian Islands was passed. As a result, thousands of Asian laborers migrate to the continental United States.
December 10, 1898	Spain cedes the Philippines and Guam to the United States with the Treaty of Paris, which ends the

	Spanish-American War. This is the start of Filipino migration to the United States.
February 4, 1899	The Philippine-American War begins. The war is officially declared over on July 4, 1902.
Summer 1899	A ship sailing from Hong Kong to San Francisco has two cases of bubonic plague on board.
December 31, 1899	The Board of Health begins a controlled burn of a few targeted buildings in Honolulu's Chinatown after the bubonic plague was diagnosed on the island. On December 31, the first building was burned, followed by more buildings during the first week of January 1900. On January 20, 1900, while the wooden buildings between Smith Street and Nuuanu Avenue on Beretania Street were being burned, the fire got out of control and several unintended buildings caught on fire. The fire spread from the steeple of Kaumakapili Church to the nearby structures, and in the end, the majority of the buildings in Honolulu's Chinatown were destroyed and an estimated 4,000–4,500 people were left homeless.
January 8, 1900	Twenty-seven men from Okinawa arrive in Hawai'i aboard the SS *City of China*. They are taken to the Ewa Plantation where they would work.
March 6, 1900	A San Francisco City health officer autopsies a corpse of a Chinese man and finds organisms in the body that resemble the plague. In April 1901, a cleanup operation of Chinatown is undertaken, scouring approximately 1,200 houses and 14,000 rooms.
March 16, 1900	President William McKinley appoints William Howard Taft to head the second Philippine Commission.
April 30, 1900	The Hawaiian Organic Act makes all U.S. laws applicable to Hawai'i, thus ending contract labor in the islands. Under this act, the Chinese in Hawai'i are required to apply for certificates of residence, and they are prohibited from entering any other U.S. territory or the mainland.

May 7, 1900   The first large-scale anti-Japanese protest takes
                     place in San Francisco. It was organized by various
                     labor groups.

May 19, 1900   San Francisco orders the quarantine and compul-
                     sory inoculation of all Japanese and Chinese upon
                     discovery of the bubonic plaque victim in
                     Chinatown.

June 14, 1900   The Hawaiian Islands officially becomes a U.S.
                     territory, and all islanders become American citi-
                     zens. President William McKinley appoints San-
                     ford B. Dole the first governor.

August 2, 1900   In response to the growing anti-Japanese senti-
                     ment, the Japanese Foreign Ministry stops issuing
                     passports to laborers headed for the United States
                     and Canada.

January 9, 1901   Peter Ryu, the first recorded Korean immigrant to
                     Hawai'i, arrives on a Japanese ship, the *Kongkong
                     Maru*.

July 4, 1901   William Howard Taft becomes the first civil gover-
                     nor of the Philippines.

1902   The Hawaiian Sugar Planters' Association hires David
                     W. Deshler in Korea to recruit Korean laborers.

1902   Congress extends the Chinese Exclusion Act, but
                     without a termination date.

July 2, 1902   The U.S. Senate passes the Philippine Organic Act,
                     which sets up terms for the civil government estab-
                     lished in 1901 under the governorship of William
                     Howard Taft. The act allows for "self-govern-
                     ment" while maintaining U.S. control.

July 4, 1902   President Theodore Roosevelt declares an end to
                     the Philippine-American War.

December 22, 1902   The first group of Korean laborers leave Korea for
                     Hawai'i aboard the SS *Gaelic*.

January 13, 1903   One hundred twenty Korean men, women, and chil-
                     dren arrive at Honolulu Harbor on the SS *Gaelic*.

February 11, 1903   Five hundred Japanese and 200 Mexican laborers
                     become the charter members of the Japanese Mexi-
                     can Labor Association in Oxnard, California.
                     Kozaburo Baba serves as president. This is the first

	farmworkers' union in California, but the American Federation of Labor refuses to recognize a non-white union.
April 4, 1903	Thirty-five Okinawans arrive in Honolulu aboard the SS *Hong Kong Maru*.
August 26, 1903	Congress passes the Pensionado Act to train Filipino students in the U.S. institution of higher education.
October 11, 1903	Federal immigration officials and the police raid Boston's Chinatown without search warrants and arrest 234 Chinese, including American-born citizens who allegedly had no registration certificates on their persons. Only 50 are found to be in the country without proper documentation.
November 3, 1903	One hundred Filipino pensionados arrive in California. By 1912, 209 Filipino men and women would be educated through the Pensionado program.
1904	The Chinese Exclusion Extension Act makes Chinese exclusion permanent.
November 4, 1904	Syngman Rhee, leader of the Independence Club in Korea, moves to the United States.
November 18, 1904	The Hawaiian Sugar Planters' Association's trustees adopt a resolution stating that all skilled positions on the plantations would be filled by "American citizens, or those eligible for citizenship."
December 1904	Two thousand plantation laborers go on strike at Waialua.
1905	Section 60 of California's Civil Code is amended to make marriage between "whites" and "Mongolians" "illegal and void."
February 23, 1905	The *San Francisco Chronicle* front-page headline reads, "The Japanese Invasion: The Problem of the Hour."
May 7, 1905	A Japanese and Korean Exclusion League is established.
May 10, 1905	China begins a nationwide boycott against U.S. products to protest anti-Chinese discrimination in the United States.
May 14, 1905	The Asiatic Exclusion League is established in San Francisco by 67 labor unions. Eventually, over

	200 labor unions would join the league to restrict Asian immigration to the United States.
November 17, 1905	With the Japan-Korea Treaty, Japan declares Korea its virtual protectorate.
1906	The Hawaiian Sugar Planters' Association (HSPA) begins recruiting workers from the Philippines after their access to Chinese, Japanese, and Korean labor was limited by immigration legislation. Fifteen laborers are sent to Olaʻa Plantation on the Big Island. In 1909, 554 Filipino laborers arrive in Hawaiʻi, followed by 2,653 in 1910, 1,363 in 1911, 4,319 in 1912, and 3,258 in 1913. By 1930, about 100,000 Filipino workers had migrated to Hawaiʻi.
April 18, 1906	The San Francisco earthquake and fire destroys government documents, which open the way for Chinese immigrants to come as "paper sons" claiming birthrights.
October 11, 1906	The San Francisco Board of Education passes a resolution ordering Japanese and Korean children to be placed in a segregated school with already segregated Chinese.
February 1907	President Theodore Roosevelt's administration persuades the San Francisco Board of Education and mayor to rescind the segregation order.
February 24, 1907	The Gentlemen's Agreement between the United States and Japan is concluded in the form of a Japanese note agreeing to deny passports to laborers who want to migrate to the United States.
March 13, 1907	The San Francisco Board of Education formally withdraws its segregation order.
March 14, 1907	President Theodore Roosevelt signs Executive Order 589 prohibiting Japanese with passports from Hawaiʻi, Mexico, or Canada from reentry to the United States.
September 1907	Shortly after the Bellingham riot, the Japanese and Korean Exclusion League was renamed the Asiatic Exclusion League to include the growing South Asian immigrant community.
September 4, 1907	A mob of 400–500 white working men in Bellingham, Washington, gather to drive a community of

	South Asians out of the city. Many of the South Asians are Sikhs but are mistaken as Hindu. By the end of the day, 125 South Asians are driven out of town, six are hospitalized, and roughly 400 are held in jail for "protective custody."
September 7, 1907	A riot against Asians in the Chinese and Japanese section of Vancouver, British Columbia, erupts.
September 8, 1907	Fighting between South Asian and white workers erupts at West's Mill, Aberdeen, Washington.
October 31, 1907	White gunmen make a nighttime attack on a South Asian bunkhouse. One man, Bhiningwan Singh, dies of gunshot wounds.
November 2, 1907	A "demonstration" intended to scare the "Hindus" drives out South Asians from Everett, Washington.
January 27, 1908	Seventy South Asians are driven out of Live Oak, California, by a white mob.
February 18, 1908	The Gentlemen's Agreement is fully in effect.
March 23, 1908	Chang In-hwan, a Korean patriot, shoots and kills Durham Stevens, who supported Japanese occupation of Korea. The Korean Women's Association is established in San Francisco.
1910	Japanese "picture brides" arrive in the United States. The Gentlemen's Agreement of 1907 stopped the issuance of passports to Japanese laborers wanting to go to America or Hawai'i. However, a loophole in the agreement allowed wives and children of Japanese laborers already residing in the United States to immigrate. As a result of the loophole, many Japanese picture brides are able to migrate to Hawai'i and the United States.
January 21, 1910	The U.S. government opens Angel Island Immigration Station on Angel Island in the San Francisco Bay.
March 21, 1910	A "race riot" between white and South Asian laborers injures two South Asians at St. John, Oregon.
August 22, 1910	Korea is formally annexed by Japan through the Japan-Korea Annexation Treaty.

November 28, 1910	Sara Choe, the first Korean picture bride, arrives in Hawai'i from Korea.
January 1, 1912	The Republic of China (Taiwan) is established, and Sun Yat-sen of the Kuomintang (the KMT or Nationalist Party) is proclaimed provisional president.
February 12, 1912	China's last emperor, Pu Yi, is forced to abdicate his throne.
September 1912	The Sikhs purchased land on South Grant Street and built a *gurdwara*, or temple, in Stockton, California. The Khalsa Diwan Society is established on May 27, 1912.
May 19, 1913	The California State legislature passes the Webb Act, or Alien Land Act. This act prohibits "aliens ineligible to citizenship" from buying land or leasing it for longer than three years.
June 1913	Fifteen Korean fruit pickers are driven out of Hemet, California, by angry unemployed white workers.
November 1, 1913	The Hindu Association is established in San Francisco.
July 28, 1914	World War I begins. It would last until November 11, 1918. In spite of racial discrimination against Asian Americans, many would serve in the war and be awarded naturalization for their military service.
February 5, 1917	The Immigration Act of 1917 restricts immigration of anyone born in a geographically defined "Asiatic Barred Zone" excluding the Japanese and Filipinos. The Gentleman's Agreement already restricted immigration of Japanese laborers, and the Philippines was an American colony so they were considered American nationals and had unrestricted entry. On December 14, 1916, President Woodrow Wilson had vetoed the bill, but Congress overrode his veto. The act prohibits immigration from all of Asia and India by drawing an imaginary line from the Red Sea in the Middle East all the way through the Ural Mountains: people living east of

	the line are not allowed entry to the United States. This act also includes a literacy test requirement.
April 2, 1917	President Woodrow Wilson asks Congress to declare war on Germany. The United States soon formally enters World War I.
July 29, 1918	Syngman Rhee establishes the New Church, a Korean Christian Church in Hawai'i.
November 11, 1918	The armistice treaty formally ends World War I.
December 19, 1918	Judge Horace W. Vaughn of the U.S. District Court for Hawai'i rules that Japanese, Chinese, and Korean veterans of World War I are eligible for naturalization under the act of May 8, 1918. As a result, 398 Japanese, 99 Koreans, and four Chinese are granted citizenship by November 14, 1919. Unfortunately, their citizenship is revoked by the *Toyota v. United States* decision on May 25, 1925.
March 1, 1919	Koreans in Korea protest Japanese occupation with a nationwide nonviolent demonstration.
April 14–16, 1919	One hundred fifty Koreans attended the first Korean Liberty Congress in Philadelphia to advocate Korean independence and make public the plight of Koreans under Japanese occupation.
August 1919	Pablo Manlapit forms the Filipino Labor Union in Hawai'i.
January 19, 1920	Pablo Manlapit, head of the Filipino Labor Union, unilaterally issues an order for Filipinos to strike and urges the Japanese to join them. By February 1, a united strike that included 8,300 Filipino and Japanese strikers, 77 percent of the entire plantation workforce on Oahu, brings the plantation to a stop. The strike lasts six months.
January 19, 1920	The 1913 California Alien Land Law is amended to close a loophole that permits Asian immigrants to own or lease land under the names of their native-born children.
March 1, 1920	The Japanese Foreign Ministry stops issuing passports to picture brides. Only women who are accompanying their husbands to the United States are issued passports.
February 26, 1921	Arizona passes an Alien Land Law.

March 8, 1921	The Washington state legislature passes an Alien Land Law.
April 1921	Texas passes an Alien Land Law.
May 19, 1921	President Warren G. Harding, pressured by the Immigration Restriction League, signs the Johnson Act, also known as the Emergency Quota Act of 1921 or the Immigration Act of 1921, into law. It is the first quota immigration act that limits the annual number of immigrants to 3 percent of the number of foreign-born persons of most nationalities living in the United States in 1910.
July 19, 1921	White vigilantes deport 58 Japanese laborers from Turlock, California, driving them out by truck at gunpoint.
1922	New Mexico passes an Alien Land Law.
September 22, 1922	The U.S. Congress passes the Cable Act, which strips any women of European or African ancestry of their citizenship if they married an "alien ineligible to citizenship." They could regain their citizenship through the naturalization process if they divorced their alien husbands, or if he died. The act is repealed in 1936.
November 13, 1922	The U.S. Supreme Court, in *Takao Ozawa v. U.S.*, upholds the 1790 Naturalization Act and rules that Japanese (and other Asians) are ineligible for naturalized citizenship: naturalization is limited to "free white persons and aliens of African nativity."
1923	Idaho, Montana, and Oregon pass Alien Land Laws.
February 19, 1923	The U.S. Supreme Court, in *U.S. v. Bhagat Singh Thind*, upholds the 1790 Naturalization Act and declares South Asians ineligible for naturalized citizenship.
November 12, 1923	The U.S. Supreme Court, in *Terrace v. Thompson*, upholds the constitutionality of Washington's Alien Land Law.
November 12, 1923	The U.S. Supreme Court, in *Porterfield v. Webb*, upholds the constitutionality of California's Alien Land Law.
November 19, 1923	The U.S. Supreme Court, in *Webb v. O'Brien*, rules that cropping contracts between a citizen with legal

	rights, and a noncitizen with no legal rights are illegal because it is a ploy that allows Japanese to possess and use land in California.
November 19, 1923	The U.S. Supreme Court, in *Frick v. Webb*, forbids aliens "ineligible to citizenship" in California from owning stocks in corporations formed for farming.
May 16, 1924	President Calvin Coolidge signs the Immigration Act of 1924 into law, establishing a national origins quota that limits the number of immigrants by country and excludes all immigrants from Asia, except for Filipinos who were "nationals" due to the Philippines' status as a U.S. protectorate.
November 4, 1924	Nevada passes an Alien Land Law.
1925	Kansas passes an Alien Land Law.
April 18, 1925	The Chinese Hospital, the first in the United States devoted to the health needs of Chinese immigrants and residents, opens its doors in San Francisco.
May 25, 1925	The U.S. Supreme Court, in *Chang Chan et al. v. John D. Nagle*, rules that Chinese wives of American citizens are not entitled to residence and therefore not allowed to enter the United States in accordance with the Immigration Act of 1924.
May 25, 1925	The U.S. Supreme Court, in *Hidemitsu Toyota v. U.S.*, rules that a "person of the Japanese race, born in Japan, may not legally be naturalized."
June 6, 1927	The U.S. Supreme Court, in *Weedin v. Chin Bow*, rules that a person born aboard to an American parent or parents who have never lived in the United States cannot be a citizen of the United States.
November 1927	A group of white workers drive out Filipino farm laborers from Yakima Valley, Washington.
November 21, 1927	The U.S. Supreme Court, in *Gong Lum v. Rice*, rules for separate but equal facilities for Mongolian children in Mississippi.
1928	The Wenatchee Valley Anti-Filipino Riot takes place.
February 20, 1928	The U.S. Court of Appeals, Ninth Circuit, in *Lam Mow v. Nagle, Commissioner of Immigration*,

	rules that children born of Chinese parents on American vessels on high seas were not born in the United States, and are thus not citizens.
May 18, 1928	Congressmen Richard J. Welch and Senator Hiram Johnson of California introduce a House bill designed to exclude Filipinos from the United States.
1929	The Exeter Anti-Filipino Riot takes place.
October 29, 1929	Stock market crash, known as "Black Thursday," triggers the Great Depression.
January 10, 1930	The Northern Monterrey Chamber of Commerce passes an anti-Filipino resolution to discourage hiring Filipino laborers.
January 19 to January 23, 1930	An anti-Filipino riot takes place in Watsonville, California, involving disputes between Filipino American farm workers and local residents opposed to immigration. Fermin Tober was killed; seven suspects were arrested, but none were convicted of any crime.
February 26, 1930	Los Angeles Superior Court judge J. K. Smith rules that Filipinos are of the "Mongolian race," which invalidates more than 100 interracial marriages since 1921.
March 3, 1931	An amendment to the Cable Act declares that no American-born woman who was stripped of her citizenship (by marrying an alien ineligible to citizenship) can be denied the right of naturalization at a later date.
January 27, 1933	The California District Court of Appeals rules in *Roldan v. Los Angeles County* that Filipinos are part of the "Malay" race, not "Mongolian," and therefore upholds the lower court ruling that they can marry whites. However, shortly afterward, the California Assembly amended the Civil Code to include "Malay" among the "races" prohibited from marrying whites.
March 24, 1934	The U.S. Congress passes the Tydings-McDuffie Act (also known as the Philippines Independence Act) that makes the Philippines an independent country in 10 years, in addition to starting to limit

	immigration of Filipinos to the United States to only 50 a year.
August–September 1934	The Filipino Labor Union leads some 6,000–7,000 white and Filipino lettuce pickers in the Salinas Valley, California, on strike for higher wages and union recognition. Thirty armed vigilantes forced 500 Filipinos from their camp at gunpoint, while 300 lettuce pickers packed their belongings to flee Salinas.
July 10, 1935	The Filipino Repatriation Act is signed into law by President Franklin D. Roosevelt, following the passage of the Tydings-McDuffie Act. Since the passage of the Tydings-McDuffie Act, some 45,000 Filipinos were still residing in the United States. This act provided free transportation for Filipinos to return to the Philippines—except for those residing on Hawai'i. Only 2,200 men accept the offer.
July 7, 1937	Japan invades China.
November 6, 1937	Japan and Nazi Germany sign the Anti-Comintern Pact directed at the Soviet Union.
September 22, 1940	Japan is granted rights to station troops in Indochina from the Vichy French government. By 1941, Japan extended its control over the whole of French Indochina
September 27, 1940	Germany, Italy, and Japan sign the Tripartite Pact, which is known as the Axis alliance.
May 19, 1941	The Viet Minh, the League for the Independence of Vietnam, is founded.
December 7, 1941	Japan attacks U.S. military bases at Pearl Harbor, Hawai'i. Over 3,500 U.S. servicemen are wounded or killed.
December 8, 1941	President Franklin D. Roosevelt brings a declaration of war on Japan to Congress, which passes it.
February 19, 1942	President Franklin D. Roosevelt passes Executive Order 9066, authorizing the secretary of war to delegate a military commander to designate military areas "from which any and all persons may be excluded." Executive Order 9066 would be chiefly enforced against Japanese Americans.

March 18, 1942	President Franklin D. Roosevelt passes Executive Order 9102, creating the War Relocation Authority that forcefully relocated Japanese Americans from their homes to internment camps.
March 21, 1942	Congress passes Public Law 503 to punish anyone defying orders to carry out Executive Order 9066.
March 27, 1942	The Second War Powers Act repeals the confidentiality of census data, allowing the FBI to use this information to round up Japanese Americans; and changes naturalization restrictions to allow persons serving the U.S. military during World War II to become naturalized.
March 28, 1942	Attorney Minoru Yasui turns himself in for arrest at the Portland, Oregon, police station to test the discriminatory curfew policies issued by General John L. DeWitt.
April 2, 1942	The state of California fires all Japanese Americans in the state's civil service.
April 20, 1942	One hundred forty-one South American civilians of Japanese ancestry arrive at San Francisco aboard the *Etolin* at the request of the U.S. government who wanted to employ them for future prisoner exchanges. By 1943, a total of 2,100 persons, mostly from Peru, would be transported into U.S. custody.
May 16, 1942	University of Washington student Gordon Hirabayashi turns himself in to the authorities to test the constitutionality of the curfew and detention orders.
May 30, 1942	Fred Korematsu is arrested in Oakland, California for violating orders to report for detention.
October 30, 1942	The U.S. Army completes its transfer of all Japanese American detainees from 15 temporary centers to 10 permanent War Relocation Authority detention camps: Manzanar, Poston, Gila River, Topaz, Granada, Heart Mountain, Minidoka, Tule Lake, Jerome, and Rohwer.
November 18, 1942	Japanese American detainees protest at the Poston War Relocation Center in Arizona.
December 6, 1942	James Ito and James Kanagawa are killed when military police fire into a crowd during a protest

	at the Manzanar War Relocation Center in California.
June 21, 1943	The Supreme Court rules in *Hirabayashi v U.S.*, declaring that the curfew law imposed on persons of Japanese ancestry was constitutional.
June 21, 1943	The Supreme Court rules in *Yasui v U.S.*, declaring that Congress in enacting Public Law 77-503 authorized the implementation of Executive Order 9066 and provided criminal penalties for violation of orders of the military commander as constitutional.
July 15, 1943	The War Relocation Authority designates Tule Lake, California as a segregation center for Japanese American detainees who would not sign the loyalty oath.
December 17, 1943	The Magnuson Act is signed into law, repealing the Chinese Exclusion Act, allowing Chinese to become naturalized citizens, and giving China a quota of 105 immigrants per year.
September 7, 1944	The Western Defense Command issues Public Proclamation No. 24 revoking exclusion orders and military restrictions against Japanese Americans.
December 18, 1944	In *Korematsu v U.S.*, the U.S. Supreme Court rules that, based solely on one's ancestry, one group of citizens may be singled out and relocated from their homes and imprisoned for several years without trial.
December 18, 1944	In *ex parte Endo*, the U.S. Supreme Court rules that the War Relocation Authority has no authority to detain a "concededly loyal" American citizen.
January 2, 1945	The War Department announces that the exclusion orders are withdrawn after the Supreme Court rules in the *Endo* case that "loyal" citizens could not be detained without trial.
May 7, 1945	Nazi Germany surrenders unconditionally to the Allies. Japan fights on alone.
August 6, 1945	The United States drops the atomic bomb on Hiroshima.
August 9, 1945	The United States drops the atomic bomb on Nagasaki.

August 19, 1945	The Viet Minh successfully seizes power in Hanoi, which they would later declare the capital of the Democratic Republic of Vietnam.
August 25, 1945	Emperor Bao Dai is forced to abdicate to Ho Chi Minh and the Viet Minh.
September 2, 1945	Japan formally surrenders to the Allies on board the battleship USS *Missouri*. After the capitulation of Japan to Allied forces, Ho Chi Minh and his People's Congress establish the National Liberation Committee of Vietnam to create a provisional government. Japan transfers all power to Ho Chi Minh and the Viet Minh. Korea is divided at the 38th Parallel: the Soviet Union has a military presence in the North, while U.S. military forces are in the South.
October 15 to December 15, 1945	All War Relocation Authority Internment camps are closed except for Tule Lake Center.
December 28, 1945	Congress enacts the War Brides Act, which would be signed into law by President Harry S. Truman. This act would allow 722 Chinese and 2,042 Japanese women (European women also) who married American servicemen to come to the United States between 1946 and 1953.
February 16, 1946	Ho Chi Minh writes a letter to President Harry S. Truman asking for support of the United States in Vietnam's independence. The United States would not respond to his letter.
March 20, 1946	The Tule Lake "Segregation Center" closes.
June 29, 1946	Congress enacts the Alien Fiancées Act, also known as the G.I. Fiancées Act, granting fiancées of American servicemen during World War II a special exemption from immigration quotas to enter the United States.
June 30, 1946	The War Relocation Authority program officially ends.
July 2, 1946	President Harry S. Truman signs the Luce-Celler Act into law, which grants naturalization rights to Filipinos and South Asians.
July 4, 1946	The Philippines gains independence from the United States. This had been promised by the passage of the Tydings-McDuffie Act of 1934.

December 19, 1946	The First Indochina War starts when Viet Minh forces attack French forces at Hanoi.
December 23, 1947	President Harry S. Truman grants full pardons to 267 Japanese American draft resisters who had violated the Selective Training and Service Act of 1940.
June 5, 1948	With the Halong Bay Agreements, a unified State of Vietnam is created replacing Tonkin (North Vietnam), Annam (Middle Vietnam), and the Republic of Cochinchina (South Vietnam) under the auspices of the French Union. Former emperor Bao Dao is installed by the French as head of state. Shortly after, President Harry S. Truman recognizes the Associated States of Vietnam and agrees to send aid ($15 million of more than $2.6 billion sent over the next five years).
June 25, 1948	President Harry S. Truman signs the Displaced Persons Act into law. This act helped individuals who were deemed to be victims of persecution by the Nazi government or who were fleeing persecution, or who could not return to their country because of fear of persecution based on race, religion or political opinions. This act focused on individuals from Germany, Austria, and Italy, the French sector of either Berlin or Vienna or the American or British Zone and individuals from Czechoslovakia after World War II. This act would also influence subsequent policies on refugees, especially those fleeing Communist countries, including refugees from Hungary, Cuba, China, Vietnam, Laos, and Cambodia.
March 8, 1949	Bao Dai signs the Elysée Agreement, confirming the independence of Vietnam as an Associated State of the French Union. As part of the agreement, the French pledge to assist in the building of a national anti-Communist army.
October 1, 1949	Chinese Communist leader Mao Zedong declared the creation of the People's Republic of China.
January 18, 1950	The People's Republic of China recognizes Ho Chi Minh's government, the Democratic Republic of Vietnam.

January 30, 1950	The Soviet Union recognizes Ho Chi Minh's government, the Democratic Republic of Vietnam.
June 25, 1950	North Korea invades South Korea, initiating the Korean War.
June 27, 1950	President Harry S. Truman deploys the Seventh Fleet to the waters off Taiwan to prevent the spread of the conflict in Korea to neighboring countries.
June 29, 1950	The first U.S. ground troops are deployed in Korea.
August 3, 1950	A U.S. Military Assistance Advisory Group (MAAG) of 35 men arrives in Saigon to evaluate French requests for military assistance, to support in training South Vietnamese troops, and to advise on strategy. By the end of the year, the United States is bearing half the cost of France's war efforts in Vietnam.
April 17, 1952	The California Supreme Court finds California's Alien Land Law of 1913 unconstitutional.
June 27, 1952	The Immigration and Nationality Act of 1952, also known as the McCarran-Walter Act, revises and consolidates all previous laws regarding immigration and naturalization. The act upholds the national origins quota system, which limited the number of immigrants allowed to enter the United States annually by country. It eliminates the Asiatic Barred Zone, allots each Asian country a minimum of 100 visas annually, and creates a preference system that would determine eligibility based on skills and family ties in the United States.
July 27, 1953	The United States, North Korea, and China sign an armistice, which ends the Korean War but fails to bring about a peace. To date, the Republic of Korea (South) and Democratic Peoples' Republic of Korea (North) have not signed a peace treaty.
October 22, 1953	Laos gains independence from French rule.
November 9, 1953	Cambodia gains independence from French rule.
April 7, 1954	Responding to the impending defeat of the French by the Viet Minh, President Dwight D. Eisenhower coins one of the most well-known Cold War phrases when he suggests the fall of French Indochina to the Communists could generate a

	"domino" effect in Southeast Asia. The "domino theory" would dominate U.S. thinking and foreign policy about Vietnam and Southeast Asia for the next decade.
May 7, 1954	Ho Chi Minh's Viet Minh forces defeat the French at Dien Bien Phu. The battle continued for 55 days. Three thousand French troops were killed, 8,000 were wounded. The Viet Minh suffered much worse, with 8,000 dead and 12,000 wounded. This battle shattered France's resolve to carry on the war.
July 20, 1954	The Geneva Conference on Indochina declares a demilitarized zone at the 17th Parallel, with South Vietnam under the leadership of Prime Minister Ngo Dinh Diem, and North Vietnam under Communist rule.
September 1954	An exodus takes place from North Vietnam to South Vietnam of some 850,000 North Vietnamese—mostly Catholics. Conversely, 80,000 residents in South Vietnam move to the North.
October 24, 1954	President Dwight D. Eisenhower pledges support to Prime Minister Ngo Dinh Diem and military forces.
November 6, 1956	California Proposition 13 is approved, repealing California's 1913 Alien Land Law by popular vote.
November 6, 1956	Dalip Singh Saund, from the Imperial Valley of California, is the first Sikh/Punjabi American elected to the U.S. Congress from the 29th California District, which then comprised Riverside and Imperial Counties.
July 8, 1959	Major Dale R. Buis and Master Sergeant Chester M. Ovnand are the first two Americans to die in the Vietnam War when guerillas strike at Bien Hoa.
May 5, 1960	The United States says it will increase the number of military advisers in South Vietnam, from 327 to 685 men.
November 8, 1960	John F. Kennedy barely defeats Richard M. Nixon in the presidential election.
December 20, 1960	The Viet Cong, or National Liberation Front, is formed.

May 12, 1961	During his tour of Asian countries, Vice President Lyndon B. Johnson meets with South Vietnamese president Ngo Dinh Diem in Saigon. Johnson refers to Diem as "the Churchill of Asia" while assuring Diem that he is crucial to U.S. objectives in Vietnam.
1962	The U.S. military begins spraying of chemical defoliants, Agent Orange or Herbicide Orange, on South Vietnam. The goals of the defoliant are: to reduce the Communist forces' cover; to deny the Communist forces' use of crops needed for subsistence; and to clear sensitive areas, such as around military base perimeters. Between 1962 and 1971, 77 million liters of defoliant would be sprayed.
November 6, 1962	Daniel K. Inouye becomes a U.S. senator, and Spark Matsunaga becomes a U.S. congressman, both representing Hawai'i.
June 11, 1963	Sixty-six-year-old Buddhist monk Thich Quang Duc sets himself on fire to protest the South Vietnamese government's intolerance toward religions and other discriminatory policies. Thich Quang Duc's self-immolation was captured in a photograph in *Life* magazine.
November 1, 1963	With implicit approval of the United States, operatives within the South Vietnamese military overthrow Ngo Dinh Diem. He and his brother, Ngo Dinh Nhu, are shot and killed in the aftermath.
November 22, 1963	President John F. Kennedy is assassinated in Dallas, Texas.
August 2, 1964	The USS *Maddox*, a destroyer located some 30 miles off the coast of North Vietnam in the Tonkin Gulf, is allegedly torpedoed by three North Vietnamese gunboats. No casualties and little damage are reported as a result of the attack.
August 4, 1964	The USS *Maddox* is allegedly attacked again by North Vietnamese gunboats.
August 5, 1964	In response to the two attacks on the USS *Maddox*, President Lyndon B. Johnson requests from Congress a resolution against North Vietnam.
August 7, 1964	The Gulf of Tonkin Resolution is debated by Congress and approved. It authorizes President

	Lyndon B. Johnson to "take all necessary measures to repel any armed attack against forces of the United States and to prevent further aggression." The resolution passes unanimously in the House of Representative, and by a margin of 82–2 in the Senate. The resolution allows President Johnson to wage all-out war against North Vietnam without ever securing a formal declaration of war from Congress.
November 3, 1964	Lyndon B. Johnson wins the presidential election in a landslide victory over Republican Barry Goldwater of Arizona.
November 3, 1964	Patsy Takemoto Mink becomes the first Japanese American woman to serve in Congress as a representative from Hawai'i.
February 7, 1965	The Viet Cong attacks the U.S. Air Force base at Pleiku, South Vietnam, killing eight Americans and wounding more than 100.
February 13, 1965	In response to the attack at Pleiku, President Lyndon B. Johnson authorizes Operation Rolling Thunder, a sustained American bombing offensive in North Vietnam.
March 8, 1965	The first American combat troops arrive in Vietnam.
April 7, 1965	The United States offers North Vietnam economic aid in exchange for peace, but the offer is summarily rejected.
September 1965	Hurricane Betsy destroys Manila Village, a Filipino settlement in Barataria Bay, established in the late nineteenth century for catching and drying shrimp.
October 3, 1965	The U.S. Congress passes the Immigration and Nationality Act, which eliminates national origins quotas. Twenty thousand people per country are allowed entry annually. Priority is given to those with skills and/or family residing in the United States.
December 31, 1965	The number of U.S. troops in Vietnam exceeds 200,000.
December 31, 1966	The number of U.S. troops in Vietnam reaches 385,000 men, plus an additional 60,000 sailors stationed offshore. By the end of the year, more than

	6,000 Americans have been killed, and 30,000 have been wounded.
December 31, 1967	U.S. troops in Vietnam are increased to 485,000.
January 30–31, 1968	During the Tet holiday, Lunar New Year, the Viet Cong launch an attack on Hue and more than 100 other South Vietnamese cities and towns. American forces are able to recapture most areas, but the attack delivers a disastrous blow to public support for the war.
March 16, 1968	In the hamlet of My Lai, U.S. Charlie Company kills some 200 Vietnamese civilians. Only one member of the division is found guilty of war crimes. The massacre fuels increasingly anti–Vietnam War public sentiments.
March 31, 1968	President Lyndon B. Johnson declines a bid for reelection.
April 4, 1968	Dr. Martin Luther King Jr. is assassinated at the Lorraine Motel in Memphis, Tennessee.
November 1, 1968	After three and a half years, Operation Rolling Thunder ends.
November 6, 1968	The Black Student Union and the coalition of other student groups known as the Third World Liberation Front lead a strike at San Francisco State College (now University) to demand the establishment of ethnic studies programs and classes.
November 6, 1968	Republican Richard M. Nixon is elected president of the United States. President Nixon promises to achieve "Peace with Honor" in Vietnam.
March 18, 1969	President Richard M. Nixon approves "Operation Breakfast," a covert bombing of Cambodia, to destroy Communist supply routes and base camps in Cambodia. It is conducted without the knowledge of Congress or the American public, and lasts 14 months.
March 20, 1969	The student-led protest at San Francisco State College (now University) ends with a settlement to establish the country's first and still only School (now College) of Ethnic Studies. Asian American Studies is one of the programs, along with American Indian Studies, Black Studies (now Africana

	Studies), and La Raza Studies (now Latina/o Studies).
November 3, 1969	President Richard M. Nixon gives a public speech on the policy of "Vietnamization." The goal of the policy is to transfer the burden of defeating the Communists onto the South Vietnamese army and away from the United States.
March 8, 1970	Prince Norodom Sihanouk is ousted as Cambodia's chief of state in a bloodless coup backed by the United States, by pro-Western Lieutenant General Lon Nol, premier and defense minister, and First Deputy Premier Prince Sisowath Sirik Matak.
June 13, 1971	The *New York Times* publishes a series of daily articles based on the information contained in the Pentagon Papers, which was given to them by Daniel Ellsberg, a military analyst who had worked on the study. Ellsberg came to oppose the war, and decided that the American public should be made aware of the information contained in the Pentagon Papers because it revealed a legacy of deception concerning U.S. policy in Vietnam, on the part of both the military and the executive branch.
January 1, 1972	Only 133,000 U.S. troops remain in South Vietnam.
February 21, 1972	President Richard M. Nixon visits China.
June 16, 1972	The Watergate break-in takes place.
December 13, 1972	Peace negotiations between North Vietnam and the United States break down in Paris.
January 8, 1973	Peace negotiations between North Vietnam and the United States resume in Paris.
January 27, 1973	All warring parties in the Vietnam War sign a cease-fire. It is signed in Paris by Henry Kissinger and Le Duc Tho.
January 21, 1974	The U.S. Supreme Court in *Lau v. Nichols* rules that school districts with children who speak little English must provide them with bilingual education. The court says, "The failure of the San Francisco school system to provide English language instruction to approximately 1,800 students of Chinese ancestry who do not speak English, or to

	provide them with other adequate instructional procedures, denies them a meaningful opportunity to participate in the public educational program and thus violates 601 of the Civil Rights Act of 1964."
August 8, 1974	President Richard M. Nixon resigns.
November 5, 1974	March Kong Fong Eu is elected California's secretary of state.
April 17, 1975	The Communist Party of Kampuchea (CPK), otherwise known as the Khmer Rouge, takes control of Cambodia. The CPK would create the state of Democratic Kampuchea in 1976 and rule the country until January 1979. While in power, the Khmer Rouge commits a genocide of its own people: the numbers of Cambodians who died under the Khmer Rouge remains a topic of debate: Vietnamese sources say three million, while others estimate one million to two million deaths.
April 23, 1975	President Gerald Ford announces, in a speech at Tulane University, that the Vietnam War is "finished."
April 29, 1975	U.S. Marines and Air Force helicopters begin massive airlift of American civilians out of Saigon. In total, over 1,000 Americans and 7,000 South Vietnamese refugees are airlifted out of Saigon.
April 30, 1975	Fall of Saigon.
May 12, 1975	*Time* magazine declares Ho Chi Minh "The Victor."
May 24, 1975	The Indochina Migration and Refugee Assistance Act is passed. The act reimburses state governments for the expenses of state resettlement programs for Vietnamese refugees. Under this act, more than 130,000 refugees from Vietnam, 4,600 from Cambodia, and 800 from Laos enter the United States.
December 2, 1975	The Pathet Lao establishes the Lao People's Democratic Republic after forcing King Savang Vatthana to abdicate and capturing Vientiane.
1976	Approximately 10,200 refugees from Laos flee to Thailand and are admitted to the United States.

February 19, 1976	President Gerald Ford rescinds Executive Order 9066, 34 years after World War II.
January 21, 1977	President Jimmy Carter extends a full and unconditional pardon to nearly 10,000 men who evaded the Vietnam War draft.
1978	Tens of thousands of "boat people"—mostly Sino-Vietnamese refugees—flee Vietnam, mostly by boat, and end up in neighboring Southeast Asian countries.
January 7, 1979	Vietnamese troops capture Phnom Penh.
June 1979	More than 54,000 Sino-Vietnamese refugees arrive by boat in neighboring Southeast Asian countries and Hong Kong.
July 1979	At an international conference in Geneva, Switzerland, the Orderly Departure Program (ODP) is established under the auspices of the United Nations High Commissioner for Refugees (UNHCR). The goal was to encourage refugees to leave their country safely, instead of the dangerous voyage by boat. On September 14, 1994, registration for the ODP was closed. Under the ODP from 1980 until 1997, 623,509 Vietnamese are resettled abroad, of whom more than 450,000 went to the United States. Refugee camps open in Thailand to house some 160,000 Cambodian and 105,000 Laotian refugees. UNHCR would assist another 350,000 Cambodian refugees who lived in Thailand outside of the camps, and some 100,000 Cambodians who fled to Vietnam.
March 17, 1980	President Jimmy Carter signs the Refugee Act into law. This act establishes the Office of Refugee Resettlement. It also adopts the definition of "refugee" used in the United Nations Protocol, and provides regular and emergency admissions of refugees.
June 19, 1982	Twenty-seven-year-old Chinese American Vincent Chin is brutally murdered in Detroit by two white men, Ronald Ebens and Michael Nitz, who mistook him for a "Japanese." Ebens and Nitz blamed Chin for losing their jobs in the auto industry. Chin was struck repeatedly with a bat, including blows

	to the head. Chin was taken to the Henry Ford Hospital, where he was unconscious and died after four days in a coma on June 23.
June 23, 1983	The Commission on Wartime Relocation and Internment of Civilians reports that Japanese American internment was not justified by military necessity and that internment was based on "race prejudice, war hysteria, and a failure of political leadership." The commission recommends an official government apology; redress payments of $20,000 to each of the survivors; and a public education fund to help ensure that this would not happen again.
October 4, 1983	The Federal District Court of San Francisco reverses Fred Korematsu's original conviction and rules that the U.S. government had no justification for issuing the internment orders.
March 25, 1985	Chinese-Cambodian Dr. Haing S. Ngor wins the Oscar for best supporting actor for his role in *The Killing Fields*.
November 6, 1986	The U.S. Congress enacts the Immigration Reform and Control Act, which includes civil and criminal penalties on employers who knowingly hire undocumented "aliens."
May 4, 1987	President Ronald Reagan proclaims Asian/Pacific American Heritage Week.
December 22, 1987	The U.S. Congress enacts the Amerasian Homecoming Act, easing immigration of Amerasian children born during the Vietnam War, or "war babies"—mostly the offspring of American fathers and Vietnamese mothers. By 2009, about 25,000 Vietnamese Amerasians and 60,000 to 70,000 of their relatives would enter the United States under this law.
August 8, 1988	The Civil Liberties Act is signed into law by President Ronald Reagan. This act provides for individual payments of $20,000 to each surviving Japanese American internee and a $1.25 billion education fund among other provisions.
September 1989	Vietnam completes its troop withdrawal from Cambodia.

October 9, 1990	The first nine redress payments are made at a Washington, D.C., ceremony. Rev. Mamoru Eto of Los Angeles, who at the time is 107 years old, is the first to receive his check.
November 29, 1990	The Immigration Act is enacted, increasing the annual visa cap to 700,000 annually. The act also creates the Diversity Immigrant Visa program.
December 1991	The United States lifts a ban on travel to Vietnam.
April 29, 1992	The United States eases its trade embargo on Vietnam.
April 29 to May 4, 1992	Korean businesses are looted and burned as a result of riots in Los Angeles due to outrage over the Rodney King verdict.
December 14, 1992	President George H. W. Bush allows U.S. companies to open offices, sign contracts and do feasibility studies in Vietnam.
February 3, 1994	President William Clinton announces the lifting of the trade embargo in Vietnam.
July 1, 1997	At midnight on this day, Hong Kong is returned to China and becomes a Special Administrative Region.
2011	California governor Jerry Brown signs the California Dream Act, AB130 and AB131, into law on June 25, 2011, and October 8, 2011, respectively. The California Dream Act allows undocumented youth access to financial aid benefits if they were brought to the United States under the age of 16, attended school regularly, and meet state GPA requirement for in-state tuition and financial aid.
2012	Asians surpass Hispanics as the largest group of new immigrants in the United States. An estimated 18.2 million Asians are recorded as residing in the United States, making them the fastest-growing racial-ethnic group in the country.
2013	A comprehensive immigration reform is introduced to the U.S. Congress. If enacted, the bill would create a DREAM Act that provides a path towards naturalization for undocumented persons living in the United States.

NOTE

1. In my attempt to verify this reference to an "East Indian" found in the *Virginia Magazine of History and Biography*, I contacted the Virginia Historical Society. The reference to the "East Indian" is not confirmed because the commenter never identified, specifically, the list to which s/he referred. However, the reference to a "Turk" is confirmed. In *Cavaliers and Pioneers*, Volume 1, a "Mr. Georg Menifye" reflects his patent for 1,200 acres in James City County. The transaction was dated February 25, 1636. Menifye—a name that appears to have been spelled many ways—received the land in return for transporting 24 persons from England to Virginia. Among those persons was "Anth. (a) Turk"—apparently referring to someone named only as Anthony, who was known as a Turk.

_____ *Part I* _____

Pre-1965

Chapter 1

Chinese in America

The Chinese characters for "America" consist of the compound "*mei*" meaning beautiful, and "*guo*" meaning country. Therefore, regardless of dialect, the Chinese call America "beautiful country" (*mei gok* in Cantonese, and *mei guo* in Mandarin). California was called *gam san* (*jinshan* in Mandarin) meaning "gold mountain." This reveals an interesting irony in the perception of America versus the lived experienced of America by Chinese migrants and Chinese Americans.

The Chinese were the first Asian immigrants to come to the United States in significant numbers. To date, the Chinese have lived in America for over 150 years.

FACTORS OF CHINESE MIGRATION

By 1800, China faced a bleak future. Its military was weak and unable to protect its people from Western colonial powers. Its rulers and cultural consciousness was too strong to surrender to the political visions of Chinese modernizers. According to Benson Tong, "in the absence of modernization, its people were forced to look elsewhere for a livelihood"; thus began the movement of Chinese migrants to America (2000, 22). Tong argues that "China's educated elite spent so much of their time and energy trying to attain the status and prestige of the scholar-official class that it had to sideline endeavors that might have fostered economic and technological change" (2000, 22). The Chinese economy was lackluster, and the spirit of entrepreneurship was dulled due to a combination of factors—no government investment in infrastructure for trade; high government taxes; and a lack of private investments. In addition, the Qing court and

Chinese quarter of San Francisco, California, 1880s. (Culture Club/Getty Images)

the feudal system was in decline (Chen 1980, 7). This made China suscep-tible to internal rebellion and external invasion by Western colonial forces.

Population growth and pressure exacerbated China's inability to protect its people from internal and external pressures. By 1800, the population of China totaled 300 million, representing a twofold increase since the 1660s (Tong 2000, 18). Agricultural land did not develop with this population growth, because so much of China consisted of arid and mountainous land. Between 1661 and 1812, the population increased by more than 100 percent, while arable land had increased by less than 50 percent (Tong 2000, 18). For instance, in the southern maritime province of Guangdong, one of the fastest-growing provinces in China, population growth increased by 79.5 percent, while China's total national average increased by 47 percent between 1787 and 1850 (Tong 2000, 21). Population growth became a sig-nificant social, economic, and political problem for China because the eco-nomic system did not develop, and the impact of the global Industrial Revolution was not significantly felt. The displaced Chinese, the poor, and the unemployed had to result to social vices, such as banditry or rebellion, or move to survive: unrest and suffering was widespread. Against such a backdrop, both migration and emigration became viable, even necessary possibilities for survival.

Population growth exacerbated harsh economic conditions. The British Opium Wars of 1893–1842 and 1856–1860 forced China to pay large indemnities to the Western imperialist colonial powers, and it drained the Chinese spirit as opium was illegally smuggled into China to advance British economic interest. For years, China successfully pushed back Western influence and kept them out of China's market. However, by the early nineteenth century, British smugglers "had opened the market wide" by introducing the addictive narcotic—opium—that penetrated all sectors of Chinese society, from the poor laborer to the social elites of the gentry class (Chang 2004, 14). The impact of forced illegal opium trade in China had a totalizing destructive effect. Iris Chang describes the impact, noting, "Whether they smoked opium through a pipe or sucked it in tablet form, heavy addicts fell into a near-comatose stupor, gradually decaying into living skeletons ... Millions of Chinese were wasting away, slowly dying from the poison" (2004, 14). The Chinese government attempted to stop the importation of opium into China but did not succeed. The Qing court assigned Lin Zexu, a special commissioner, to stop the smuggling of opium into China. Lin confiscated 20,000 chests of opium and destroyed it out at sea. In response, the British government launched a series of attacks against China. This provided Britain a reason to force open China's doors: British forces captured one port city after another: Canton (Guangzhou), Amoy (Xiamen), Foochow (Fuzhou), and Ningbo, Shanghai, and Nanking (Nanjing). In 1842, Britain imposed the Treaty of Nanking, which forced China to open five of its ports (Canton, Amoy, Fuzhou, Ningbo, and Shanghai) to international trade, pay a total of $33 million in indemnities, cede Hong Kong to Britain, and allow the opium trade; this would be the first of many unequal treaties China would be forced to sign (Chen 1980, 8–9). More importantly, instead of importing opium from India, and to keep profit at home, poppies were brought into China. "Soon poppies were blooming all over the country. Chinese opium production soared, and Indian imports dropped, as Indian opium could not penetrate the interior. Domestic opium proved to be an immeasurably worse problem than the Indian" (Huang 2001, 108–10). Other Western powers followed on the heels of Britain's example in "ravaging, humiliating, and exploiting enfeebled China" (Chen 1980, 8). The United States claimed its share of China and its riches through the Treaty of Wangxia, which gave it most-favored-nation treatment in trade and extraterritoriality (exemption from Chinese laws) for American nationals in China, and the right to be tried by the U.S. consular court. With each defeat, China was burdened by new indemnities, which the Qing court squeezed from the people.

The Western invaders, and later Japan, drained the Qing dynasty of silver, which resulted in the Qing government's high taxation on the peasant farmers, who were unable to pay their taxes, which resulted in them losing their land. Once displaced from their land, they were unable to find employment elsewhere because China's industrial sector was underdeveloped, a result of foreign competition imposed on China after the Opium Wars had undermined domestic industries such as silk production. In fact, Guangdong produced many mass-produced goods, but cheap foreign goods flooded the local markets, limiting the demand for Chinese-made goods such as premodern Chinese handicrafts (Chen 1980, 8). The rapid growth of the colonized islands of Macao and Hong Kong, by as early as the mid-1850s, captured much trade from Guangdong. By 1870, free trade and competition from other coastal ports in China exacerbated the unemployment rate for the urban proletariat in Guangdong. Unemployment, high taxation, growing population pressure, and natural disasters such as flooding deepened the problems of hunger and poverty in the Guangdong province. Tong notes that one flood in Guangdong was so severe that, according to one imperial account, the "rivers and the sea and the streams, have joined in one sheet over the land for several hundred *li* [one *li* equals a third of a mile]" (2000, 23). The hardest-hit population was subsistence-based peasantry, who also bore the heaviest taxation. These immigrants defied Chinese law, since the Ming and Qing dynasties forbade overseas travel under punishment of death (Chen 1980, 10–11). They were willing to take the risk in light of the turmoil in the economy, hostile ecological and climatic conditions, overpopulation, and oppression by their government and invaders, which led to destitution and deprivation. All they needed to do was reach the Portuguese colony of Macau or the British colony of Hong Kong and then, away from the reaches and jurisdiction of the emperor, hop on a ship headed for California's gold country.

GOLD MOUNTAIN DREAMS

The greatest outflow of Chinese immigrants occurred between the 1840s and 1900. An estimated two and a half million people left China, and went to Hawai'i, the United States, Canada, Australia, New Zealand, Southeast Asia, the West Indies, South and Central America, and Africa. During this early period, the majority traveled to the Kingdom of Hawai'i and the mainland United States. Civil unrest and political and military chaos pushed Chinese immigrants out of their country to seek sanctuary elsewhere. Virtually all the Chinese who emigrated came from only five small regions in the two provinces of Fujian and Guangdong and the island of Hainan. Three of the groups settled mainly in Southeast Asia, while the other two traveled across the Pacific to Hawai'i and the United States. A vast majority of the first wave of Chinese immigrants who landed in California during the nineteenth century came from Guangdong Province. The Guangdong natives in the United States can, in turn, be divided into three subgroups, each speaking its own Chinese dialect. According to Chen, from the 1840s to the turn of the century, the main sources of emigration to the United States were: (1) *Sam yup* (*sanyi*) people who came from three districts—Nanhai, Panyu, and Shunde, including Guangzhou, the capital of Guangdong Province—in the Pearl River delta; (2) *Sze yup* (*siyi*) inhabitants who hailed from four districts—Xinhui, Taishan, Kaiping, and Enping; (3) other areas of Guangdong Province, including Hua Xian, Sanshui, Sihui, Qingyuan, Zhongshan, Zhongxin, Boluo, Dongguan, Baoan, Huaji, Guangning, Gaohe, Yangchun, Yangjiang, Guanghai, Mei Xian, and Jieyang; and (4) Hong Kong (1980, 17–18). Murray Lee notes, "Between 1848 and 1881, 95 percent of the over 300,000 Chinese who came to America were Cantonese" (2011, 17).

To the Cantonese migrants, emigration represented a means for a better life in the face of population pressure, economic hardship, political

Chinese grocery store in San Francisco's Chinatown, about 1904. Between 1848 and 1882, waves of Chinese immigrants came to California, Oregon, Washington, and Idaho in search of gold. Although their search was for gold, many ended up in coal mines, railroad construction, and service work (e.g., cooks, laundry workers, and shop keepers). Chinese pioneers began to establish Chinatowns, either by necessity or by choice, and started to recreate and reproduce a perception of community. (Library of Congress)

upheaval, religious persecution, and natural disasters. Although aspiring immigrants had many places to choose from, places where gold had been reportedly discovered—most notably California, Australia, and the Fraser River valley of British Columbia—were the most alluring. "Gold Mountain" was more than just a designation; it was an aspiration, an idea for riches and renewed life. Gold Mountain was any place, not just California, where gold or money or work were available; where wealth was possible.

GAM, GOLD

The discovery of gold at Sutter's Mill in 1848 provoked a distant gaze toward the West Coast. This includes the Pacific Northwest and British Columbia as well. Australia was also a central object of the gold gaze. San Francisco was known as "Old Gold Mountain" (Jiujinshan) while Australia was known as "New Gold Mountain" (Xinjinshan). Between 1848 and 1882, waves of Chinese migrants came to California, Oregon, Washington, and Idaho in search of gold, predominantly from the southern provinces of Guangdong (also known as Canton) and Fujian. Although their search was for gold, many ended up in coal mines, railroad construction, and service work (e.g., as cooks, laundry workers, and shopkeepers). Chinese pioneers began to establish Chinatowns, either by necessity or by choice, and started to recreate and reproduce a perception of community. A high percentage of these immigrants were young men in their working prime, chosen by their families to journey to Gold Mountain (Mandarin, *Jinshan*; Cantonese, *Gam San*), overblown with hopes of making it rich and returning home after several years aboard. San Francisco was a major port of entry for Chinese migrants during the early period of the gold rush. Jack Chen notes that three Chinese migrants arrived in San Francisco in 1848, followed by another 323 in 1849, and 450 in 1850 (1980, 11). According to Ronald Takaki, by 1851, there were 2,716 Chinese immigrants residing in the United States; by 1852, there were 20,026 (1989, 79).

In 1876, the Pacific Mail Steamship Company began regularly scheduled runs between Hong Kong and San Francisco. As a result, between 1870 and 1883, an average of 12,000 Chinese migrants were arriving through the port of San Francisco each year. Before the steamship, the voyage of 7,000 miles took from 55 to 100 days. With the advent of the steamship, and the famous China route that began in 1867 and lasted until the turn of the century, the time taken to reach San Francisco was shortened to weeks. The steamships could hold more passengers than the traditional sailing ships. Emigration was further encouraged when the price of the tickets for the steamship dropped threefold. By 1870, 63,000 Chinese immigrants were living on American soil—between 75 and 80 percent living in California, with sizable communities in Idaho, Montana, and other areas in the Southwest and New England. For this reason, along the West Coast but primarily in California, there were many Chinese communities of various sizes, as far south as Baja California and San Diego, and northward to Vancouver, Canada.

A major pull factor in their decision to leave their villages for distant lands since the late eighteenth century was the exaggerated tales of the riches of America, on Gold Mountain. The people of Guangdong had been exposed to American influences by way of Yankee traders and missionaries. Early Chinese immigrants in the nineteenth century who chose to journey to Gold Mountain were known as *gam san haak* (Cantonese for "travelers to Gold Mountain") and found only *hek fu* ("taking in pain") (Takaki 1998, 80; Tong 2000, 21). Prejudice, disfranchisement, and social exclusion marked their daily existence and Gold Mountain dreams. This movement of Chinese laborers is concomitant with the rise of the global capitalistic economy. Tong notes, "the global expansion of European and American capitalism had necessitated the movement of workers, capital, and technology across borders so that investors and businesspeople could tap into the natural resources and markets of the underdeveloped countries. The eventual immigration of those from Guangdong to Gold Mountain was part of a larger diaspora that involved as many as 2.5 million between 1840 and 1900" (2000, 22–23). It was, as Murray Lee describes, "part of a worldwide Chinese migration pattern" (2011, 17).

EARLY IMMIGRATION

The travelers were mainly poverty-stricken young men. Some of them were married, were generally illiterate, or had very little schooling, but all were inspired by the tales of Gold Mountain and had dreams of gold. There was not just gold to be mined, but employment opportunities as well. The Chinese entered into contract, a form of forced slave labor to afford their passage to Southeast Asian countries, the Kingdom of Hawai'i and the mainland United States. For example, arrangements for their Pacific passage were made by an emigration broker, a labor recruiter who represents the sugar plantation owners in Hawai'i. They were offered "free passage" to the island in exchange for their labor. The terms of the contracts usually lasted five years and included shelter, food, and medical care. On a sugar cane plantation in Louisiana, Chinese laborers signed their contracts with their thumbprints, stipulating:

1. The worker owes the recruiter $100, for travel, which is to be deducted from future wages;
2. The contract was for five years, with a month wage of $7;

3. Working hours were from sunrise to sunset, with one hour off for breakfast and lunch;

4. At cane-pressing time, the height of the season, workers had to work at night. Workers get 50 cents for six hours of night time work;

5. The workers also had to do domestic work in the homes of the plantation owners (Chen 1980, 25).

The other way to finance their passage was through the "credit-ticket system." Here, a broker would loan money to the migrant, who would later pay off the loan with interest out of his earnings. The Chinese laborers fell victim to the "coolie trade" because they were exploited under the terms of their contacts and treated harshly, no better than African slaves kidnapped and forced into labor through coercion in Cuba, Peru, and elsewhere in the Americas (Jung 2006, 34). Thus, mixed in with "gold seekers" were "freedom seekers." Jack Chen says, "Among the earliest immigrants in 1848 were twenty-five Chinese who, finding themselves tricked into near slavery in Peru, escaped to freedom in America and joined the Gold Rush" (1980, 13).

Chinese emigration also included merchants. They were venture capitalists seeking new opportunities in a foreign land (Kwok 1988, 16). Like the peasant laborers, this class of people were also mostly, if not all men. Single women did not travel alone to distant foreign lands. The married ones often stayed home to care for their families and elders. They also stayed behind because the family simply could not afford their passage. Because husbands and sons were separated from wives and families, the Chinese migrants are described as *sojourners*. Sojourners are people on the move, involved in temporary migration, who plan to eventually return to those they left behind. "During the first decade of immigration to the United States as many as a third of them did so" (Tong 2000, 25). This practice, known as "return migration," also characterized turn-of-the-century European immigration to the New World. However, two-thirds of the Chinese migrants remained—for legal, financial, or personal reasons—in the United States, to live, work, and settle.

HAWAI'I SUGAR PLANTATIONS

Before 1900, Hawai'i was an independent monarchy. Hawai'i's lucrative sugar industry entered the world market in the 1940s, replacing small local farms with plantation fields, improved refinement of sugar processing, and increased output (Okihiro 2009, 115). Historian Gary Okihiro notes that "By 1846 there were eleven sugar plantations, two run by Chinese who were pioneer sugar producers, and sugar exports advanced quickly from 4 tons in 1836 to 180 tons in 1840 and nearly 300 tons in 1847" (2009, 115). Hawai'i's sugar industry was fueled by the growing population of California and Oregon. The American Civil War also fueled the development of Hawai'i's sugar industry, as the North was cut off from the South's raw material. The North thus became a steady market for higher-priced imported sugar and cotton (Okihiro 2009, 115). In the 1850s, the price for a pound of sugar in the North increased from 6.95 cents to 10.55 cents. In 1864, it reached its peak at 17.19 cents (Okihiro 2009, 115). This created a great demand for sugar and, by extension, sugar plantations. The need for cheap labor surely influenced the sugar plantation owners' recruitment of contract workers from China, the Pacific Islands, Japan, Korea, and the Philippines as well as Puerto Rico, Europe, and California. Starting around 1852, the plantation owners imported Chinese laborers in large numbers.

CHINESE IN HAWAI'I VERSUS CALIFORNIA

The experience of the Chinese in Hawai'i is much different than their co-ethnic experience over on the mainland. Chinese laborers in Hawai'i were more likely to have their wives with them. According to Eleanor Nordyke and Richard Lee, in 1900, of the 25,767 Chinese in Hawai'i, 3,471, or 13.5 percent were female, but of the 89,683 Chinese on the U.S. mainland, only 4,522, or 5 percent, were female (1989, 209–10). One reason for the differences in sex ratio is the ethnic makeup of the two groups of immigrants. The Chinese in California were mainly Punti, whereas most of their counterparts in Hawai'i were Hakka. Hakka society did not practice foot-binding, and Hakka women had greater freedom of mobility. Moreover, the immigration conditions and policies also affected the sex ratio difference between Hawai'i and the mainland. Since 1864, the *Pacific Commercial Advertiser* expressed angst about the predominantly male Chinese population and encouraged plantation owners to import Chinese women, as a way to control the men and the social problems and vices that result from a bachelor society—a society of single, unmarried men. The plantation owners believed that Chinese women could be used to control the men, better than any regulation that they can enforce. The plantation owners saw that Chinese women were strong instruments that could be used to control the Chinese men. Women who immigrated to Hawai'i did so under the same circumstances as Chinese men: labor contracts. They were supposed to engage in "light labor" only and not be separated from their husbands. Chinese women were paid less than their male counterparts.

CHINESE WOMEN IN HAWAI'I VERSUS CALIFORNIA

The combination of missionary concern and employer self-interest did not encourage the immigration of Chinese women into the mainland, as it had in Hawai'i. In fact, the opposite occurred, because employers viewed Chinese male laborers as sojourners, as temporary and migratory. California employers wanted a workforce of single men. They wanted a mobile workforce that could move from one location to the next for construction and harvesting. Chinese men therefore worked on the railroad and as migrant farm laborers. The differences in gender ratio of the Chinese community in Hawai'i and California influenced the way they were perceived: on Hawai'i, they were not seen as competitors in the labor market, whereas in California, they were. This difference in perception led the Chinese to become a racialized group, and thus, targets of prejudice, hostility, and violence. By the 1880s, the white community in California represented 87 percent of the population and saw Chinese women and their families as a threat to white racial purity and what they considered to be a "white man's country."

Besides coming as wives, Chinese women were also imported to America and forced into the lucrative prostitution trade, regardless of the final destination: Hawai'i or California. Chinese prostitutes lived and worked as slaves to their owners and usually did not survive more than six years. The prostitutes ranged in age from 16 to 25. The majority could not read the terms of the contracts they were forced to sign with their thumbprint. The lowest-level prostitutes were forced to work and live in cribs, rooms no larger than four by six feet. They were forced to sell themselves to poor laborers, teenage boys, sailors, and drunks for a little as 25 to 50 cents. If infected with disease, they were left to die and thrown out. Prostitutes forced to work in the mining camps lived short, harsh lives. Prostitutes who revolted were physically punished. Some would try to run away, but their owners would track them down because they were highly valued. Their condition was, in large measure, a result of the demographics of the society, immigration policies, and economic restrictions.

Chinese women were viewed as exotic curios on the East Coast, but things were different on the West Coast as gold started to run low with increasing competition. The rising hostility toward Chinese immigration on the West Coast correlates with the racialized and debased descriptions of Chinese women in the media. In 1870, of the 3,536 Chinese women in California, 2,157, roughly 60 percent, were prostitutes. Because the Chinese population in California consisted mostly of men, Chinese prostitutes were in high demand. The Chinese prostitute problem was employed to fuel anti-Chinese sentiments, and it resulted in the passage of the 1875 Page Law. The Page Law was designed to halt the flow of Chinese prostitutes to America, who were seen as a great threat to white manhood, health, morality, and family life (Tong 2000, 28). "Chinese men, bereft of family life and denied conjugal ties, sought prostitutes or *baak chai* (a derogatory Cantonese phrase for 'one hundred men's wife')—as they did opium smoking and gambling—for entertainment. Applied stringently, the Page Law excluded wives and single women with legitimate claims. Immigration officials believed that prostitutes typically posed as wives, sisters, or daughters of sojourners already in America. Officials consequently assumed that all Chinese women seeking entry into the United States were potential prostitutes" (Tong 2000, 28).

In San Francisco, Chinese prostitutes became the first immigrant group in the host society to be targets for removal or confinement in geographic locality. This movement to isolate Chinese prostitutes in the municipality of San Francisco extended into a larger effort to isolate all Chinese in the United States. By the mid-1890s, an unexpected health concern made it possible for city health officers to force the Chinese into a specific geographical locality. The bubonic plague provided them with the reason they needed to isolate the Chinese.

The Burlingame Treaty (1868) between China and the United States repealed the century-old prohibitory emigration law of the Qing government and secured the right of Chinese to open and voluntary migration to the United States. More importantly, the treaty offered Chinese immigrants in America, equal protection of all legal rights enjoyed by other foreigners residing in the United States. By the early 1870s, the U.S. federal courts interpreted that the treaty also provided for the rights of the Chinese to live and work in America. The treaty's spirit of equality and fair treatment for the Chinese was soon overturned as anti-Chinese sentiments along the Pacific Coast swelled.

ANTI-CHINESE EXCLUSION, 1840–1882

Gold on Gold Mountain was not as plentiful as the embellished tales described. The very first wave of Chinese immigrants who landed in the port of San Francisco were viewed favorably, as celestials and strangers who eventually will become good Americans. When California celebrated its admission into the Union in 1850, the Chinese participated in the ceremonies alongside whites. Justice Nathaniel Bennett declared that even though the Chinese were born and raised under different governments, that day, they stood as brothers, respected as equals, who share one country, one hope, and one destiny (Takaki 1998, 80). This quickly changed as the nativist cry got louder and louder. White miners demanded that the Chinese, along with the Mexican, Hawaiian, French, and Chilean miners, be banned from mining. "Within just several years of the discovery of gold, 2,400 Chinese, an estimated two-thirds of the Chinese in America, were laboring in the mines of the American West" (Tong 2000, 32). Competition intensified, and the Chinese miners became the targets of hostility and faced rigid racial prejudice from competing white miners as well as from local and state governments. The best example of this is the California state legislature's passage of the Foreign Miner's Tax of 1852, which was chiefly enforced against Chinese miners, who often had to pay more than once (Chinn, Lai, and Choy 1969, 24). In theory, the Foreign Miner's Tax was ostensibly imposed on all miners who did not desire to become naturalized citizens. Lawmakers knew, of course, that the Chinese could not gain citizenship, since the 1790 Nationality Act excluded nonwhites from being able to become a naturalized citizen. The Foreign Miner's Tax remained intact until the passage of the Civil Rights Act of 1870. By that time, the state of California had collected $5 million from the Chinese, a sum representing 25–50 percent of the state revenue. In 1855, the California state legislature passed a law known as "An Act to Discourage the Immigration to this State of Persons Who Cannot Become Citizens Thereof." This law imposed on the master or owner of a ship who imported people ineligible to become naturalized citizens a landing tax of $50 for each passenger who arrived by ship.

By the late 1850s and early 1860s, there were 24,000 Chinese miners, two-thirds of whom were mining in California. Many of the Chinese miners

Harper's Weekly illustration of Chinese immigrants at the San Francisco Custom House in 1877. (Library of Congress)

organized themselves into small groups, composed of up to 40 members, while others formed their own companies. Most of the Chinese miners were also independent prospectors. Chinese miners in Yuba County obtained their placer claims through preemption rather than purchase. Chinese miners filed a required application in the county's record's office and marked the boundaries of their claim in the preemption claim procedure.

As a result of exclusion from mining, and of gold becoming scarcer during the mid-1860s, the Chinese left the mines and ventured into fishing. Eventually, Chinese fishing activities stretched from the Oregon boundary down to Baja California and also along the Sacramento River delta. By the 1870s, a number of them concentrated on catching and processing shrimp in the San Francisco Bay, while others collected abalone off the coast of Southern California. A large portion of Chinese immigrants established their residence along the California coast and began the business of gathering, drying, and exporting seafood resources, namely seaweed (Ulva), kelp, and abalone back to China. One of these thriving communities was in Cambria, San Luis Obispo County. Prior to the official establishment of the little community of Cambria in 1866, the Chinese immigrants in California were already living along the coastal bluffs in San Luis Obispo County. The Chinese seaweed farmers found the rocky coastal area of San Luis Obispo County ideal for their trade. The Ulva (a sea lettuce) already grew but competed with many other forms of algae. In order to encourage luxurious and fast growth, the Chinese made sure the rocks preferred by the Ulva were plentiful and strategically placed to receive the full benefit of wave action and sun. The selected rocks were thoroughly cleaned by scorching or burning, originally accomplished by pine shavings smoldering in a wire basket held against the rocks. In later years, a blow torch was used, eliminating the job of scraping the dead algae away.

RAILROADS

Besides the venture into the fishing industries, large numbers of Chinese workers were employed in the railroad industries. In February 1865, 50 Chinese workers were hired by the Central Pacific Railroad to help lay the tracks for the transcontinental line leading east from Sacramento. The Chinese laborers were praised by Leland Stanford, the company's president, and Charles Crocker, the company's superintendent, as hardworking, amiable, and quiet—workers who can learn any skill quickly and efficiently. They even went as far as to suggest that Chinese workers were more productive and reliable compared to white workers. The Chinese laborers were trained for all aspects of railroad construction, including blasting through mountains, driving horses, and handling rocks with picks and shovels.

Animosity and hostility from white railroad laborers developed, which resulted in their demand that the company stop hiring Chinese laborers.

Within a two-year period, the company employed 12,000 Chinese laborers, roughly 90 percent of their workforce. The railroad employed the "dual wage system," paying Asian workers less than white workers as a means to keep wages for both groups low. The dual wage system results in "ethnic antagonism" whereby white workers demanded restrictions on Asian workers, which later resulted in immigration exclusion. Not only were the Chinese laborers fast workers, but their employment saved the company a lot of money because the Chinese laborers were paid $31 a month, while their white coworkers were paid $45 a month. Because the Central Pacific managers wanted to accelerate construction, they forced Chinese workers to work through the winter of 1866. Time was a big concern for the company because the amount of payment it received in land and subsidy from the federal government was determined on the miles of tracks they were able to build. The Chinese workers lived and worked in tunnels under the snow. Snowslides and landslides occasionally buried the camps and crews. In the spring, the thawing corpses, motionless, with shovels and picks

Chinese laborers work on the U.S. Central Pacific Railroad during the late 1800s. (Library of Congress)

in their hands, were discovered. That spring, Chinese workers went on strike and demanded eight-hour days and $45 a month: 5,000 workers went on strike. The strike was advertised through a Chinese-language print. The Central Pacific managers blamed their rival Union Pacific for masterminding the strike. This allowed them to negate the possibility that the Chinese workers were capable of acting on their own benefit and behalf. As a possible solution to the Chinese strike, the Central Pacific sent a wire to New York, inquiring about the feasibility of sending 10,000 blacks to replace the striking Chinese (Takaki 1998, 86). Superintendent Crocker responded to the Chinese strikers by cutting off their food supplies, which worked because weeks later, virtually imprisoned in their camps on the mountains of the Sierras, the starving strikers went back to work. In 1869, the transcontinental railroad was completed ahead of schedule. The completion of the transcontinental railroad is a symbol of America's Manifest Destiny. The construction of the Central Pacific Railroad line was a Chinese achievement, but this fact remains unnoticed and invisible.

AFTER THE RAILROAD

Released from railroad construction, the Chinese laborers moved into agriculture. In California's Sacramento–San Joaquin River delta region, they constructed irrigation channels, reclaimed swamplands, and built the levees, dikes, and ditches. As tenant farmers or sharecroppers, the Chinese introduced new varieties of fruits and vegetables for the local markets. The majority were laborers who toiled in orchards, vineyards, and hop fields. By 1870, the Chinese constituted 18 percent of all farm laborers in California; by 1880, they represented 86 percent of the agricultural laborers. The dual wage system was also employed in this industry. Employers paid Chinese laborers lower wages than white workers. The Chinese workers were trapped in a racially based dual wage system, where they were paid less than white workers for doing the same job. In 1880, Chinese pickers in Santa Clara County, California, went on strike, demanding increased compensation for the fruit they harvested. The 1882 Chinese Exclusion Act reduced the supply of Chinese farm laborers, so they recognized the increased need for their labor and demanded higher wages as a result.

Other ex-miners began working in the salmon canneries on the coastal bays and streams from central California to western Alaska. "In Alaska in 1902, the peak year of Chinese employment there, over 5,300 of the cannery work force of 13,800 were Chinese" (Newell 1988, 636). Others traveled to the Pacific Northwest after being recruited to build the North Pacific line or to run lumber mills. Still others worked in small businesses—laundries, restaurants, and dry-goods stores owned by Chinese merchants. During the

1870s, Chinese workers were recruited to replace the emancipated black slaves for plantation work and railroad building in the southern states of Louisiana, Mississippi, and Florida. The Chinese did not stay on the plantations long. As early as 1871, the *New Orleans Times* notes that Chinese preferred to work in the small trades and industries in the city rather than toil in the fields. By 1880, there were a recorded 50 Chinese in Mississippi, 133 in Arkansas, 489 in Louisiana, and 95 in New Orleans, working as laundryman, cigar makers, shoemakers, cooks, and woodcarvers. Chinese workers were also recruited to the Northeast, specifically Massachusetts, New Jersey, and Pennsylvania, as scabs to break striking shoemakers, steam launderers, and cutlery makers—most of whom were Irish immigrants. By then, there were 500 Chinese in New York, and about 900 in Boston (Tong 2000, 33).

San Francisco, also known as *Dai Fow* (Cantonese for "Big City") became a city with employment opportunities. "Ethnic antagonism," which pitted one ethnic group against another to keep wages low, resulted in anti-Chinese sentiments and violence against them, drove many into self-employment. The Chinese laundry was chief among them. The Chinese laundryman was an American phenomenon. It does not exist in China; in fact, there were no laundries in China during that period. Back in China, women do the washing, not men. Opening a laundry in the United States required little capital because the materials were simple: a stove, trough, dry room, sleeping area, a sign, and some English skills. Besides low capital-investment demands, the Chinese were pushed into this line of work because it was one of the few that were open to them besides restaurants. In 1900, one out of four employed Chinese males worked as a laundryman.

After the railroad and mining, the Chinese population became an urban population because many were "driven out" of rural areas as a result of economic competition and racial discrimination. San Francisco's Chinese population went from 2,719 in 1860 to 12,022 in 1870. Similarly, Los Angeles's Chinese population went from 605 in 1880 to 1,817 in 1890 (Tong 2000, 33). In the 1870s, the urban Chinese population moved into manufacturing and once again found themselves caught in a racially segregated labor market with low wages. Often Chinese laborers occupied menial positions in the woolen mills, paper mills, knitting mills, and tanneries, while European Americans took the skilled jobs. In instances where they held the same position as whites, they were paid less for the same work. In the early 1880s, Chinese men earned one dollar a day as factory workers, while white men earned two dollars (Tong 2000, 34).

Throughout much of this early period, anti-Chinese sentiments informed much of the public policies and popular racism that discriminated against the Chinese living in America.

1882–1965

By 1882, the Chinese population in the United States was about 110,000, or one-fifth of one percent, of the total U.S. population. When Chinese laborers were no longer needed, political agitation against the Chinese intensified, and the U.S. Congress enacted a series of very harsh laws, beginning in 1882, that were designed to exclude Chinese immigrants and deny their naturalization rights and basic civil liberties (Lee 2011, 298). In the spring of 1882, the Chinese Exclusion Act was passed by Congress and signed by President Chester A. Arthur. Section 14 of the Act declares, "hereafter no State court of the United States shall admit Chinese to citizenship; and all laws in conflict with this act are hereby repealed." Section 15 states, "That the words 'Chinese laborers,' wherever used in this act, shall be construed to mean both skilled and unskilled laborers and Chinese employed in mining." By 1888, the act was extended to include all Chinese, not just laborers. It was renewed by the Geary Act of 1892 and extended indefinitely in 1902. The Chinese Exclusion Act was the first U.S. law ever passed to prevent immigration and naturalization on the basis of race, which later was extended and expanded to include other Asian immigrants, such as the Japanese, Koreans, and Indians. The exclusionist policies led to an immediate and sharp decline in the Chinese population: from 105,465 in 1880, to 89,863 in 1900, to 61,639 in 1920.

This demographic decline resulted in the steady disappearance of Chinatowns throughout the United States. For example, the Chinese communities in California towns such as Cambria, Riverside, Yosemite, Hanford, Mendocino, Santa Barbara, Ventura, and San Luis Obispo slowly disappeared as the remaining Chinese moved northward to San Francisco or southward to Los Angeles, two cities with major Chinese centers and more possibilities for employment. Chinatown communities in Evanston, Wyoming; Silver City, Idaho; and Walla Walla, Washington, gradually disappeared as well. It is estimated that by 1900, nearly 45 percent of Chinese immigrants resided in the San Francisco Bay Area. At the same time, those years witnessed an increasing number of Chinese American families, which resulted in a new generation of acculturated English-speaking Chinese Americans who grew up between the 1930s and 1940s. In the 1880s, cities and towns with a Chinatown were scattered throughout the West, though the Chinatown might consist of only a street or a few stores and its inhabitants might number only a few hundred. Eventually, these enclaves disappeared altogether. By 1940, only 28 cities with Chinatowns could be identified; by 1955, only 16. Enforcement of the exclusion laws by immigration officials resulted in additional exclusionary measures that doubly hindered Chinese immigration, but also reinforced the popular conceptions and construction of the

Chinese as "Orientals," "perpetual foreigners" who threatened the American landscape.

RESISTANCE TO ANTI-CHINESE HOSTILITIES

In response to the systemic decimation and exclusion, the Chinese Six Companies, also known as the Chinese Consolidated Benevolent Association (CCBA), who advocated for Chinese rights in the United States, sent a letter to President Ulysses Grant in 1876, reminding the president of the Chinese contributions to America's development and expansion. The Chinese Six Companies also publicly denounced mob violence against the Chinese. The Chinese also employed the U.S. court system in their protest. In 1855, Chan Yong applied for citizenship in San Francisco's federal district court and was denied citizenship on the basis of the 1790 Naturalization Law, which limited naturalization rights to "whites" only. Since the Chinese were not "white," they were therefore unable to become naturalized citizens. In 1862, Lin Sing sued the San Francisco tax collector, challenging a $2.50 capitation tax levied on the Chinese on the basis that it was unconstitutional. The California Supreme Court, in *Lin Sing v. Washburn*, ruled that while the Chinese could be taxed as "other residents," they could not be set apart as "special subjects of taxation" (California Supreme Court 1906, 534–85). This was a victory for the Chinese as the California Supreme Court ruled in their favor based on the fact that the state law was unconstitutional.

In 1868, the Chinese Six Companies lobbied for inclusion of a provision to protect the Chinese immigrants in America, in the negotiations between the United States and China. They argued that federal protection of the Chinese would protect Chinese lives and properties in the United States, but also promote Chinese investments in the country and promote trade between America and China. The Burlingame Treaty of 1868 recognized the "free migration and emigration" of the Chinese to the United States as visitors, traders, and permanent residents (Odo 2002, 31). It also provided the Chinese with rights and privileges of movement and residency as subjects of the "most favored nation." The flow of immigration (encouraged by the Burlingame Treaty) was stopped by the Chinese Exclusion Act. The Chinese population in the United States gradually declined until the Exclusion Act was repealed in 1943 with the passage of the Magnuson Act. Anti-Chinese sentiments and discrimination extended to the top ranks of the U.S. government; in 1888, President Grover Cleveland, who supported the Chinese exclusion, pronounced the Chinese "an element ignorant of our constitution and laws, impossible of assimilation with our people and dangerous to our peace and welfare" (Spence 1991, 215).

The Civil Rights Act of 1870 contained language that included the Chinese in America. This act nullified the decision in *People v. Hall*

(1854), which made it illegal for Chinese to testify against a white person in court (Odo 2002, 19). On August 9, 1853, George Hall, a white miner, accompanied by his brother and one other man, assaulted and robbed a Chinese placer miner on the Bear River in Nevada County, California. Ling Sing left his tent after hearing the sound of gunfire and was shot and killed by Hall. The sheriff arrested Hall and his companions. Hall was later tried and found guilty based on the testimony of three Chinese witnesses. The judge sentenced Hall to death by hanging. However, the chief justice of the California Supreme Court, Hugh Murray, overturned the conviction on the basis that "Asiatics" were "Indians" and therefore unable to testify against a white man in court. Murray argued that "Asiatics" long ago traveled over the Bering Strait and "descended" into Indians. Indians were not allowed to testify in court against a white man, so since "Asiatics" (in this case, the Chinese eyewitnesses) were Indians, they too, cannot testify in court against a white man.

DRIVING OUT THE CHINESE

Fear of the bubonic plague at the beginning of the twentieth century fueled anti-Chinese sentiments and the efforts to "drive them out" or to confine them to a certain geographic locality (Pfaelzer 2007). In 1894, the plague was found in Canton and Hong Kong. In 1896, the San Francisco board of health ordered that all passengers arriving from China and Japan be detained and quarantined because the plague was present there. Two cases of the plague discovered in Honolulu's Chinatown resulted in the removal of 4,500 Chinese into a quarantine camp. In San Francisco, there was suspicion that a Chinese man died of the plague because his autopsy revealed enlarged lymph nodes, so Surgeon General Walter Wyman ordered San Francisco's Chinatown to be placed under quarantine. Health and city officials immediately cordoned off Chinatown and forbade travel outside of California without a certificate of health. Growing anti-Chinese sentiment that resulted from economic competition and racism coupled with the fear of the bubonic plague resulted in large-scale efforts to "drive out" the Chinese residents in smaller rural townships, most often by burning down their places of residence. This pushed Chinese immigrants to urban areas such as San Francisco.

1906 SAN FRANCISCO EARTHQUAKE AND FIRE, ANGEL ISLAND, AND PAPER SONS

Due to exclusionary immigration laws, the majority of Chinese men in the United States believed they would never be able to bring their wives and or family to America. However, on April 18, 1906, things changed. Early that

The 1906 San Francisco earthquake impacted the Chinese American community and migration in significant ways. View of Chinatown reduced to rubble after the 1906 San Francisco earthquake and fire. The near-total destruction of Chinatown prompted local politicians to draft a plan that would have moved Chinatown to a less desirable area near the Presidio. However, when the Chinese government threatened to cut off trade with the city, the plan was dropped. The fire that resulted from the earthquake destroyed many government documents, which opened up a way for Chinese migrants to enter the United States as "paper sons." (Library of Congress)

morning, an earthquake shook the city. Fires broke out and destroyed much of the city along with the municipal records. Without records, the Chinese living in the United States could claim they were born here and thus were citizens who could sponsor their wives and children in immigrating to the United States. Before the earthquake and fire, the number of Chinese women remained around 5 percent or less of the total Chinese population. According to Takaki, in 1900, there were 4,522 Chinese women living in America. After the earthquake and fire, Chinese women began arriving in much larger numbers: in 1910, 219 women arrived; in 1915, 356 women arrived; in

1920, 573 women arrived; in 1922, 1,050 women arrived; and by 1924, 1,893 women arrived. In the years 1907–1925, roughly 10,000 Chinese women came to the United States (Takaki 1998, 235). A 1924 immigration act stopped the inflow of Chinese women because it prohibited entry of immigrants who were ineligible to become citizens, and the act also instituted a permanent quota that provided preferences to immigrants from certain parts of Europe.

Meanwhile, Chinese sons were also entering the United States. U.S. law stipulated that children of American-born citizens were automatically granted citizenship status, even if they were born in foreign countries. These Chinese children of self-proclaimed American-born Chinese fathers were legally allowed to enter the United States. Many sons came, while others were imposters known as "paper sons" and sometimes "paper daughters." Immigration officials knew of the paper sons and did not trust that all Chinese women were wives of Chinese American men, so they were detained at Angel Island.

Angel Island is the largest island in the San Francisco Bay. Nearly 300,000 immigrants passed through Angel Island Immigration Station during its heyday. Angel Island Immigration Station's goal was to exclude the entry of Chinese, then Japanese, Koreans, Indians, and other Asian immigrants. While detained on Angel Island, real sons and paper sons, along with mothers and wives, were asked a series of questions to determine whether or not the kin relationship was real or fake. According to Robert Barde, questions were asked such as: What is your mother's name? What kind of feet does she have? Had your father any brothers or sisters? What are their names? What is the name of your father's or husband's native village? How long has he been away? How many floors did your house have? On what floor did you live? What feast did you celebrate? Who attended the celebration? (2008, 29–36).

IMPACT OF WORLD WAR II

For Chinese immigrants, living in America was difficult. Attempts to settle and create families was not easy, especially with the passage of alien land laws that made it illegal for immigrants ineligible to become naturalized citizens from buying and owning real estate. In 1913, California passed its first alien land law (the Webb-Heney Bill). This law also stipulates that aliens ineligible for citizenship may not lease land for agriculture for terms longer than three years. This, along with violence and attacks fueled by anti-Chinese sentiments, pushed Chinese laborers out of the agricultural industries and into the urban ghettos of San Francisco's Chinatown. Throughout the 1920s, 1930s, and into the 1940s, Chinatowns in urban communities grew and became tourist economies. Their survival in Chinatowns was forced, as they were not allowed to make homes elsewhere in the United

States. The majority were also employed in self-service industries such as restaurants, laundries, and so on. American-born Chinese children were also forced to attend segregated schools.

World War II and the postwar period witnessed great social changes for Chinese living in America. The United States and China became allies during World War II, which brought about changes in restrictive immigration policies that resulted in the repeal of the Chinese Exclusion Act in 1943 with the passage of the Magnuson Act. The Magnuson Act repealed 61 years of official racial discrimination against the Chinese. This allowed for a modest increase in Chinese immigration, especially after the Chinese Communist revolution of 1949 sent many Chinese in search of refuge abroad. The postwar period was also when Chinese gained naturalization rights and, eventually, the end of antimiscegenation laws prohibiting the marriage of a Chinese to a white person. The culmination of progressive social change was realized with the passage of the 1965 Immigration and Nationality Act, which lifted national origin quotas and allowed for large-scale Chinese immigration to the United States to resume.

The Chinese immigrants' first wave was fairly homogenous in that they came from the Pearl River delta region of Canton China, and consisted mostly of men. In addition, most were sojourners with peasant backgrounds and low levels of education. There was a small merchant class in the mix. The Hart-Celler Act of 1965 transformed the homogenous Chinese American society into a heterogeneous one, reflecting diversity in religious, social, economic, educational, linguistic, and ethnic backgrounds. The majority before 1965 spoke Taishan and Canton dialects. Today, there is an increase in Mandarin, Chaozhou, Fujianese, Hakka, and Shanghai dialects among the Chinese American populations whose countries of origins include mainland China, Hong Kong, Taiwan, Singapore, and Malaysia. There is also a sizable sector of the population who are ethnic Chinese from Southeast Asia (mainly from Vietnam and Cambodia) who entered the United States as refugees after the fall of Saigon in 1975. Chinese immigrants from Taiwan, Hong Kong, and Singapore come from higher social-cultural backgrounds with higher educational levels. As such, they tend to enter into professional white-collar jobs.

A gender imbalance was evident in the male-to-female ratio in the Chinese American communities. The passage of the Page Law in 1857 made the gender imbalance even more distinct. During and after World War II, more and more Chinese immigrants were admitted into the United States as war brides. After the Communist victory in China in 1949, hundreds of refugees and their families entered the United States as political refugees. The overall increase in Chinese women led to the increase in American-born Chinese between the 1940s and 1960s. As such, in 1960, over 60 percent of the

Chinese American population was American-born. Further indications of growth are evident in the increase in population by 28.5 percent from 2000 to 2006.

REFERENCES

Barde, Robert E. *Immigration at the Golden Gate: Passenger, Ships, Exclusion, and Angel Island*. Westport, CT: Praeger, 2008.

California Supreme Court. *Reports of Cases Determined in the Supreme Court of the State of California*, Vol. 20. San Francisco: Bancroft-Whitney Company, 1906.

Chan, Sucheng. *Asian Americans: An Interpretive History*. New York: Twayne, 1991.

Chang, Iris. *The Chinese in America*. New York: Penguin, 2004.

Chee, Maria W. L. *Taiwanese American Transnational Families: Women and Kin Work*. London: Routledge, 2005.

Chen, Jack. *The Chinese of America: From the Beginnings to the Present*. San Francisco: Harper & Row, 1980.

Chinn, Thomas H., Mark Lai, and Philip Choy, eds. *A History of the Chinese in California: A Syllabus*. San Francisco: Chinese Historical Society of America, 1969.

Choy, Philip. *Canton Footprints: Sacramento's Chinese Legacy*. Sacramento, CA: Chinese American Council of Sacramento, 2007.

Choy, Philip. *San Francisco Chinatown: A Guide to Its History and Architecture*. San Francisco: City Lights Books, 2012.

Chung, Sue Fawn. *In Pursuit of Gold: Chinese American Miners and Merchants in the American West*. Champaign: University of Illinois Press, 2011.

Chung, Sue Fawn, and Priscilla Wegars, eds. *Chinese American Death Rituals: Respecting the Ancestors*. New York: AltaMira Press, 2005.

Daniels, Roger. *Asian America: Chinese and Japanese in the United States since 1850*. Seattle: University of Washington Press, 1988.

Echenberg, Myron. *Plague Ports: The Global Urban Impact of Bubonic Plague, 1894–1901*. New York: New York University Press, 2007.

Hing, Bill O. *Making and Remaking Asian American through Immigration Policy 1850–1990*. Stanford, CA: Stanford University Press, 1993.

Hsu, Madeline Y. "Exporting Homosociality: Culture and Community in Chinatown America, 1882–1943." In *Cities in Motion: Interior, Coast, and Diaspora in Transnational China*, edited by David Strand, Sherman Cochran, and Wen-Hsin Yeh. Berkeley, CA: Institute of East Asian Studies, 2007.

Huang, Shaoxiong. "Opium and Warlordism." In *Modern China and Opium: A Reader*, edited by Alan Baumler. Ann Arbor: University of Michigan Press, 2001.

Jung, Moon-Ho. *Coolies and Cane: Race, Labor, and Sugar in the Age of Emancipation*. Baltimore: Johns Hopkins University Press, 2006.

Kingston, Maxine Hong. *China Men*. New York: Vintage Books, 1980.

Kwok, D. W. Y. "By History Remembered." In *Sailing for the Sun: The Chinese in Hawaii 1789–1989*, edited by Arlene Lum, 10–25. Honolulu: Hawaii National Bank, 1988.

Kwong, Peter. *Chinatown, New York: Labor and Politics, 1930–1950*. New York: Monthly Review Press, 1979.

Kwong, Peter. *The New Chinatown*. New York: Hill and Wang, 1996.

Kwong, Peter, and Dusanka Miscevic. *Chinese America: The Untold Story of America's Oldest New Community*. New York: New Press, 2007.

Lai, Him Mark. "Historical Development of the Chinese Consolidated Benevolent Association/Huiguan System." *Chinese America: History and Perspectives* (1987): 13–51.

Lee, Anthony. *Picturing Chinatown: Art and Orientalism in San Francisco*. Berkeley: University of California Press, 2001.

Lee, Erika. *At America's Gates: Chinese Immigration during the Exclusion Era, 1882–1943*. Chapel Hill: University of North Carolina Press, 2003.

Lee, Erika, and Judy Yung. *Angel Island: Immigrant Gateway to America*. Oxford: Oxford University Press, 2010.

Lee, Jonathan H. X. "Chinese Immigrants." In *Multicultural America: An Encyclopedia of the Newest Americans*, edited by Ronald Bayor. Santa Barbara, CA: Greenwood, 2011.

Lee, Murray. *In Search of Gold Mountain: A History of the Chinese in San Diego, California*. Virginia Beach, VA: Donning Company Publishers, 2011.

Loewenstein, Louis K. *Streets of San Francisco: The Origins of Street and Place Names*. Illustrated by Penny deMoss. San Francisco: Lexikos, 1984.

Lum, Arlene, ed. *Sailing for the Sun: The Chinese in Hawaii 1789–1989*. Honolulu: Hawaii National Bank, 1988.

Lydon, Sandy. *Chinese Gold: The Chinese in the Monterey Bay Region*. Aptos, CA: Capitola Book Company, 1985.

Nash, Robert. "The Chinese Shrimp Fishery in California." PhD diss., University of California, Los Angeles, 1973.

Newell, Dianne. "The Rationality of Mechanization in the Pacific Salmon-Canning Industry before the Second World War." *Business History Review* 62:4 (Winter 1988): 626–55.

Nordyke, Eleanor, and Richard K. C. Lee. "The Chinese in Hawai'i: A Historical and Demographic Perspective." *Hawaiian Journal of History* 23 (1989): 196–216.

Odo, Franklin, ed. *The Columbia Documentary History of the Asian American Experience*. New York: Columbia University Press, 2002.

Okihiro, Gary Y. *Pineapple Culture: A History of the Tropical and Temperate Zones*. Berkeley: University of California Press, 2009.

Pan, Erica Y. Z. *The Impact of the 1906 Earthquake on San Francisco's Chinatown*. San Francisco: Peter Lang, 1995.

Pfaelzer, Jean. *Driven Out: The Forgotten War against Chinese Americans*. Berkeley: University of California Press, 2007.

Spence, Jonathan. *The Search for Modern China*. London: Norton, 1991.

Takaki, Ronald T. *Strangers from a Different Shore: A History of Asian Americans.* Rev. ed. Boston: Little, Brown, 1998.

Tong, Benson. *The Chinese Americans: The New Americans.* Westport, CT: Greenwood Press, 2000.

Wong, K. Scott. *Americans First: Chinese Americans and the Second World War.* Philadelphia: Temple University Press, 2005.

Yeh, Chiou-ling. *Making an American Festival: Chinese New Year in San Francisco's Chinatown.* Berkeley: University of California Press, 2008.

Zesch, Scott. *The Chinatown War: Chinese Los Angeles and the Massacre of 1871.* Oxford: Oxford University Press, 2012.

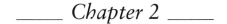

Chapter 2

Japanese in America

Japanese Americans are descendants of immigrants who came from Japan, or Nippon, meaning "source of the sun." They are also many who are from Okinawa and self-identify as Okinawan instead of Japanese American. Since they follow on the heels of Chinese immigrants, their experience reveals many similarities; yet, because of Japan's rapid industrialization and modernization during the Meiji period (1868–1912), it was also very different from the Chinese American experience. The origins of the first-generation Japanese Americans, or *Issei*, began with Japanese laborers being recruited to work on Hawai'i sugar plantations. Their American-born children are called *Nisei*, or second generation; the third generation is called *Sansei*, the fourth is called *Yonsei*, and so on. *Nikkei* refers to all Japanese Americans regardless of generation or citizenship status, and *Kibei* refers to those children born in the United States but educated in Japan.

On the U.S. mainland, the Japanese communities formed around agriculture. Japanese immigrants entered the United States in the greatest numbers from 1886 to 1908, with a second wave of mostly women immigration peaking between 1916 and 1920. Until the 1970s, Japanese Americans were the largest single ethnic group among Asian Americans and their history in Hawai'i was longer, more sustained, and more significant than anywhere else in America.

FACTORS OF JAPANESE MIGRATION

During the Meiji period, thousands of people were displaced because their land was taken out of cultivation or their homes were taken away. By 1870, the U.S. Census indicates that 55 Japanese immigrants were living in the United States. In 1880, the U.S. Census shows 148 Japanese immigrants living in the United States, 86 of whom resided in California. Most of this early immigration was considered illegal by Japanese law. Pressure from its growing displaced population resulted in the Japanese government lifting its ban on emigration and allowing Japanese laborers to go to Hawai'i to work on sugar plantations starting in 1884. On January 8, 1900, the first group of 27 Okinawans arrived on the shores of Honolulu on the SS *China* (Nakasone 2002, xi). The Japanese laborers went to Hawai'i and the United States as contract laborers. They signed contracts for agricultural employment in exchange for passage. As such, they were like the Chinese who were mostly *dekaseginin*, or "sojourners" who were young men who intended to work for a limited time and then return to Japan with their earnings from aboard.

Since Chinese laborers were excluded from immigration with the passage of the 1882 Chinese Exclusion Act, businesses on the mainland United States were in need of cheap labor as well. Eight years after Chinese exclusion, there were 2,039 Japanese living in the United States (Fryer 2010, 371): two decades later, there were 72,257 Japanese in America (Takaki 1989, 180). San Francisco, Seattle, and Portland were major ports of entry for Japanese immigrants. Roughly 76 percent of the Japanese immigrants settled along the Pacific Coast: this trend continued for four decades. There were sizable populations of Japanese immigrants in Colorado, Utah, and New York, where the population reached 1,000 (Fryer 2010, 371).

Early Japanese immigrants remained primarily single and male. In the 1900 U.S. Census, 23,916 of 24,326 Japanese immigrants were male and only 410 were female. The ratio of women to men shifted when after 1908, the United States and Japan signed the "Gentlemen's Agreement" that restricted the migration of unskilled laborers from Japan to the United States, but did not cut off the migration of wives or family members of permanent residents. The period from 1908 to 1924 was dominated by the arrival of "picture brides." These were women who migrated to join husbands they had married either during a return trip to Japan or by proxy. This period also initiated the rapid growth of the second generation of Japanese Americans and the growth of Japanese American communities.

Though the Japanese immigrants were aware of the experience of the Chinese before them and hence attempted to do things differently, they inherited much of the resentment directed toward the Chinese because both were Asian and nonwhite. Even so, the Japanese transitioned from being *dekaseginin* to citizens, in light of nativist perceptions that to be American is to be "white."

HAWAI'I SUGAR PLANTATIONS

Since the 1850s, sugar was king in Hawai'i. According to Gary Okihiro, the number of plantations growing sugar in Hawai'i grew from 20 in 1875 to 63 in 1880; sugar export increased from 25 million pounds in 1875 to 250 million pounds in 1980 (2009, 115–16). Starting in 1852, Chinese contract laborers were recruited to work on the plantations. By 1865, the Chinese laborers were leaving the plantation for other work. As well, Japanese laborers were recruited to replace the Chinese, and over time, they became the largest group of plantation workers. Stanley Easton and Lucien Ellington note that on May 17, 1868, the *Scioto* left Yokohama for Honolulu with 148 Japanese: 141 men, six women, and two children. There were "samurai, cooks, sake brewers, potters, printers, tailors, wood workers, and one hairdresser" (Easton and Ellington 2011). The plantation owners pitted the ethnic groups against one another to keep wages low. Japanese laborers were brought in to replace the Chinese laborers who attempted to demand high wages and better living conditions. Korean and Filipino laborers were later brought in to replace Japanese laborers who also demanded higher wages and better living conditions. All Asian laborers were subordinate to the white plantation managers and foremen, even though Asian laborers constituted roughly 70 to 85 percent of the workforce (Takaki 1989, 138). Contract laborers continued until 1900, when federal law terminated that practice. Immediately, planters formed the Hawaiian Sugar Planters' Association to systematically keep wages low through wage fixing agreement (Takaki 1989, 141).

JAPANESE IN HAWAI'I VERSUS CALIFORNIA

Unlike the Chinese workers before them, a significant percentage of Japanese women workers immigrated over with the men. Despite the harsh conditions, immigrant workers established ethnic communities. Plantation owners pitted the Chinese workers against the native Hawaiian workers, the Japanese workers, and white workers by paying them different wages for the same work. On Hawai'i, the Japanese were not a minority group, but on the mainland, they were. Japanese immigrants were needed as laborers in Hawai'i. Because fertile land was owned by the "Big Five" corporations, and small business opportunities such as retail stores were operated by the plantations, the Japanese population in Hawai'i focused on unionization and organized labor strikes to improve their social and economic standards of living. Japanese workers, Gary Okihiro contends, "saw themselves in class terms and recognized that their strength lay in collective action" (1991, 42). Japanese American labor organizations led to the island's largest sugar strikes in 1909 and 1920.

Things were different over on the mainland. Takaki argues that the Japanese discovered certain possibilities that existed on the mainland to a greater extent than on the islands: opportunities for small businesses and small farms (1989, 180–97). The first Japanese-owned farm in California was established on May 27, 1869. Followers of Lord Matsudaira Katamori established the Wakamatsu Tea and Silk Farm Colony on 600 acres on the Sacramento River at Placerville (Zhao 2009, 14). They introduced mulberry trees, silk cocoons, tea plants, and bamboo roots to California. In less than two years, the colony failed because the dry California weather was not conducive to their cultivation.

In California, the Japanese immigrants were aware that the Chinese immigrants attempted to be a part of the general economy in manufacturing and trade occupations, which provoked anti-Chinese violence, policies, and ultimately exclusion. The Japanese therefore withdrew from manufacturing and entered instead into related enterprises. So, instead of shoe manufacturing, they were into shoe repair (Takaki 1989, 198). Thus the Japanese focused on entrepreneurial opportunities such as restaurants, barber shops, billiard halls, saloons, and grocery stores, and operated buses and delivery wagons because labor unions were among the staunchest opponents of Japanese inclusion. In fact, their members belonged to anti-Japanese organizations such as the Asiatic Exclusion League, whose mission was to protect white workers by excluding all Japanese and Koreans from coming to the United States. Other nativist groups, like the Sons of the Golden West, the Grange Association, and the American Legion pressured politicians to deport Asian immigrants and to segregate them into ghettos of laboring underclass (Tateishi 1984, xiv). Despite the racial economic exclusion, the Japanese immigrants focused on ethnic enterprise and by extension ethnic solidarity as a viable means of livelihood (Takaki, 1989, 180). However, their success only fueled anti-Asian, anti-Japanese sentiments even though they developed ethnic community and economy for survival. Even more cyclical and frustrating is the nativist conclusion that the Japanese immigrants were unassimilable because they developed ethnic communities and economies.

The Japanese immigrants faced a lot of racism and social prejudice. Some, as Takaki notes, were called "chinks," revealing that they inherited the anti-Chinese sentiments. Additionally, they were also called "Yellow Jap" or "Dirty Jap" and were told to "go home" (Takaki 1989, 181). They were refused service at restaurants and in barber shops, and found it difficult to rent homes or buy houses. According to Lon Kurashige, the real issue was not the number of Japanese immigrants in the United States at the time, but rather the assumption that they were cheap labor that would undermine the "standard of living for white workers, propelling American society into a downward spiral of economic, moral and racial degeneration" (2002, 17). Moreover, "[t]he rhetoric, and the resulting anti-Japanese policies, embodied the worst sort of paranoia in American politics, as even states with few Japanese or any other residents of color took pains to secure the future of their white populations" (Kurashige 2002, 17).

Japanese farming in the late nineteenth century was fueled by industrialization coupled with the nationalization of the railroad, and modernization
as exemplified by the refrigerated car, which resulted in an increase need
for fresh agricultural produce. In addition, the development of California's
irrigation system with water from Colorado also spurred Japanese farming
(Street 2004, 520). Historian Sucheng Chan notes that by the "first years
of the twentieth century, fully two-thirds of the Japanese in California
(about 16,000 individuals) earned a living as farm laborers" (1991, 38). In
1900, the federal census recorded only 29 Japanese leased land in California;
by 1910, that number jumped to 1,816 (Street 2004, 517). Japanese farmers
belonged to prefectural associations, known as *kenjinkai*, and agricultural
associations, or *nogyo kumiai,* who pooled their resources together to form
tanomoshi, or credit-rotating systems, that allowed members to have the
capital needed to start a small business or farm. One big factor in transforming the Japanese population from *dekaseginin,* or sojourners, to settlers was
their entry into agriculture and utilization of mutual-support systems, which
allowed them to coordinate crop production, fix prices, exchange information, provide financial assistance, arbitrate disputes, stabilize rent, and
establish marketing organizations (Kurashige 2002, 19; Street 2004, 520).

JAPANESE IMMIGRATION, EXCLUSION, AND CITIZENSHIP

Japanese American communities faced increasing restrictions against
immigration, citizenship, property, and basic civil rights over the first four
decades of the twentieth century. First, as Japanese immigrants began entering the United States, they found a society already ordered by racial hierar-
chies, segregation, and the recent passage of the 1882 Chinese Exclusion
Act. It did not take long for Japanese immigrants to become targets of
race-based attacks and exclusionist efforts to cut off immigration from
Japan. In 1902, white workers successfully got the Chinese Exclusion Act
of 1882 extended, and wanted to include the Japanese.

On October 11, 1906, the San Francisco municipal school board directed
all school principals to send Chinese, Japanese, and Korean students to
"Oriental Schools." This action led to an international geopolitical event
as the government of Japan voiced their protest to Washington. Washington
was careful in its dealing with Japan because it was a rising military power in
Asia. President Theodore Roosevelt forced the San Francisco municipal
school board from segregating Japanese American children, which allowed
them to attend school with white children. However, Roosevelt agreed to
the Gentlemen's Agreement, signed in 1907 and implemented in 1908,
which restricted the migration of unskilled laborers from Japan. Furthermore, Roosevelt prohibited Japanese laborers holding passports for
Hawai'i, Mexico, or Canada from re-migrating to the U.S. mainland.

The state of California agreed not to pass overtly anti-Japanese legislation in the future. Roger Daniels points out that the Gentlemen's Agreement was "sold" to Californians as "tantamount to exclusion," but it was not. Instead, under its terms, the Japanese American population would double in less than 20 years because Washington agreed that Japanese already residing in America could send for their wives and family members left behind (Daniels 1988, 126). However, by 1924, the immigration policy changed, banning entry to all aliens ineligible to become citizens, which ended all Japanese immigration. The Immigration Act of 1924 is considered to be the ultimate triumph of the Native Sons of the Golden West (Kimball and Noel 2005).

Laws and discriminatory policies were passed that further politically racialized the Japanese as "Other" and noncitizen. In 1913, the California legislature passed a law that denied Japanese residents the ability to own property. Japanese immigrants were able to subvert that law by purchasing property in their children's name since they were born in America and were thus American citizens according to the 14th Amendment and *United States v. Wong Kim Ark*, 169 U.S. 649 (1898). Many Issei parents purchased land in their children's names. When tested in court, the California State Supreme Court upheld the right of even the youngest Nisei, second-generation children, to own property as a right of citizenship. The test case involved two-year-old Tetsubumi Yano, who was born in the United States to Japanese immigrant parents. Yano's family owned 14 acres of land in her name, and the court ruled that Yano's parents should be allowed to serve as her guardians (*Estate of Tetsubumi Yano* [1922] 188 Cal. 645, 648). This only angered many white Californians and fueled a call for a total ban on Japanese immigration. By 1920, however, a new anti-Japanese legislation corrected that loophole. The right to own property, or to establish a home, a business, or farm, was directly tied to the rights of the Issei to become naturalized citizens.

CITIZENSHIP

In 1922, the U.S. Supreme Court confirmed in *Takao Ozawa v. United States* that Japanese immigrants were not eligible to become naturalized citizens. Takao Ozawa immigrated to the United States in 1894 as a student, graduated from Berkeley High School and then attended the University of California at Berkeley. He was a self-described "assimilated" American who primarily spoke English in his home. In October 1914, Ozawa applied for U.S. citizenship at the U.S. District Court in Hawai'i. The court rejected his application on the grounds that he was of the Japanese race, and not white. Ozawa filed a lawsuit that gradually made its way to the U.S. Supreme Court. The court's ruling in November 1922 declared that first-generation Japanese Americans, the Issei, were ineligible of becoming naturalized citizens.

The 1870 Naturalization Act limited naturalization rights to only "white persons and persons of African descent." Ozawa did not challenge the constitutionality of the law; rather, he sought to have Japanese classified as "white" (Haney López 1996, 56–57). Ozawa told the court, "My skin is white, I am a white person. I've lived in this country more than twenty-eight years. I deserve citizenship" (Haney López 1996, 58). Unable to become a naturalized citizen, Ozawa's right to be fully American was compromised.

In 1913, California passed its first Alien Land Law, restricting aliens ineligible for citizenship from owning land. The law was challenged in the courts, so it was amended several times and was replaced in 1920. The Alien Land Law expanded to states throughout the West from 1920 to 1923 to include a ban on long-term leases or rental of land to aliens ineligible for citizenship. These laws specifically targeted Asian immigrants. Japanese farmers were prohibited from owning land until after World War II, when the Supreme Court declared California's Alien Land Law unconstitutional in *Oyama v. California* (1984).

JAPANESE WOMEN IN AMERICA

Japanese women in Hawai'i and on the mainland had double duty: they had to work the fields as well as do the house work. Many immigrated to the United States as "picture brides." Picture bride marriages originated with arranged marriages that had their origins, within aristocratic circles, and in the samurai class during feudal times, before the modern Meiji Era in Japan. It became accepted even among peasants in rural communities. With the introduction of photography from the West, exchanging photos introduced couples when it was difficult to meet in person. This also allowed the "go-between" or *nakōdo* to bring a photograph. This could save embarrassment if one party were rejected; the matter could then be quietly resolved.

Japanese immigration to Hawai'i, in the earliest period between 1885 and 1910, included four times as many men as women. When the men in Hawai'i wanted to begin families, they returned to their villages and had families arrange marriages. But the trip was long and expensive, and many wrote their parents to find suitable wives or asked *nakōdo* for assistance. Go-betweens generally conducted research to ensure the socioeconomic status of the intended couple, their educational backgrounds, and their family histories. The peak period for this "picture bride" practice was after the Gentlemen's Agreement of 1907–1908, which restricted Japanese laborers from entering the United States until the passage of the Immigration Act of

A group of first-generation Japanese immigrants gathering at a garden club meeting, Oregon, July 1924. (Underwood Archives/Getty Images)

1924, which banned entry to "aliens ineligible to citizenship" and virtually ended all immigration from Japan.

The Gentlemen's Agreement significantly increased in the number of Japanese women who immigrated to Hawai'i and the U.S. mainland (Daniels 1988, 126). Over 20,000 picture brides were married to Japanese men in Hawai'i in absentia through families back home or *nakōdo* and the years from about 1910 to 1924 are often referred to as the "picture bride period" or *yobiyose*-jidai, "the period of summoning families" (Daniels 1988, 126). The influx of picture brides marked the transition from a society of largely single male transients to communities of permanent residents, especially on the West Coast. Due to the high levels of Japanese women immigrating to the United States, Washington asked Japan to stop issuing passports to picture brides in 1921, with the "Ladies Agreement."

In 1900, out of the total population of 24,326 Japanese immigrants in the United States, only 985 were female (24 males for every female). By 1910, the female population had increased to 9,087; by 1920, there were 22,193 women. Of course, not all the arranged marriages succeeded. In some cases, men sent photos from years earlier to disguise their ages or even photos of younger friends. Some grooms never showed up at the immigration station. In other case, women arrived as *kari-fūfu* (temporary spouse) simply to gain entry into the United States. Many immigrants then remarried. The system allowed adventurous women to join the workforce at a time when labor immigration was restricted but spouses were still allowed. The exclusion act of 1924 closed this loophole almost entirely until well after World War II ended in 1945. In the meantime, the picture bride system permitted a large and flourishing community of Japanese American families to develop in the United States.

THE JAPANESE AMERICAN EXPERIENCE AND WORLD WAR II

The bombing of Pearl Harbor by Japanese forces on the morning of December 7, 1941, marked a bitter turning point in Japanese American history. President Franklin D. Roosevelt signed Executive Order 9066 on February 19, 1942, authorizing the exclusion of Japanese—including Okinawan—Americans from the West Coast. The order granted the federal government the ability to create military zones, including the authority to remove individuals—mostly American citizens and residents of Japanese descent—from areas that were deemed threats to national security. Immediately after Pearl Harbor, the Federal Bureau of Investigation (FBI) identified and captured Japanese American community leaders from California, Oregon, and Washington—states that were designated critical zones of national security. These early detainees, arrested by the FBI as early as December 1941, were sent to facilities such as the Department of Justice internment camps in Santa Fe, New Mexico; Crystal City, Texas; and Fort Missoula, Montana. They were held without bail, without being formally charged, and without knowing what crime they were being accused of committing.

On March 18, 1942, President Roosevelt issued Executive Order 9102, establishing the War Relocation Authority (WRA) for the purposes of relocating Japanese Americans named in Executive Order 9066. In total, 112,000 Japanese Americans were forced to leave their homes and property and move into government detention facilities euphemistically called "Assembly Centers" and "Relocation Centers." They were sent to 10 camps located in far-flung regions, each housing 10,000 to 20,000 Japanese Americans: Rohwer and Jerome, Arkansas; Gila River and Poston, Arizona; Manzanar and Tule Lake, California; Amache, Colorado; Minidoka, Idaho; Topaz, Utah; and Heart Mountain, Wyoming (Gesensway and Roseman 1988, 44). The relocation began in the summer of 1942 and was completed by November. The Japanese American evacuees "boarded decrepit, sluggish trains. . . . Their journeys lasted up to ten days. Black shades covered the train windows day and night. . . . Their movement was restricted to a narrow strip alongside the train by armed guards, who aimed guns" at them (Gesensway and Roseman 1988, 43–44). All facilities were surrounded by barbed wire and military guard towers. The WRA described the relocation

Seventy years have passed since Japanese Americans were shipped off to wartime camps, and advocates are trying to stop time, if for a moment. The Japanese American National Museum established an online archive of personal stories from community members who survived the camps in the hopes of getting the now-octogenarian Nisei generation to share their experiences before it is forgotten. Today, Manzanar and other internment camp sites are pilgrimage destinations for those who wish to reconnect with history and memories. (AP Photo)

center as a "pioneer community" that offered its inhabitants basic housing and federal government protection (Gesensway and Roseman 1988, 44). Remarkably, Executive Order 9066 did not relocate Hawaiian Japanese, who made up nearly one-third of the population of the islands where the attack took place.

Some individuals were placed under government control in a variety of other facilities ranging from Department of Justice internment centers to segregation facilities and even federal penitentiaries. Additionally, 2,264 individuals of Japanese ancestry were sent by 12 countries in Latin America for detention in the United States during the war: 1,800 of them were Japanese Peruvian (Gardiner 1981). While the exact purpose of this international transfer of individuals was unclear, common speculations included a plan to use Japanese Latin Americans for hostage-exchange purposes.

The relocation of Japanese American families marked an end to Japanese American farmers. The Western Growers Protective Association supported the order as it meant the elimination of competition (Okihiro and Drummond 1992, 171). In their absence, Japanese American land and property were simply taken over by other farmers and families. After the war, only a few were able to return to their property, restore their farms, and reestablish their businesses.

Several years after the initial relocation, public opinion began to shift concerning the need for incarcerating Japanese Americans who never demonstrated any disloyalty to the United States. Secretary of War Henry Stimson, who approved the proposal to organize an all-Nisei combat team in 1943, withdrew his support of Executive Orders 9066 and 9102 in 1944, claiming that the relocation program was based on misinformation and public hysteria (Coombs 1992, 90).

To date, scholars still debate the terminology that best describes the facilities used to detain Japanese Americans. Although the word *internment* is commonly used to refer to the confinement of all Japanese Americans, only those aliens arrested by the FBI and held under the authority of the Department of Justice were housed in internment camps. During the war, some had already begun using the term "concentration camp" to describe the facilities that held the majority of Japanese Americans; but today the use of this term is less common due to its close association with the death camps that housed Jews and other groups targeted by Nazi Germany for extermination. Other common terms are detention facilities, confinement centers, or virtual prisons, but none are precisely accurate. What scholars can agree on is the power that the government wielded by creating facilities that were extra-legal and outside the boundaries of U.S. constitutional law.

Soldiers of Honor and Heroism

In light of having their loyalty to the United States questioned, having their civil rights stripped away without due process, and being racialized as enemies from within, Japanese Americans acquiesced to their situation as a way to show that they were in fact "good" and "patriotic" Americans. The 442nd Regimental Combat Team and 100th Infantry Battalion best exemplified this. Both were comprised of all Nisei soldiers. The 100th Infantry Battalion consisted of former members of the Hawai'i National Guard, activated Army Reservists, and regular Army personnel (Hawaii Nikkei History Editorial Board 1998, 3). The 100th earned the nickname "The Purple Heart Battalion" for their heroism and tremendous casualties.

The 442nd Regimental Combat Team was also considered to be one of the most decorated unit of its size in U.S. Army history during World War II. Their moto was "Go for Broke" because they wanted to prove Japanese American loyalty to the United States (Burgan 2007, 50). The team consisted of 4,000 Japanese American soldiers. The majority of them were volunteers

Members of the 442nd Regimental Combat Team in the Vosges Forest, France. In its most famous action, the 442nd rescued the "Lost Battalion," an American regiment cut off and surrounded by German troops in the Vosges Mountains. (Center for Military History)

from Hawai'i, and some were drafted while in the internment camps. Indeed, camp administrators encouraged volunteers, suggesting that it would be a good way to prove their loyalty as Americans. They also worked closely with the WRA officials in Washington "to create among internees as positive an image of military conscription as possible by establishing a series of public rituals to validate service in the American military forces" (Hayashi 2004, 180). The existence of the 442nd Regimental Combat Team fighting on the European front was cited by some in the army and the Japanese American community as undermining the lawful justification for the internment camps. In fact, President Franklin D. Roosevelt contradicted his order to intern 112,000 Japanese Americans when he supported the creation of an all–Japanese American combat unit, saying "The principle on which this country was founded and by which it has always been governed is that Americanism is a matter of the mind and heart; Americanism is not, and never was, a matter of race and ancestry" (Fuchs 1990, 227–28).

Though Japanese Americans served the United States bravely, the 442nd Regimental Combat Unit was segregated from the rest of the troops. The military and the president argued that segregating them allowed them to stand out, whereas if they were scattered among millions of other soldiers, they would go unnoticed. The unit fought in Italy before moving on to France. In France, they liberated Bruyères from German forces, during which 200 died and 600 were wounded. The 442nd and the 100th Infantry Battalion joined forces on June 11, 1944. The 100th was designated the First Battalion of the 442nd but kept its original name, the 100th Infantry Battalion.

By the end of the war, the 442nd and 100th suffered "an unprecedented casualty rate of 314 percent" and received 18,143 individual decorations (Jeffers 2008, 245). Together the 442nd and 100th received many honors for their heroism in war: one Congressional Medal of Honor, 52 Distinguished Service Crosses, 560 Silver Stars, 28 Oak Leaf Clusters to the Silver Star, 4,000 Bronze Stars, 1,200 Oak Leaf Clusters to the Bronze Star, and "perhaps most telling of the sacrifices made by these gallant soldiers, 9,486 Purple Hearts" (Jeffers 2008, 245–46).

No-No Boys

The internment camp administrators began to employ the loyalty questionnaire as a way to determine the loyalty of internees who were over 17 years of age to see if they would leave the camps to work. As well, it was a means of replenishing the 442rd and 100th units' casualties. In a survey for Japanese American civilians from the Department of War and the War Relocation Authority in 1943, two questions generated the most conflict. Question 27 asked, "Are you willing to serve in the armed forces of the United States on combat duty, wherever ordered?" And Question 28 asked, "Will you swear unqualified allegiance to the United States of America and faithfully defend the United States from any and all attack by foreign or domestic forces, and foreswear any form of allegiance to the Japanese Emperor?"[1]

Questions 27 and 28 evoked anger, frustration, and resistance, most notably among young Japanese American men. Some mainland Nisei youth saw no reason to fight for a government that had dispossessed them and their families of their civil rights and private properties. As well, among older Japanese Americans and Japanese American women, the questions caused uncertainty because they knew about military age and gender restrictions. Question 28 asked them to renounce their allegiance and citizenship to Japan and its emperor, but since they were not allowed to become naturalized citizens of the United States, many feared they would be stateless.

In some camps, leaders met to discuss how the two questions should be answered. Issei and Kibei who supported Japan, and as a way to protest the treatment of Japanese Americans since Pearl Harbor, encouraged the Nisei to answer no to both questions. Those who qualified their answers to both questions were considered to have answered no. Men answering no to both questions became known as the "No-No Boys." About 10 percent of draft-age Issei and Nisei Japanese Americans interned by the U.S. government during World War II answered no to both questions. The loyalty test caused strain on Japanese American families. Some simply answered yes to avoid being separated from their families. During the war period, No-No Boys were consider pariahs of the community who brought them shame. The Japanese American Citizens League (JACL) did not support them during the war. However, decades later, the National Japanese American Citizens League supported U.S. Army second lieutenant Ehren Watada's right to a fair trial after he refused to deploy to Iraq in 2006. And the Honolulu JACL endorsed Watada's refusal to obey military orders that he deemed illegal. Breaking ranks with his comrades in a highly potent gesture, John Masunaga, then 83 and a veteran of the highly decorated 442nd Regimental combat team, also supported Watada.

Draft Resisters

Often times confused with No-No Boys are draft resisters. In total, 310 Japanese Americans resisted the draft. However, unlike the No-No Boys, they answered yes to Questions 27 and 28. The JACL promoted voluntary service or at least compliance with the draft as a way for Japanese Americans to prove their loyalty and be accepted by mainstream American society. Punishment for resistance varied. For instance, Judge Louis A. Goodman dismissed all charges against the resisters from Tule Lake, saying, "it is shocking to the conscience that an American citizen be confined on the ground of disloyalty and then, while so under duress and restraint, be compelled to serve in the armed forces or be prosecuted for not yielding to such compulsion" (Inada 2000, 320). On October 7, 1944, in federal court in Phoenix, Arizona, Judge Dave M. Ling charged 112 resisters from Poston (Colorado River), just "one cent" and ruled their time served. Their attorney, Abraham Lincoln Wirin, paid their fines with one dime, a dollar bill, and two pennies that he borrowed from his assistant (Chin 2002, 479). On average, though, resisters were sentenced to anywhere from six months to five years in federal prison, with the average resister receiving a one- to two-year sentence. All Japanese American draft resisters were pardoned by President Harry S. Truman in December 1947 when the presidential commission determined that the resisters were drafted under unreasonable circumstances. Within the Japanese American communities, however, the reconciliation process was much slower. Some resisters had trouble finding employment after the war, were asked to move out of their communities, or were refused marriage, but all were nearly forgotten or ignored by history. In July 2000, at its biennial convention, the JACL adopted a resolution to recognize the wartime draft resisters as "resisters of conscience" and apologized to them for having failed to acknowledge their civil right to protest the treatment of Japanese Americans during World War II (Harth 2001, 10).

Fighting in the Courts

Japanese Americans challenged their treatment during World War II in formal ways by challenging the discriminatory laws in the courts. Four cases made it all the way to the Supreme Court: *Yasui v. United States* (1943), *Hirabayashi v. United States* (1943), *Korematsu v. United States* (1944), and *Ex parte Mitsuye Endo* (1944).

Minoru Yasui was born in Oregon to Issei parents. On March 28, 1942, Yasui deliberately broke the curfew by walking around downtown Portland after hours and presenting himself to the police station. Yasui was a member of the Oregon bar and was an army second lieutenant in the infantry reserve. Executive Order 9066 limited the movement of Japanese Americans to home

American lawyer Minoru Yasui (1916–1986) at Topaz in 1983, the detainment camp where he was held during World War II because of his "Japanese Ancestry," Abraham, Utah. (Carl Iwasaki/Time Life Pictures/ Getty Images)

and work by establishing a curfew between 9:00 p.m. and 6:00 a.m. Through Pubic Proclamation Number 3 issued on March 24, 1942, the curfew was justified as a means of securing the country from risk of espionage and acts of sabotage. Yasui waived his rights to a trial by jury and was found guilty: he was fined $5,000 by a federal judge and sentenced to one year in the Multnomah County Jail in Portland. He was transferred to the Minidoka War Relocation Center in 1944. While serving his sentence, he filed an appeal to the Ninth Circuit Court. The Supreme Court heard the case in May 1943 and issued its ruling on June 21, 1943. The ruling, authored by Chief Justice Harlan Fiske Stone, upheld the constitutionality of the curfew and the War Powers Act.

In a similar case, a student in Seattle named Gordon Hirabayashi was arrested for breaking the curfew and challenging exclusion from the West Coast. Hirabayashi claimed his Fifth Amendment rights to "due process under the law" were violated by the exclusion and curfew orders. Hirabayashi's case would be the first case to test the laws in May 1943. Moreover, it was the first case to challenge the laws based on race because it only applied to one ethnic group—Japanese Americans. Hirabayashi's lawyer argued that he was a citizen of the United States, was born in the United States, had no ties to Japan, had never been to Japan, and had no relations with anyone living in Japan. However, the court ruled that national security was paramount during times of war. The curfew the court argued was a "protective measure." The court was able to avoid more complex legal issues with exclusion, registration, and relocation by focusing their ruling on Hirabayashi's violation of the curfew law.

Fred Korematsu challenged the exclusion from the West Coast as well. Korematsu refused to obey the relocation order and was arrested for violating the Civilian Exclusion Order Number 34. He was found guilty in federal court on September 8, 1942. His conviction was upheld on January 7, 1944, by the Ninth Circuit Court of Appeals. Korematsu then appealed to the U.S. Supreme Court. Korematsu's case completed Hirabayashi's case by forcing the court to address the constitutionality of force relocation and exclusion. On December 18, 1944, the court issued its ruling, with five justices affirming the lower court's ruling. Justice Hugo Black wrote the majority opinion and said that national security concerns outweighed Korematsu's constitutional rights. Three justices—Owen Roberts, Frank Murphy, and Robert Jackson—wrote dissenting opinions. Justice Roberts argued that relocation was akin to imprisonment. Furthermore, without evidence of disloyalty, and because there were no trials, Japanese Americans' Fifth Amendment rights had been violated. Justice Murphy concurred with Justice Roberts, but went on to add that the policies were acts of racism against Japanese Americans. Justice Jackson dissented on the grounds that since the relocation orders targeted only Japanese Americans whose parents were born in Japan, the order was unconstitutional because it was based on "inherited guilt."

Mitsuye Endo was a Japanese American woman who was born in Sacramento. On May 15, 1942, she was forced to leave her home and job as a stenographer for the State Highway Commission in Sacramento. She was relocated to Tule Lake Relocation Camp in Northern California. Sacramento is the state capital, so under Public Proclamations Numbers 1 and 2, it was classified as a sensitive military zone. Hence, any persons of Japanese descent within the zone were put under strict curfew or ordered to be relocated to less sensitive areas. At the time of her relocation, Endo was an American citizen and her brother was a member of the U.S. Army. On July 1942, Endo filed a writ of habeas corpus demanding that the government present evidence for her arrest. She asked that the court grant her freedom and release her from Tule Lake Relocation Camp. Endo's lawyers argued that her detention was illegal due to the length of time she had been detained without being charged. The lack of due process, they argued, was a federal abuse of the War Powers Act, which violated the 14th Amendment's "equal protection under the law" clause because Italian Americans and German Americans were not targets of relocation or curfew and their home countries were officially at war with the United States.

Only Endo's case received a favorable ruling during the war. The Supreme Court agreed with her on all counts. Before the Supreme Court's ruling was able to be put in effect, Endo was released from camp on the basis of a citizenship review. In 1983, Korematsu had his conviction overturned under a writ of error called *coram nobis* at the federal court level. The Korematsu case in particular remains unchallenged at the Supreme Court level and continues to be used as precedent for cases that require "strict scrutiny" because they have the potential of affecting only a specific population of people. Hirabayashi's conviction on the exclusion count was overturned in 1986. Then in 1988, his conviction for curfew violation was overturned, also under *coram nobis*. His attorney argued that the court had made an error based on inaccurate information regarding the scope of disloyalty among Japanese Americans in the state of Washington. The federal appeals court agreed and issued Hirabayashi a formal apology for the original convictions.

CIVIL RIGHTS AND REDRESS

After World War II, Japanese Americans worked hard to restore their lives and recover from the devastation of having been imprisoned without due process and without having been charged with any crimes. Many did not want to talk about their experiences. Nisei became notorious for keeping their wartime experiences from their sansei children. However, it is the sansei generation who would fight for their rights, and the rights of their elders, to be recognized and treated as fully American.

The social and political climate during the postwar period was one of civil rights and ethnic pride. While the JACL was disparaged for cooperating with the U.S. government in all of their policies during World War II, lawyers and lobbyists for the JACL worked diligently to overturn laws banning interracial marriage, legalizing segregation, and restricted rights to citizenship and immigration based on race. The end of race-based immigration quotas following the passage of the 1965 Immigration Act allowed immigration from Japan to be restored; yet the number of new Japanese immigrating to the United States remained low due to a booming postwar economy in Japan. Those Japanese who did immigrate to the United States after the war often came because of family ties, such as marriage to a U.S. soldier, and became the first generation of Japanese immigrants no longer barred from naturalized citizenship due to racial discrimination and restrictions.

From the late 1960s through the 1970s, the JACL, the National Coalition for Redress/Reparations, the National Council for Japanese American Redress (NCJAR), and Japanese American politicians such as Senator Daniel Inouye, Senator Spark Matsunaga, Congressman Norman Mineta, and Congressmen Robert Matsui, lawyers, and activists worked unstintingly to achieve redress for Japanese Americans interned during the war. Some, like the NCJAR, sought redress through the courts, while others lobbied Congress. On April 20, 1988, after years of hard work, the U.S. Senate passed the Civil Rights Act by a vote of 69–27 (Daniels et al. 1992, 221). The act acknowledged that the U.S. government had committed a grave injustice against all those who were interned. Each surviving individual received a tax-free payment of $20,000 as a token payment for the losses incurred because of their internment. Some people returned the checks out of protest, arguing that money could never repay them for all that they had suffered and lost. One of the most significant outcomes of redress was the resurgence of stories about internment camp experience from the Nisei generation. Oral history projects boomed as people began talking more openly about what really happened during the war, including conflicts over the draft resisters, the loyalty questionnaire, those who answered "no-no" to the loyalty questionnaire, those who renounced their citizenship, and about the collaboration between the JACL and the government. Having achieved redress, many Japanese Americans felt vindicated and could finally tell their stories to children and to the public without feeling shame or guilt. As well, the redress campaign brought the generations together.

NOTE

1. A later version of Question 27 asked Japanese American women if they were willing to serve in the Women's Auxiliary Army Corps or the Army Nurse Corps. And a narrower version of Question 28 asked Issei if they would obey "the laws of the United States" and not "interfere with the war effort."

REFERENCES

Burgan, Michael. *The Japanese American Internment: Civil Liberties Denied*. Minneapolis, MN: Compass Point Books, 2007.
Chan, Sucheng. *Asian Americans: An Interpretive History*. New York: Twayne, 1991.
Chin, Frank. *Born in the USA: A Story of Japanese America, 1889–1947*. Lanham, MD: Rowman & Littlefield Publishers, 2002.
Coombs, F. Alan. "Congressional Opinion and War Relocation, 1943." In *Japanese Americans: From Relocation to Redress*, edited by Roger Daniels, Sandra Taylor, Harry Kitano, and Leonard Arrington. Seattle: University of Washington Press, 1992.
Daniels, Roger. *Asian America: Chinese and Japanese in the United States since 1850*. Seattle: University of Washington Press, 1988.
Daniels, Roger. *History of Indian Immigration to the United States: An Interpretative Essay*. New York: Asia Society, 1989.
Daniels, Roger. *Prisoners without Trial: Japanese Americans in World War II*. New York: Hill and Wang, 2004.
Daniels, Roger, Sandra Taylor, Harry Kitano, and Leonard Arrington, eds. *Japanese Americans: From Relocation to Redress*. Seattle: University of Washington Press, 1992.
Easton, Stanley, and Lucien Ellington. "Japanese Americans." *Multicultural America*, 2011. http://www.everyculture.com/multi/Ha-La/Japanese-Americans.html (accessed June 11, 2014).
Estate of Tetsubumi Yano. Supreme Court of California. Sac. No. 3191. https://casetext.com/case/estate-of-tetsubumi-yano#.VBCLN2O_6pQ (accessed September 10, 2014).
Fryer, Heather. "The Japanese American Experience: History and Culture." In *Asian American History and Culture: An Encyclopedia*, edited by Huping Ling and Allan Austin. Armonk, NY: M. E. Sharpe, 2010.
Fuchs, Lawrence H. *The American Kaleidoscope: Race, Ethnicity, and the Civic Culture*. Middletown, CT: Wesleyan University Press, 1990.
Gardiner, C. Harvey. *Pawns in a Triangle of Hate: The Peruvian Japanese and the United States*. Seattle: University of Washington Press, 1981.

Gesensway, Deborah, and Mindy Roseman. *Beyond Words: Images from America's Concentration Camps*. Ithaca, NY: Cornell University Press, 1988.

Haney López, Ian. *White by Law: The Legal Construction of Race*. New York: New York University Press, 1996.

Harth, Erica. *Last Witnesses: Reflections on the Wartime Incarceration of Japanese Americans*. New York: Palgrave Macmillan, 2001.

Hawaii Nikkei History Editorial Board, compiler. *Japanese Eyes, American Heart: Personal Reflections of Hawaii's World War II Nisei Soldiers*. Honolulu, HI: Tendai Educational Foundation, 1998.

Hayashi, Brian Masaru. *Democratizing the Enemy: the Japanese American Internment*. Princeton, NJ: Princeton University Press, 2004.

Inada, Fusao, ed. *Only What We Could Carry: The Japanese American Internment Experience*. Berkeley, CA: Heyday Books, 2000.

Jeffers, H. Paul. *Command of Honor: General Lucian Truscott's Path to Victory in World War II*. New York: Penguin Books, 2008.

Kimball, Richard, and Barney Noel. *Native Sons of the Golden West*. Charleston, SC: Arcadia, 2005.

Kurashige, Lon. *Japanese American Celebration and Conflict: A History of Ethnic Identity and Festival, 1934–1990*. Berkeley: University of California Press, 2002.

Nakasone, Ronald, ed. *Okinawan Diaspora*. Honolulu: University of Hawai'i Press, 2002.

Odo, Franklin, ed. *The Columbia Documentary History of the Asian American Experience*. New York: Columbia University Press, 2002.

Okada, John. *No-No Boy*. Seattle: University of Washington Press, 1976.

Okihiro, Gary Y. *Cane Fires: The Anti-Japanese Movement in Hawai'i, 1865–1945*. Philadelphia: Temple University Press, 1991.

Okihiro, Gary Y. *Island World: A History of Hawai'i and the United States*. Berkeley: University of California Press, 2008.

Okihiro, Gary Y. *Pineapple Culture: A History of the Tropical and Temperate Zones*. Berkeley: University of California Press, 2009.

Okihiro, Gary Y., and David Drummond. "The Concentration Camps and Japanese Economic Losses in California Agriculture, 1900–1942." In *Japanese Americans: From Relocation to Redress*, edited by Roger Daniels, Sandra Taylor, Harry Kitano, and Leonard Arrington. Seattle: University of Washington Press, 1992.

Street, Richard S. *Beasts of the Field: A Narrative History of California Farmworkers, 1769–1913*. Stanford, CA: Stanford University Press, 2004.

Takaki, Ronald T. "Ethnicity and Class in Hawaii: The Plantation Labor Experience, 1835–1920." In *Labor Divided: Race and Ethnicity in United States Labor Struggles, 1835–1960*, edited by Robert Asher and Charles Stephenson. Albany: State University of New York Press, 1990.

Takaki, Ronald T. *Pau Hana: Plantation Life and Labor in Hawaii*. Honolulu: University of Hawai'i Press, 1983.

Takaki, Ronald T. *Strangers from a Different Shore: A History of Asian Americans*. Rev. ed. Boston: Little, Brown, 1989.

Tateishi, John. *And Justice for All: An Oral History of the Japanese Detention Camps*. Seattle: University of Washington Press, 1984.

Togo, Kazuhiko. "The Contemporary Implications of the Russo-Japanese War: A Japanese Perspective." In *The Treaty of Portsmouth and Its Legacies*, edited by Steven Ericson and Allen Hockley. Lebanon, NH: Dartmouth College Press, 2008.

Toji, Dean S. "The Rise of the Nikkei Generation." In *The New Face of Asian Pacific America: Numbers, Diversity and Change in the 21st Century*, edited by Eric Lai and Dennis Arguelles. San Francisco: AsianWeek, 2003.

Zhao, Xiaojian. *Asian American Chronology: Chronologies of the American Mosaic*. Santa Barbara, CA: ABC-CLIO, 2009.

_____ *Chapter 3* _____

Koreans in America

Americans of Korean descent, or *hangukgye migugin*, come from the Choson, or "land of morning clam." Korea is a peninsular country whose history dates back four millennia. Korea is contiguous to the northeastern corner of China and is surrounded by Russia, China, and Japan. As such, Korea's history for centuries is marked by invasions by neighboring countries. For much of the late sixteenth, seventeenth, and eighteenth centuries, Korea sealed itself off from the outside world and was dubbed by Westerners as the "Hermit Kingdom." This period of isolation was a period of relative peace and calm.

By the late nineteenth century, internal problems, a weakening government, and international colonial pressures dragged the hermit out of its shell. An increasingly vulnerable Korean Court sought to fend off the expansionist advances of foreign envoys and their warships beginning in the 1860s, but to no avail. Japan used "gunboat" diplomacy to coerce Korea into signing the Treaty of Kanghwa of 1876. The United States, with the diplomatic support of China, convinced the Korean Court to sign the Treaty of Chemulpo of 1882, which stipulated that "there shall be perpetual peace and friendship between the President of the United States and the King of Choson (Korea) and the citizens and subjects of their respective governments. If other powers deal unjustly or oppressively with either government, the other will exert good offices, on being informed of the case, to bring about an amicable arrangement, thus showing their friendly feelings" (quoted in L. Kim 2003, 174). The treaty established diplomatic relations between Korea and the United States, opening the way for Korean immigration to Hawai'i at the turn of the century that was fueled by Japanese colonization (I. Kim 2004, 14–15).

FACTORS OF KOREAN MIGRATION

Following on the heels of Chinese and Japanese immigration to the United States, Korean immigrants were similar and different in several ways. They were fewer in numbers: compared to the 50,000 Chinese who arrived between 1853 and 1900, and the 18,000 Japanese who arrived between 1885 and 1907, approximately 7,200 Koreans arrived between 1903 and 1905. Then, an additional 2,600 arrived between 1905 and 1924, 600 of whom were political refugees and students who were involved in the anti-Japanese independence movement. Similar to the Chinese and Japanese immigrants before them, Korean immigrants did not have the intentions of permanently settling in the United States (Choy 1979, 77).

The history of Korean immigration to the United States developed in three waves. The first wave unfolded in two phases. The first phase occurred between 1903 and 1905 and consisted primarily of male laborers for the plantations of Hawai'i; in total, roughly 7,226 laborers arrived (I. Kim 2004, 13). Following on their heels were 1,100 "picture brides"—Korean brides who were brought to the United States in arranged marriages through the exchange of pictures, from 1910 to 1924 (Park 1997, 8). The second wave unfolded from 1951 to 1964, during the post–Korean War period. In total, 14,027 Koreans arrived; they consisted of young Korean women married to American service personnel, their children, and Korean War orphans —many Amerasians fathered by American servicemen—adopted by American families (S. Kang 2002, 46; Park 1997, 8). This included a small number of students and professional workers. The third wave occurred as a result of the passage of the Immigration Act of 1965 and consisted mainly of Korean immigrants who came over for "family reunification."

First Wave

Similar to the Chinese and Japanese immigrants before them, Korean immigrants were recruited as laborers to work on the sugar plantations of Hawai'i. Korean immigration was pushed by several factors. From 1888 to 1889, Korea suffered from a devastating drought that caused a great famine that lasted until 1902 (L. Kim 2001, 28). Additionally, modernizing policies of the Korean officials of the Yi Dynasty outraged many peasants. Lili Kim documents that Korean men protested the requirement to cut off their "top-knots" and wear Western clothing, proclaiming that "they would rather cut off their heads than cut off their hair" (2001, 28). Hyung June Moon notes that between 1901 and 1902, the situation in Korea was dire because of famine, drought, flood, and various epidemics (1976, 43–44). The Korean government could not resolve, nor did it want to solve, the social and economic problems that plagued it. Therefore, when Horace N. Allen, a

Presbyterian missionary and medical doctor who entered Korea in October 1884, suggested allowing Koreans to immigrate to Hawai'i for work, the emperor and the Korean officials listened (Moon 1976, 44–46).

Allen found favor with the Korean royal family because he successfully treated the prince well. This resulted in the Korean Court treating Christian missionaries well, and eventually Christianity's spread among Koreans. Allen visited the United States in 1902 while serving as American minister to Korea. While heading back to Korea, Allen stopped in San Francisco and Honolulu and met with representatives of the Hawaiian Sugar Planters Association (HSPA). Allen would become the plantation owners' chief ally in recruiting laborers from Korea (L. Kim 2003, 173). Allen met with HSPA representatives at their request: the purpose of the meeting was to discuss the HSPA's interest in recruiting Koreans because, by then, Japanese workers, who comprised two-thirds of the total labor force in the islands, had become militant and were engaging in work stoppages and spontaneous strikes. Andrew Lind argues that the plantation owners recognized "that the desired control over the work force could be more readily exercised if it did not consist exclusively of a single ethnic group" (1982, 13). Thus, importing Koreans would offset what plantation owners called the Japanese "labor monopoly" (Chan 1990, xl). Allen agreed to assist the HSPA in recruiting Korean laborers as a way to repay a favor to George Nash, governor of Ohio, who lobbied for him to get the ministerial post. Additionally, Governor Nash's stepson, David W. Deshler, operated a number of enterprises in Japan and Korea, with whom Allen had acquaintance (Patterson 1988, 27). Wayne Patterson notes that "Allen's enthusiasm was hardly surprising, as his entire diplomatic career in Korea had been devoted to obtaining franchises for American businessmen" (1988, 21). In a letter to Governor Sanford B. Dole of Hawai'i, Allen discussed the benefits of hiring Korean laborers, saying, "The Koreans are a patient, hard-working, docile race; easy to control from their long habit of obedience" (cited in L. Kim 2001, 27). In another letter to Doe, Allen added that Korean laborers are a more "teachable race than the Chinese" (cited in L. Kim 2001, 27).

Upon Allen's return to Korea, he lobbied Emperor Kojong and secured an "emigration franchise" for David Deshler. Allen played on Kojong's nationalism, saying that since the Americans wanted Korean workers and not Japanese (or Chinese) workers, Korea would gain new international prestige. Additionally, Kojong agreed because famine stalked several northern provinces in 1902 (Yans-McLaughlin 1990, 49). Deshler setup a bank, the East-West Development Company, in which the HSPA would be the sole depositor to lend money to the immigrants because they would need to have money—$50—in their possession as proof that they were free immigrants, and not contract laborers, upon their arrival in Hawai'i. Hawai'i became annexed by the United States in 1900; thus it had to observe the prohibition against importing contract laborers, which was outlawed since 1885 (L. Kim 2001, 32). Deshler established branch offices throughout major port cities— Inchon, Mokpo, Pusan, Masan, Wonsan, Chinampo, Seoul, and Pyongyang (Moon 1976, 47). The company published advertisements listing the reasons for emigrating to Hawai'i:

WE HEREBY ANNOUNCE THE FOLLOWING BY THE ORDER OF THE
TERRITORIAL GOVERNMENT OF HAWAII, U.S.A.

1. We announce that we are pleased to offer various benefits to those who want to go to the Hawaiian islands by themselves or with families.
2. The climate in Hawaii is temperate and delightful throughout the year. So it will please everyone.
3. School education is very liberal and every island has an educational system in order to teach English, free of charge.
4. For the farmers, it is very easy to find jobs throughout any season and especially for those who are healthy and well-conducted, there are steady jobs available and (all persons) shall be protected by law.
5. Wages shall be $15.00 per month by American gold (30.00 yen by Japanese gold or 57.00 won by Korean money) and working hours will be ten hours everyday except Sundays.
6. Lodging, fuel, water and medical expenses will be provided by the employers. (Cited in Moon 1976, 47–48; see also Yi 2007, 42)

At first, few Koreans responded to the recruitment efforts. Then, a Methodist missionary, Reverend George Heber Jones, persuaded members of his congregation in Inchon that life for them as Christians would be "more pleasant in Hawai'i, because it was a Christian land" (Yans-McLaughlin 1990, 49). "Another missionary, Homer Hulbert, who published the *Korea Review*, also urged Koreans to emigrate in the pages of his magazine" (Yans-McLaughlin 1990, 49). Half of the Korean immigrants who left in December 1902 were from Jones's church. The first group to arrive was the 102 Koreans—56 men, 21 women, and 25 children—aboard the USS *Gaelic*, a U.S. merchant ship, on January 13, 1903. By 1905, there were 7,843 Koreans in Hawai'i—6,701 men, 677 women, and 465 children under 14 years of age (Yang 1978, 16).

The first wave of Korean laborers who emigrated between 1903 and 1905 were primarily young men. They were mostly brought in as strikebreakers to replace Japanese workers who demanded better wages "after they had served their time as contract laborers" (Park 1997, 9). Additionally, 1,000 were recruited to work in the henequen plantations of Mexico (Chan 1990, xxxix). As a result of the missionaries' role in the recruitment of

Korean laborers, nearly 40 percent who emigrated to Hawai'i were converts to Protestant Christianity. The class origin of these early Koreans is unclear; a few came from the *yangban* (elite class), but the majority seemed to have been peasants, former soldiers, artisans, urban workers, and unemployed men (Park 1997, 9; Patterson 1988, 103–33).

Life and labor on the plantations was back-breaking, closely regulated, and long as Korean plantation worker, Hyung-soon Kim describes: "We were treated no better than cows or horses. ... Every worker was called by number, never by name. During working hours, nobody was allowed to talk, smoke or even stretch his back. A foreman kept his eyes on his workers at all times. When he found anyone violating working regulations, he whipped the violator without mercy" (Takaki 1983, 74). According to Yong-ho Ch'oe, on average, they worked 60 hours a week: Their work in the fields started at 6:00 a.m. and ended at 4:30 p.m., with a 30-minute lunch break. Most of the Korean male laborers worked as field hands and received 65 cents a day in 1905, which increased to 73 cents in 1910 (Ch'oe 2007, 23). Korean plantation workers in Hawai'i were typically "contracted" for terms of three to five years with a single plantation owner to pay back the costs of recruitment and passage to the United States. The owners segregated and paid field laborers differential wages according to "race," pitting one group against another in a dual wage system. To keep up their spirits, Korean laborers wrote traditional poetry and sang folk songs while working in the fields, describing the terrible conditions of labor and overbearing bosses in a foreign tongue that overseers could not understand. Like other Asian workers, they had no real opportunities to advance because only whites could hold positions of power and authority.

Due to the harsh working conditions on the plantations, Korean laborers did not stay at the plantations for very long. Between 1903 and 1907, over a thousand Korean laborers immigrated from Hawai'i to the mainland United States. In 1905, the movement of Koreans from Hawai'i to the mainland ended abruptly. There are several reasons for this: first, the Korean government stopped emigration because reports indicate Koreans were being mistreated in Mexico; second, the Japanese government pressured Korea to stop sending Korean laborers to the islands because they were used as scabs against the Japanese; and last, Koreans were racialized as being the same as the Japanese, and thus they inherited much of the anti-Japanese sentiment prevalent on the mainland. Thus, on March 14, 1907, President Theodore Roosevelt issued Executive Order 589, based on the Gentlemen's Agreement, prohibiting the "movement of Oriental immigrants from Hawaii to the American mainland" (Patterson 1988, 174). Through the Gentlemen's Agreement, Japan agreed to stop issuing passports to laborers who wanted to migrated to the United States and Hawai'i; Koreans were impacted because they traveled with Japanese passports.

By 1910, nearly one-third of the male laborers left Hawai'i for the mainland. Some of them were able to establish small businesses, such as grocery stores, laundry shops, vegetable and fruit shops, and barber shops. On the mainland, Korean immigrants primarily resided in agricultural towns throughout California—Riverside, Lompoc, Oxnard, Redlands, Fresno, and Bakersfield (Moon 1976, 93). During this period, roughly 200 Koreans were residing in San Francisco, with 60 in Los Angeles, and working as domestics. Some moved further inland to Utah to work in the copper mines, or Colorado and Wyoming to work in the coal mines, and to Arizona and Nevada to work on the railroads. Some moved north to Alaska and found employment in the salmon fisheries. There were also some, 1,300 who returned to Korea (Patterson 1988, 173).

Life and labor for Koreans on the mainland were just as difficult as it was on the plantations of Hawai'i. Many of the Korean laborers, 60 to 80, labored and boarded together under a Korean labor "boss" who also ran a Korean hotel (Moon 1976, 105–6). While working in the agricultural fields of California, they lived in dilapidated old Chinese quarters that were segregated from the white communities. By 1912, Korean emigration resumed. During the 35 years of Japanese colonial rule, few Korean political refugees and students immigrated to the United States. By 1924, 541 Koreans were living in the United States as political refugees.

Although the Korean immigrants carried aspirations of striking it rich and returning to Korea, they remained in the United States. Two factors compounded this development: One, they were exploited on the plantations and were not able to save money as they had hoped; and Secondly, Korea became a Japanese colony.

Korea and Japanese Colonization

Japan's interest in Korea goes back to 1876, when Korea was forced to sign the Treaty of Kanghwa that opened up Korea for Japan's commercial interest (Y. Lee 1986, 13). In 1894, Japan sent military forces into Korea to quell an antiforeign revolt, which provoked a war with China. The Sino-Japanese War (1894–1895) ensued, and China was defeated. During this time, Korea's traditional ally, China, was a protectorate of several Western imperialist powers. After China's defeat in the Sino-Japanese War, Korea sought support from Czarist Russia to fend off Japan. But when Russia fell to Japan in the Russo-Japanese War (1904–1905), Korea was left without allies. After Japanese victory, Horace Allen, at the time, a U.S. minister to Korea, urged President Theodore Roosevelt to intervene to prevent Japanese colonization of Korea. Roosevelt ignored the request on the grounds that Japanese occupation of Korea would prevent Russian expansion elsewhere (Patterson and Conroy 1986, 5–6).

With its victory in the Russo-Japanese War of 1905, Japan made Korea its protectorate and placed a Japanese resident-general in Seoul, which deprived Korea of the right to supervise domestic and international policies (Togo 2008, 165). "The new executive head possessed sweeping powers to supervise Japanese officials and advisers in Korea, intervene directly in Korean decision making, issue regulations enforceable by imprisonment or fines, and use Japanese troops to maintain law and order" (Dickinson 2008, 373). The United States and Japan came to an understanding, in what is known as the Taft Katsura Agreement of July 29, 1905, that the United States would recognize Japan's interests in Korea in exchange for Japan's recognition of U.S. interests in the Philippines (Togo 2008, 165–66). The Portsmouth Treaty of September 5, 1905, ended the Russo-Japanese War and Russia's bid for influence on the Korean Peninsula. By 1910, Japan deposed the last monarch of Korea's centuries-old Choson (or Yi) dynasty and annexed Korea as a Japanese colony as part of the Treaty of Japan (Dickinson 2008, 373).

The effects of natural disasters and famine leading up to the wars and the impact of Japanese colonialism compounded the plight of the Korean people: uprooted thousands of Koreans migrated to cities and port areas in search of employment; many of them were also recruited to work on the sugar plantations of Hawai'i, as part of a divide-and-control strategy. However, by April 1905, the Korean government halted Korean emigration (Patterson 2000, 5). Several factors precipitated this policy: (1) word got back that Korean immigrants were treated poorly in Mexico and Hawai'i; (2) Japan pressured Korea to stop emigration because Korean laborers were used as scabs against striking Japanese plantation workers; and (3) the de facto Japanese protectorate wanted to stop "anti-Japanese colonial resistance" activities among the overseas Koreans (Park 1997, 9).

Korean Independence Movement

Prior to these first waves of immigration, a very small number of Korean intellectuals had already set foot in the United States. So Jae (or Chae) Pil, also known as Philip Jaisohn, arrived in 1885 and, in 1890, became the first Korean to receive U.S. citizenship. Jaisohn returned to Korea in 1896 and formed the Independence Club, *Tongnip Hyophoe* (Matray 2005, 40). Ahn Chang-ho arrived in 1899, followed by Syngman Rhee (Yi Sung-man) and Park Yong Man in 1904. These individuals and their fellow expatriates were prominent advocates of Korea's modernization and leaders in a vibrant overseas Korean independence movement. "Far from the watchful eyes of the colonizers, Koreans living in China, Cuba, Russia, Mexico, Hawai'i and the continental United States mobilized to fight the colonial powers of Japan" (L. Kim 2001, 42). Among the early Korean pioneers in Hawai'i and the U.S. mainland, "the most devastating experience of their immigrant lives was Japan's colonization of their beloved homeland in 1910" (L. Kim 2003, 172). The first wave of Korean migrants wanted to return to Korea as soon as they saved enough money, but the news and reality of Japanese colonization changed them to "accidental settlers." As a result of Japanese colonization of Korea, Korean immigrants in America felt "orphaned," as subjects of a "stateless" country with "no legitimate government to protest on their behalf" which left them "vulnerable to abuses by their employers and other nationals" (L. Kim 2003, 173).

Although relatively small in size, the overseas Korean community quickly established many organizations, albeit short-lived, that explicitly supported an independent Korea. For example, between 1905 and 1907, Koreans living in Hawai'i founded the Mutual Aid Society, the Self-Strengthening Society, and the Young and Old Alliance (I. Kim 2004, 23–24; L. Kim 2003, 174). On the mainland, branches of the organizations founded on Hawai'i were established, along with new ones, such as the Mutual Salvation Society founded in New York; the Newly Rising Alliance, founded in Seattle; and the All-Together Protecting the Nation Society, founded in San Francisco (H. Kim 2004, 66; L. Kim 2003, 174). Many of the organizations met in Korean Christian churches. They published newspapers and wrote about nationalist struggles in the United States and Korea, keeping alive the spirit of independence. Koreans mobilized and coalesced at these political organizations to cultivate Korean nationalism and fight against Japanese imperialism (Patterson 2000, 54). As such, Richard Kim argues, "Korean nationalism was ironically central to the Americanization of Korean immigrants" (2011, 6). Often overlooked, Korean women also played an important role in the independence movement, as Anne Soon Choi notes:

The efforts of Korean women in the independence movement must be recognized. Indeed, as in many other political and social movements in the United States, women served as the "rank and file" of nationalist organizations, especially in fundraising and the daily maintenance of such organizations. Thus, for young women ... older Korean immigrant women served as models for emulation and as agents of encouragement. In the 1920s, organizations such as the *Taehan Puinhoe* (Korean Women's Association), *Sinmyong Puinhoe* (Sinmyong Women's Association), *Taehan Puin Kujehoe* (Korean Ladies Relief Society), *Youngnam Puinhoe* (Youngnam Women's Association), and the Korean Young Women's Christian Association involved nearly all adult women in the islands. (Choi 2004, 145)

In December 1907, as a means to unite the various organizations, the United Korean Society was created (H. Kim 2004, 66). Two years later, in San Francisco, the Korean National Association was founded, and it elected Ahn Chang-ho its first president. Although there was an attempt to unite the various organizations, the Korean independence movement in the United States was divided into three fractions. Pak Yong-man represented the activist and militant approach; Syngman Rhee emphasized education and diplomacy; while Ahn Chang-ho called for the development of patriotic leadership (I. Kim 2004, 24–26).

Rhee and Pak began as friends. As the editor of the *Korean National Herald*, Pak invited Rhee to join the Hawaiian chapter of the Korean National Association in 1912 (I. Kim 2004, 24). Rhee received a doctoral degree in 1910 from Princeton University and had connections with U.S. officials (H. Kim 2004, 71–75). As such, Rhee firmly believed that education and diplomacy was the most pragmatic approach to secure Korean independence. On the other hand, Pak founded Kundan, a military academy, in 1914 and believed that military training and resistance was the key to fight Japan. Rhee and Pak engaged in smear campaigns against each other, whereby Rhee spread rumors that Pak was a traitor and Pak accused Rhee of mishandling the Korean National Association's finances. In 1919, Rhee and his contingent formed their own organization, the Tongihoe, or Comrade Society. The Rhee-Pak rivalry ended tragically when Rhee and his followers branded Pak a Bolshevik and petitioned immigration service to deport him on the grounds that he was a communist. Pak escaped deportation through his connections but was assassinated by "a Korean fanatic" on October 17, 1928 (L. Kim 2001, 54). Although the Korean independence organizations differed in tactical approaches in fighting Japanese imperialism, they were unified in their hatred of Japan and their desire to see Korea liberated (Moon 1976, 304).

Durham W. Stevens's Assassination

The assassination of Durham W. Stevens galvanized the Korean independence movement in the United States and publicized it to the American public. Stevens was an American diplomat who was appointed to the State Department in 1873; in 1884, he took a position as adviser to the Japan's Ministry of Foreign Affairs. Stevens's mission was to reassure American business concerns about Japan's colonization of Korea. On March 20, 1908, while traveling from Korea to Washington, D.C., Stevens made a stop in San Francisco, where he gave an interview with a *San Francisco Chronicle* reporter. In the interview, Stevens said that the Korean people benefitted greatly by Japanese colonizers and that they were incapable of self-rule. Korea was benefitting from Japanese occupation, just as the Philippines was benefitting from U.S. occupation, Stevens added. Moreover, Stevens said, "the peasants have welcomed the Japanese, while the official class has not, but even the officials are beginning to see that the only hope for the country lies in a reorganization of the old institutions" (*San Francisco Chronicle*, March 21, 1908, cited in Moon 1976, 333). A delegation of four Korean immigrants went to the Fairmont Hotel to meet with Stevens. They asked Stevens to take back his statement: not only did Stevens refused, he went on to reiterate the great work Japan was doing for Korea.

On March 23, 1908, two Korean immigrants, Chang In-Hwan and Chon Myong-won, confronted Stevens in front of the Ferry Building, and one of them, Chang In-Hwan, shot Stevens three times. In an interview, Chang In-Hwan proudly stated, "Stevens is a bad man. ... I love my country. I am a patriot and I shot Stevens because I think he is a traitor. ... I am a student here. ... I went to night school here. ... I do not care what happens to me. I hope I killed Stevens" (*Kongnip Sinmun*, March 25, 1908, cited in Moon 1976, 344). Stevens died on March 26 at Harbor hospital. Both Chang In-Hwan and Chon Myong-won were arrested and arraigned for murder.

In a display of solidarity and Korean patriotism, Koreans from many organizations in Hawai'i and across the United States, including Koreans from Mexico, Siberia, China, and Japan, donated $7,390 for their defense funds (L. Kim 2001, 47). Chang In-Hwan was convicted of second-degree murder and received a 25-year sentence, but he was released from San Quentin after serving 10 years for good behavior. Chon Myong-won was released without a trial due to a lack of evidence that the assassination was a conspiracy. The Korean independence movement in the United States thus gained national attention among the American public.

Koreans and Anti-Japanese Sentiments

Koreans residing in the United States from 1903 to 1945 largely harbored anti-Japanese sentiments (Choi 2003–2004, 69–70). Korean anti-Japanese sentiments were expressed in boycotts of Japanese businesses, volunteering to break Japanese labor strikes, a taboo on establishing relationships with people of Japanese descent in public or private, and establishing their own independent Korean identity (Moon 1976, 282–322). The animosity toward Japanese people was observable to outsiders as documented in 1930 by Charles K. Ferguson, who wrote, "The one glaring important fact about the Koreans in Los Angeles is that singly and collectively they hate the Japanese; all Japanese. They boycott them in America; they work against them at every available opportunity in the East; and they are determined about the independence of their homeland. This issue of independence enters into all Korean thinking" (cited in Moon 1976, 283). Anti-Japanese sentiments and behaviors among Koreans residing in the United States was refueled as a result of the March 1, 1919, Korean Independence Movement (H. Kim 2004, 67–68). It was the most notable and bloodiest resistance effort in Korea. Thirty-three Korean nationalists signed the Declaration of Korean Independence, and more than a million Koreans participated in a peaceful demonstration and march, shouting "Teahan Toknip Manse," "Long Live Korean Independence" (D. Kim and Ch'oe 2007, 123). Japanese colonial officials responded brutally. Between March and December, over 7,500 Koreans were killed and 15,000 injured, with nearly 45,000 arrested. An independent Korean provisional government was secretly established in Seoul in April 1919, and it elected Rhee its president (H. Kim 2004, 68).

Among the Koreans who arrived to the United States was a strong sense of nationalism because they were actively engaged in fighting Japanese colonialism at home. Similar to the Chinese, the majority of Korean immigrants were "bachelors," and some were "married bachelor," known as *chong gak*. Sucheng Chan notes that since nearly 10 percent of the immigrants were women, and 8 percent were children, this indicated that Koreans were not sojourners, but rather settlers who intended to stay (1990, xlii). Under Japanese colonial rule, which lasted until 1945, the only Koreans legally allowed to migrate to the United States were roughly 1,100 Korean "picture brides" in 1910–1924 (W. Kim 1971, 22–23).

Picture Brides

The Korean male laborers who immigrated to the United States in 1903–1905 relied on picture brides as a means to establish their families. Their arrangements were made by a marriage broker back in Korea. The first known Korean picture bride, Choe Sara, migrated to Hawai'i on November 28, 1910, and became Mrs. Yi Nae-su (Moon 1976, 123). Picture brides endured stricter and more comprehensive immigration inspection. Immigrant agents asked them questions concerning their moral character, their future husband-to-be, and his length of time in the United States. After passing the interrogation, they waited for their fiancé to go "claim" them: here, too, they would be asked questions to corroborate the information made by the picture brides. If both agreed, they would be married at the immigration station and have their photos taken (Moon 1976, 124).

The Korean picture brides were more literate and educated than their husbands. Their vision of life in Hawai'i was drastically different from the reality they would encounter. The shock and disappointment usually started with the first meeting when the picture brides met their long-awaited grooms who looked older—usually 15 to 20 years older than their photos. Working under the hot plantation sun did not help their appearance. The Korean laborers who did not have a decent suit were photographed in borrowed ones: A house servant might be photographed in front of a mansion, which would lead the bride to assume her future husband was a wealthy man (Moon 1976, 127). Some of their fiancés borrowed money for their brides' passage to America, and thus the brides immediately started to work alongside their husbands to pay off their debt.

Between 1910 and 1924, over 1,000 additional Koreans came to the United States as "picture brides." The picture bride phenomenon resulted from the U.S.-Japan "Gentleman's Agreement" of 1907–1908 that banned immigration of Japanese laborers to the United States (Park 1997, 9). This was the federal government's way of appeasing nativists in California from passing overtly anti-Japanese legislation because Japan was a raising superpower in Asia. Although it restricted the migration of unskilled Japanese laborers, it continued to allow their wives and family members to immigrate. Since Japan annexed Korea in 1910, Koreans were considered "Japanese nationals" and were thus able to bring their wives and children. The sugar barons of Hawai'i exploited this loophole with the belief that Korean workers with families would be better workers less prone to social vices and more inclined to settle down on the plantations rather than move away. Similarly, Koreans on the mainland were almost exclusively men, many of whom had left their wives and children back home. Unlike the Punjabi and Filipino immigrants, Korean men did not marry women of a different ethnic background. Antimiscegenation laws would have prohibited them from marrying white women, but they could have married Mexicans as the Punjabi and Filipino immigrants did. Hyung Moon suggests that this might be a result of the independence movement and the strong national patriotism that accompanied it (1976, 113). The immigration of the Korean picture brides did impact the early Korean American community as it signaled their shift from the sojourner to permanent settlers.

Koreans: Just Another Asian

Legislation that prevented the Chinese and Japanese immigrants from being fully American also affected Korean immigrants. The Alien Land Act of 1913 that prohibited aliens ineligible for citizenship from owning land was applied to Korean immigrants. The Naturalization Act of 1790 restricted U.S. citizenship rights to the "white race," which eliminated Asians. African Americans were protected under the Fourteenth Amendment, as were Mexicans who were born in territories seized by the United States after the Mexican-American War in 1848. Native Americans were able to obtain citizenship through the 1890 Indian Naturalization Act. A loophole in the Alien Land Law was corrected in 1920 when Californians voted to prohibit the leasing of land to Asian aliens altogether. The 1913 act restricted leasing land to three years. Chinese, Japanese, and Korean farmers operated on leased land, and, therefore, were not affected by the ownership clauses of the law, but were affected when leasing land was not an option. In response, some immigrant parents transferred ownership rights to their American-born children, who were legal U.S. citizens. Other states followed California's lead in passing restrictive land ownership laws that did not name any specific group of people by invoking the U.S. naturalization policies that discriminated against nonwhite immigrants: Arizona (1917); Washington, Missouri, Arkansas, and Louisiana (1921); New Mexico (1922); Oregon, Montana, and Idaho (1923); and Kansas (1925). Wyoming and Utah joined during World War II in 1942.

Korean American veteran Easurk Emsen Charr challenged Korean eligibility for naturalization in 1921 when he appealed to the District Court in Missouri concerning his application for U.S. citizenship based on his military service. In his autobiography, Charr says he remembers his "grand and glorious feeling ... that I was now an American soldier ... going to war alongside the Yankees. ... When I was all dressed up in my uniform, I looked and felt like a real American soldier. And wasn't I proud of myself!" (1996, 180–82). Historian Lucy Salyer notes, "The Selective Draft Act of 1917 required all men, whether alien or citizen, aged 21 to 31—by 1918 the requirement extended to those aged 18 to 45—to register with the Selective Service System. Almost 24 million men registered, of whom approximately 16 percent were noncitizens" (2004, 851). Many of the noncitizen soldiers were pressured to become naturalized citizens. In May 1918, the U.S. Congress made it possible for noncitizen soldiers to become naturalized by requiring that they demonstrate they are on "active duty" and had testaments from two superior officers of their loyalty to the United States (Salyer 2004, 852). This streamline process was not applied to all alien soldiers, as Charr's case reveals.

Although Charr served honorably in the U.S. military in the Army Medical Corps during World War I, his petition for naturalization was denied because the court declared Koreans are members of the "Mongol family" and were therefore ineligible for naturalization (Maeda 2009, 25). The Naturalization Act of 1906, as amended in 1918, provided military veterans the right to naturalization. The act allowed "any aliens" who enlisted and was expected to be honorably discharged the ability to gain citizenship without the need for a process of declaration of intent or proof of residency for the required period, but was restricted to only "free white persons and persons of African nativity or descent" to naturalize. In 1918, Congress allowed native-born Filipinos and Puerto Ricans with three years of military service to seek immediate naturalization because they were American nationals by virtue of being colonial subjects of the United States. The court acknowledged that Charr's personal qualifications were not in question but decided based on the existing statute.

Unlike the Chinese and Japanese who came from a limited locality, Korean immigrants originated from wider geographic regions. Whereas Chinese and Japanese immigrants were mostly lower-class farm laborers, the Koreans were mixed of lower class with little or no education to literate, educated upper-class Koreans, known as *yangban*. Their relatively small population in comparison to the Chinese and Japanese would mean that Koreans would not form ethnic enclaves (i.e., Chinatowns) and would therefore not be able to rely on an ethnic economy. Lastly, one significant difference, which was alluded to earlier, was that a sizable population of Koreans were converts to Protestant Christianity. Their attraction to Christianity, Wayne Patterson suggests, "indicates that they were more 'liberal' than most Koreans, having rejected to a certain extent many of the conservative tenets of Confucian Korean society in the late Choson period. This liberal nature helped them adapt more quickly to Western values" (Patterson 2000, 7).

THE KOREAN WAR AND THE SECOND WAVE

Korea was liberated from Japan on August 15, 1945, at the end of World War II, only to be divided at the 38th Parallel by the United States and the

The 7th Infantry Division attempts to neutralize enemy targets during the Korean War.

Soviet Union, leading to the emergence of two rival states on the Korean Peninsula—the U.S.-backed government of Syngman Rhee in the south and the Soviet-backed government of Kim Il Sung in the north. The newly divided competing governments both claimed authority over the entire peninsula. On June 25, 1950, the Soviet-backed Democratic People's Republic of Korea in the north launched a surprise attack on South Korea, which ignited a costly, bloody, three-year conflict known as the Korean War (1950–1953). The Korean War is often viewed as the "Forgotten War" because it is overshadowed by World War II and the Vietnam War. Three million civilians lost their lives during the three-year period (Kwon and Lee 2009, 12–13). Additionally, two million Korean troops were killed or severely injured in the battlefield. The Korea Red Cross reported that 10 million family members were separated; countless left homeless and orphaned. The war ended in a truce. No peace treaty has ever been signed, and to this day, Korea remains divided.

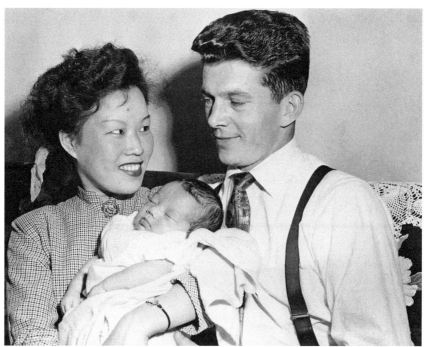

A Korean War vet claims another first. Sergeant Johnnie Morgan, who says he brought the first Korean war bride to the United States, claims another first with the birth of the first child born to a Korean bride and a GI father in the United States. Sergeant Morgan, stationed in Seattle, is shown with his wife Yoong Soon and their baby daughter Yvonne Arlene. (Bettmann/Corbis)

Korean War Brides

Immigration after the war was still highly restricted by U.S. laws. The largest groups to immigrate were those sponsored by U.S. citizens—Korean War brides and their dependants, and orphans. Between 1955 and 1977, roughly 13,000 Korean orphans—many were Amerasians—were adopted by American families: The number of war brides arriving in the United States between 1950 and 1975 is estimated at 28,205 (Hurh and Kim 1984, 49). By 1989, there were nearly 100,000 Korean War brides in the United States (Yuh 2002, 2). They followed their husbands and settled down to raise families in a strange new land, many still suffering from posttraumatic stress disorders resulting from the war. Many of the war brides were viewed as prostitutes and club hostesses by the Korean American community; hence they faced internal stigma and prejudice (Yuh 2002, 12–14). Additionally, they faced racism and prejudice from mainstream America. As a result, they formed their own community that provided them with social and cultural support (Yuh 2002, 188–221). Korean War brides played a central role in supporting their extended families and facilitating the growth of the Korean American population. War brides became American citizens and then sponsored their families. It is estimated that nearly half of all Korean Americans can attribute their immigration to the United States to a war bride.

Korean Adoptees

Approximately 200,000 Korean children to date have been adopted by families in the West, of which an estimated 150,000 were sent to the United States. Overseas adoption from Korea originally began as a rescue operation for Korean War orphans. Korean children were adopted primarily by white, middle-class families throughout the United States. Many of the adoptees were processed through the Oregon-based Holt Adoption Agency, which at first focused on Amerasian orphans but later became an important conduit for all kinds of Korean adoptions (E. Kim 2004, 180–81). Cut off from their culture and history, many struggled with identity issues in isolation, as Janine Bishop, a Korean American adoptee, recounts: "Many times I feel kind of detached from the rest of the family ... I guess that I hated feeling that I didn't belong. It's not that they made me feel I didn't belong, but I hated to think of them ever having to explain to people, like 'She's my cousin,' and people would go, 'Huh?' and they would have to say, 'Well, she's adopted' " (1996, 308). Today, Korean American adoptees are actively organizing to support each other (E. Kim 2004; Lee, Yoo, and Roberts 2004). The richly varied experiences of Korean adoptees growing up in the United States and coming to terms with the circumstances of their adoption are being revealed by adoptees in poetry, literature, documentary films, and educational forums. They have also form support groups such as the Korean American Adoptee and Adoptive Family Network, the Adopted Korean Connection, and so forth.

Compared to the first wave, second-wave Korean immigrants were demographically very different: they were mostly young women and their children. They were pushed and pulled largely due to the impact of the Korean War. The sex ratio is markedly different as well. During the first wave, the sex ratio was 10 Korean men to 1 Korean woman. In the post–Korean War era, the sex ratio was 1 male to 3.5 females (Hurh 2001, 1339). After World War II, a significant number of Korean students arrived in the United States, with 6,000 Korean students settling in the United States from 1945 to 1965.

REFERENCES

Abelmann, Nancy, and John Lie. *Blue Dreams: Korean Americans and the Los Angeles Riots*. Cambridge, MA: Harvard University Press, 1997.

Bishop, Janine. "Adopted." In *East to America: Korean American Life Stories*, edited by Elaine Kim and Eui-Young Yu. New York: New Press, 1996.

Chan, Sucheng. *Asian Americans: An Interpretive History*. New York: Twayne, 1991.

Chan, Sucheng. "Introduction." In *Quiet Odyssey: A Pioneer Korean Woman in America*, by Mary Paik Lee. Seattle: University of Washington Press, 1990.

Charr, Easurk Emsen. *The Golden Mountain: The Autobiography of a Korean Immigrant 1895–1960*. Edited and with an Introduction by Wayne Patterson. 2nd ed. Urbana: University of Illinois Press, 1996.

Cho, Grace. *Haunting the Korean Diaspora: Shame Secrecy, and the Forgotten War*. Minneapolis: University of Minnesota Press, 2008.

Ch'oe, Yong-ho. "The Early Korean Immigration: An Overview." In *From the Land of Hibiscus: Koreans in Hawai'i, 1903–1950*, edited by Yong-ho Ch'oe. Honolulu: University of Hawai'i Press, 2007.

Choi, Anne Soon. " 'Are They Koreaned Enough?' Generation and the Korean Independence Movement before World War II." *Amerasia Journal* 29:3 (2003–2004): 55–77.

Choi, Anne Soon. " 'Hawai'i Has Been My America:' Generation, Gender, and Korean Immigrant Experience in Hawai'i before World War II." *American Studies* 45:3 (Fall 2004): 139–55.

Choy, Bong Youn. *Koreans in America*. Washington, DC: Burnham Inc. Publishing, 1979.

Danico, Mary Yu. *The 1.5 Generation: Becoming Korean American in Hawai'i*. Honolulu: University of Hawai'i Press, 2004.

Dickinson, Frederick R. "Japanese Empire." In *Encyclopedia of the Age of Imperialism, 1800–1914*, edited by Carl C. Hodge. Westport, CT: Greenwood Press, 2008.

Dickinson, Frederick R. *War and National Reinvention: Japan in the Great War, 1914–1919*. Cambridge, MA: Harvard University Press, 1999.

Djun Kil Kim. *The History of Korea*. Westport, CT: Greenwood Press, 2005.

Eui-Young Yu, Peter Choe, and Sang Il Han. "Korean Population in the United States, 2000, Demographic Characteristics and Socio-Economic Status." *International Journal of Korean Studies* 6:1 (Spring–Summer 2002): 71–107.

Gwak, S. Sonya. *Be(com)ing Korean in the United States: Exploring Ethnic Identity Formation through Cultural Practices*. Amherst, NY: Cambria Press, 2008.

Houchins, Lee, and Chang-su Houchins. "The Korean Experience in America, 1903–1924." *Pacific Historical Review* 43:4 (November 1974): 548–75.

Hurh, Won Moo. *The Korean Americans*. Westport, CT: Greenwood Press, 1998.

Hurh, Won Moo. "Korean Immigrants." In *Multicultural America: An Encyclopedia of the Newest Americans*, edited by Ronald H. Bayor. Santa Barbara, CA: ABC-CLIO, 2011.

Hurh, Won Moo, and Kwang Chung Kim. *Korean Immigrants in America: A Structural Analysis of Ethnic Confinement and Adhesive Adaptation*. Cranbury, NJ: Fairleigh Dickinson University Press, 1984.

Ion, A. Hamish. *The Cross and the Rising Sun: The British Protestant Missionary Movement in Japan, Korea, and Taiwan, 1865–1945*. Vol. 2. Waterloo, Ontario, Canada: Wilfrid Laurier University Press, 1993.

Jo, Sunny. "The Making of KAD Nation," In *Outsiders Within*, edited by Jane Jeong Trenka, Julia Chinyere Oparah, and Sun Yung Shin. Cambridge, MA: Southend Press, 2006.

Kang, K. Connie. *Home Was the Land of Morning Calm: A Saga of a Korean-American Family*. Cambridge, MA: Da Capo Press, 1995.

Kang, S. Steve. *Unveiling the Socioculturally Constructed Multivoiced Self: Themes of Self Construction and Self Integration in the Narratives of Second-Generation Korean American Young Adults*. Lanham, MD: University Press of America, 2002.

Kim, Do-Hyung, and Yong-ho Ch'oe. "The March First Movement of 1919 and Koreans in Hawai'i." In *From the Land of Hibiscus: Koreans in Hawai'i, 1903–1950*, edited by Yong-ho Ch'oe. Honolulu: University of Hawai'i Press, 2007.

Kim, Elaine H., and Eui-Young Yu, eds. *East to America: Korean American Life Stories*. New York: New Press, 1996.

Kim, Eleana. "Korean Adoptees Role in the United States." In *Korean-Americans: Past, Present, and Future*, edited by Ilpyong J. Kim. Elizabeth, NJ: Hollym International Corp., 2004.

Kim, Han-Kyo. "The Korean Independence Movement in the United States: Syngman Rhee, An Ch'ang-Ho, and Pak Yong-Man." In *Korean-Americans: Past, Present, and Future*, edited by Ilpyong J. Kim. Elizabeth, NJ: Hollym International Corp., 2004.

Kim, Ilpyong J., ed. *Korean-Americans: Past, Present, and Future*. Elizabeth, NJ: Hollym International Corp., 2004.

Kim, Lili M. "Korean Independence Movement in Hawai'i and the Continental United States." In *Major Problems in Asian American History: Documents and Essays*, edited by Lon Kurashige and Alice Yang Murray. Boston: Houghton Mifflin Company, 2003.

Kim, Lili M. "The Pursuit of Imperfect Justice: The Predicament of Koreans and Korean Americans on the Homefront during World War II." PhD diss., University of Rochester, 2001.

Kim, Richard S. *The Quest for Statehood: Korean Immigrant Nationalism and U.S. Sovereignty, 1905–1945*. Oxford: Oxford University Press, 2011.

Kim, Warrant Y. *Koreans in America*. Seoul: P. Chin Chai Printing Co., 1971.

Kwon, Brenda L. *Beyond Ke'eaumoku: Koreans, Nationalism, and Local Culture in Hawai'i*. New York: Garland Publishing, 1999.

Kwon, Hyeyong, and Chanhaeng Lee. *Korean American History*. Los Angeles: Korean Education Center in Los Angeles, 2009.

Lee, Hyun Ah. "Korean Women in America: Gender-Role Attitude and Depression." PhD diss., University of Illinois at Urbana-Champaign, 2001.

Lee, Richard M., Hyung Chol Yoo, and Sara Roberts. "The Coming of Age of Korean Adoptees: Ethnic Identity Development and Psychological Adjustment." In *Korean-Americans: Past, Present, and Future*, edited by Ilpyong J. Kim. Elizabeth, NJ: Hollym International Corp., 2004.

Lee, Yur-Bok. "Korean-American Diplomatic Relations, 1882–1905." In *One Hundred Years of Korean-American Relations, 1882–1982*, edited by Yur-Bok Lee and Wayne Patterson. Tuscaloosa: University of Alabama Press, 1986.

Lee, Yur-Bok, and Wayne Patterson, eds. *One Hundred Years of Korean-American Relations, 1882–1982*. Tuscaloosa: University of Alabama Press, 1986.

Lind, Andrew W. "Assimilation in Rural Hawaii." *American Journal of Sociology* 45:2 (September 1939): 200–214.

Lind, Andrew W. "The Ghetto and the Slum." *Social Forces* 9:2 (December 1930): 206–15.

Lind, Andrew W. "Immigration to Hawaii." *Social Process in Hawaii* 29 (1982).

Maeda, Daryl J. *Chains of Babylon: The Rise of Asian America*. Minneapolis: University of Minnesota Press, 2009.

Matray, James I. *Korea Divided: The 38th Parallel and the Demilitarized Zone*. New York: Chelsea House Publishers, 2005.

Moon, Hyung June. "The Korean Immigrant in America: The Quest for Identity in the Formative Years." PhD diss., University of Nevada at Reno, 1976.

Odo, Franklin, ed. *The Columbia Documentary History of the Asian American Experience*. New York: Columbia University Press, 2002.

Park, Kyeyoung. *The Korean American Dream: Immigrants and Small Business in New York City*. Ithaca, NY: Cornell University Press, 1997.

Patterson, Wayne. *The Ilse: First-Generation Korean Immigrants in Hawai'i, 1903–1973*. Honolulu: University of Hawai'i Press, 2000.

Patterson, Wayne. *The Korean Frontier in America: Immigration to Hawai'i, 1896–1910*. Honolulu: University of Hawai'i Press, 1988.

Patterson, Wayne, and Hilary Conroy. "Duality and Dominance: A Century of Korean-American Relations." In *One Hundred Years of Korean-American Relations, 1882–1982*, edited by Yur-Bok Lee and Wayne Patterson. Tuscaloosa: University of Alabama Press, 1986.

Salyer, Lucy. "Baptism by Fire: Race, Military Service, and U.S. Citizenship Policy, 1918–1935." *Journal of American History* 91:3 (2004): 847–76.

Sunoo, Sonia Shinn. *Korean Picture Brides: 1903–1920: A Collection of Oral Histories*. Bloomington, IN: Xlibris Corporation, 2002.

Takaki, Ronald T. "Ethnicity and Class in Hawaii: The Plantation Labor Experience, 1835–1920." In *Labor Divided: Race and Ethnicity in United States Labor Struggles, 1835–1960*, edited by Robert Asher and Charles Stephenson. Albany: State University of New York Press, 1990.

Takaki, Ronald T. *Pau Hana: Plantation Life and Labor in Hawaii*. Honolulu: University of Hawai'i Press, 1983.

Takaki, Ronald T. *Strangers from a Different Shore: A History of Asian Americans*. Rev. ed. Boston: Little, Brown, 1989.

Togo, Kazuhiko. "The Contemporary Implications of the Russo-Japanese War: A Japanese Perspective." In *The Treaty of Portsmouth and Its Legacies*, edited by Steven Ericson and Allen Hockley. Lebanon, NH: Dartmouth College Press, 2008.

Tuan, Mia, and Jiannbin Lee Shiao. *Choosing Ethnicity, Negotiating Race: Korean Adoptees in America*. New York: Russell Sage Foundation, 2011.

Yang, Shara Lee. "75 Years of Progress for the Koreans in Hawaii." In *75th Anniversary of Korean Immigration to Hawaii*, edited by Samuel S. O. Son. Honolulu, HI: 75th Anniversary Publication Committee, 1978.

Yans-McLaughlin, Virginia. *Immigration Reconsidered: History, Sociology, and Politics*. Oxford: Oxford University Press, 1990.

Yuh, Ji-Yeon. *Beyond the Shadow of Camptown: Korean Military Brides in America*. New York: New York University Press, 2002.

_____ *Chapter 4* _____

Indians in America

Indian Americans, otherwise known as "Asian Indians," "South Asians," or "Eastern Indians," originate from India, Pakistan, Bangladesh, and Sri Lanka. The vast majority of Indian immigrants arrived in the United States during the late nineteenth and early twentieth centuries. Earlier, during the 1600s, Indian immigrants were brought over to the British American colony as indentured servants. After American independence from Britain, Indian immigrants entered the United States as maritime workers. By the 1880s, Indian traders arrived in the United States carrying silk, linens, spices, and other goods from India. American intellectuals were also interested in Indian religious traditions and philosophies: among them were Ralph Waldo Emerson and Henry David Thoreau. American enchantment with India reached its zenith when Swami Vivekananda, a fluent English-speaking Hindu monk, addressed the World Parliament of Religions in Chicago in 1893 (Hess 1969, 60–61). The interest he generated led to the establishment of "The Vedanta Society," which now has centers all across America. Perhaps as a result of the goodwill generated between the American and Indian peoples of this period, the American people shipped large quantities of food to India to help Indians endure the famine of 1897 caused by British colonial interest in cash crops instead of food crops. India had been colonized by Great Britain since 1857. Historian Gary Hess notes that the early Indian immigrants to Canada and by extension to the United States consisted of two groups: small entrepreneurs and unskilled laborers (1974, 578).

Indian immigration to the United States unfolded in two distinct waves. The first wave arrived in the late nineteenth century as a "by-product of Indian emigration to Canada" where they encountered discrimination and exclusionary policies that led them on a secondary migration to the United States (Hess 1969, 60). They came primarily from the Punjab (literally

An informal group portrait of immigrants from India, 1907. (Frederick C.
Howe/National Geographic Society/Corbis)

"the land of the five rivers") but included, to a lesser extent, Indians from
Bengal, Gujarat, and the United Provinces (the present state of Uttar Pra-
hesh) (Hess 1974, 578). The majority originate from the Doaba region of
the Punjab, north of the Sutlej River and east of the Beas River. As such,
the majority of them practiced the Sikh religious tradition. As Sikhs, they
wore turbans and did not cut their hair and beards. There were Muslims
and Hindus as well, all of whom spoke the Punjabi language. The second
wave began in 1946 when Congress passed the Luce-Celler Act, which
allowed Indians to become naturalized citizens. But significant numbers of
Indian immigrants did not migrate to the United States until the after the
passage of the Immigration Act of 1965.

FACTORS OF INDIAN MIGRATION

The voyage from India to the United States was costly and long. The Punjabi pioneers who decided to leave India sold land or borrowed money from
relatives to pay for their passage to Canada and the United States. First, they
traveled by train over land to reach the port of Calcutta. There, they
boarded a steamship for an 11- to 12-day journey to Hong Kong. From
Hong Kong, they boarded another ship that carried them across the Pacific
Ocean for another 18- to 19-day journey. The first significant wave of Indian
immigrants from British India arrived in 1898. Between 1898 and 1903, an
average of 30 Indian immigrants arrived in the United States. Between

1904 and 1906, it increased to 250 annually (Hess 1969, 61). Then, as Indians were targets of persecution in Canada, the number of Indians arriving in the United States increased dramatically: in 1907, 1,072, and in 1908, 1,710 (Hess 1969, 61).

FIRST WAVE

During this period, the Punjab region was undergoing rapid modernization, which displaced many people from their land. At this time, the Punjab state of India was used to growing cash crops such as indigo instead of food crops for the British colonial empire, which lead to famine for many farmers. In order to support their families, the youngest sons of families were encouraged to immigrate to the United States to locate work to support their families in India. There were 6,800 or so Indians who settled in the western region of the United States between 1899 and 1914 (Leonard 1992, 24). They constituted a relatively homogenous social group in that nearly 80–90 percent were Punjabis who were mostly men, spoke Punjabi, practiced Sikhism, and come from the martial caste and landowning families. However, they were portrayed as illiterate and backward. They were called "Hindoo" in America, which means they come from "Hindustan" or India, and illustrates how little Americans knew about India and Indians.

Similar to the Chinese immigrants before them, the Sikh workers first immigrated to work on the railroads, and then in agriculture as a result of Chinese and Japanese exclusionary policies. They were pushed by famine in their homeland, while some came as students. Still, others immigrated to work for India's independence from the yoke of British colonialism. Like the Chinese, Japanese, and Korean immigrants before them, Indian immigrants were also willing to work for low wages. In the mid-1860s, Indians were considered as a potential source of labor on the sugar plantations of Hawai'i, which was dropped by 1884 when Japan decided to permit immigration to the islands (Takaki 1989, 294). Nevertheless, by 1900, there were 2,000 Sikhs living in the Pacific Northwest and working in the lumber industry (Ciment 2010, 315). A timber mill in Astoria, Oregon, was nicknamed "Hindu Alley." Additionally, a few hundred Indians worked in lumber mills in Bellingham, Washington. By 1907, nearly 2,000 Indians, virtually all men, worked on the Western Pacific Railroad. In 1910, 1,782 Indians were admitted, mostly in San Francisco (Hess 1974, 580). "One particularly well documented Indian work group was led by Tuly Singh Johl and helped build the Marysville railway station in California" (Koritala 2011). At the same time, thousands migrated to California to work in the agricultural industry. According to the 1910 census, there were 5,424 Indian immigrants living in the United States, and about half, 2,742, residing in California (Hess 1974, 580). In 1912, the Sikhs established their first *gurdwara* in Stockton,

California. Because of discriminatory laws, immigration from India ended in 1917. Karen Leonard notes, "Federal policies and laws included the 1917 Barred Zone Act, which barred most Asians from legal immigration; the 1924 National Origins Quota Act, which set a quota of only 105 immigrants per year from India; and the 1923 U.S. Supreme Court Thind decision, which declared Indians to be Caucasians but not 'white' and therefore ineligible for U.S. citizenship" (2011, 975). Even so, Takaki notes that by 1920, some 6,400 Indians had ready entered the United States (1989, 294). The numbers dwindled between the 1920s and the 1960s as virtually no Indians immigrated to the United States.

A significant number of Indians in the early wave served in the British military in China, Southeast Asia, East Africa, Lebanon, and other places. "Punjabis serving overseas learned about the opportunities in the western United States" where it was reported that men who earned 16 cents a day in India could earn $2 a day in the United States (Leonard 1992, 30). Passage was possible via steamships that linked Hong Kong to the Philippine Islands and Canada, the United States, and Mexico. A pull factor among the first wave community were tales of the ability to earn money and obtain land in the United States. As such, immigration overseas, especially to the United States, was preferred to internal migration to other parts of India. Leonard notes, "An emigrant from the Punjab to the United States who had returned to his village asserted in the late 1920s that in America a man could do as he pleased; there was plenty of land and plenty of money" (1992, 30).

CHARACTERISTICS OF EARLY INDIAN IMMIGRANTS

Similar to the other Asian immigrants before them, Indian immigrants were predominately men: like the Chinese before them, they were primarily younger men in their 20s with little education. Some were married but came without their families, which resulted in the formation of a bachelor society. Moreover, like the Chinese, Indian immigrants who left the Punjab during this period intended eventually to return home with material riches to support their families. Antimiscegenation laws prohibited interracial marriages with white women, so the early Punjabi men married Mexican women. Leonard notes, "the Punjabi men and Mexican women looked racially similar to the county clerks issuing marriage licenses. The bi-ethnic couples produced many children, children with names like Maria Jesusita Singh, Jose Akbar Khan, and Carmelita Chand. These 'Mexican-Hindu' children, mostly Catholic and bilingual in English and Spanish, called themselves Hindus and were extremely proud of their Indian heritage" (2011, 975). Through marrying Mexican women, some Punjabi farmers were able to subvert the 1913 Alien Land Law in California because they put their wives' or U.S.-born children's names on the deeds. Tinaz Pavri documents that by

Portrait of a Sikh immigrant from India, 1917. (Frederick C. Howe/ National Geographic Society/Corbis)

"1920 Asian Indians owned 38,000 acres in California's Imperial Valley and 85,000 acres in the Sacramento Valley" (2011). Jawala Singh, who left Indian in 1905 and later became a wealthy farmer in the United States, earned the nickname "the Potato King" (Singh 2011, 1004).

The Mexican women who married Punjabi men were mainly younger women who were also farm laborers. They met each other while working in the fields and developed relationships that later resulted in marriage. In Northern California, between 1913 and 1946, 47 percent of Punjabi men married Mexican women; in central California, 76 percent of them married Mexican women; in Southern California, 92 percent married Mexican women (Takaki 1989, 310). Punjabi-Mexican unions were termed "Mexidus," which refers to a combination of Mexican and Hindu that misrepresents the identity of the immigrant Indian men, who were primarily Sikhs (Arora 2010, 344). The early community thus reflected a cultural mix of Punjabi and Mexican traditions, languages, foodways, and customs. Their children were raised to speak Spanish and English, practice the Catholic faith, and interchange Mexican tortillas for Indian rotis. It is estimated that

nearly 500 Punjabi-Mexican unions took place in the early twentieth century (Lindel 1991, B1). However, children of the Punjabi-Mexican marriages tended to marry non-Indians, thus gradually leading to the
disappearance of the first Indian American community (Watts 2010, 316).

In California, Punjabi immigrants mostly lived in rural areas and worked
in agriculture. Since agricultural work was seasonal, they moved in small
groups, with a 'boss man' who spoke English best and negotiated work on
the group's behalf (Leonard 1992, 32). The formation of the small groups
of Punjabi farmers originated as they departed India, but maintained while
in the United States as a result of the absence of women in their community.
"These democratic groupings—consisting of members who shared a
common language, values, heritage, and sense of purpose—served as surro-
gate families for the lonely Punjabi men far from home, security, and loved
ones" (Singh 2011, 1002). They moved around in groups, harvested different corps and performed various types of agricultural work during different
times of the year. In the winter months of December and January, they
pruned trees. "The Asian Indians moved around a great deal during the year
because they contracted farm work for cultivating and pruning grapes or
fruit trees, planting and harvesting rice, picking grapes and fruit" (Takaki
1989, 303). They worked 10 to 14 hours a day. They colluded with other
workers (e.g., Japanese) to deliberately slow the pace of their work in order
to extract more wages for their labor. Some Punjabi bookkeepers conspired
with the "boss man" to alter the figures in the books whereby they claimed
60 men worked, when only 50 did (Takaki 1989, 304–5).

INDIAN STUDENTS AND FREEDOM FIGHTERS

In 1885, the Indian National Congress was established. The majority of
the members were English-speaking educated Indians who wanted to
decolonize India. The Indian National Congress encouraged a small number
of students to emigrate in order to study in American universities and work
for India's independence. At the start of the twentieth century, about 100
Indian students studied in college and university campuses across America.
During the summers, it was common for Indian students in California to
work in the agricultural fields and orchards together with their compatriots.
Similar to Koreans who worked on revolutionary activities, some Indian students, together with a small group of Indian immigrants who migrated to
America as "political refugees" from British rule, saw the United States as
the ideal place to mobilize for India's independence. The independence
"movement" was known as Ghadar, which means "revolution" or
"mutiny" in Punjabi and Urdu. They also published a weekly newspaper
by the same name, and various revolutionary materials in English, Urdu,
and other Indian languages (Hess 1974, 585). The first issue of *Ghadar*

declared, "Today there begins in foreign lands . . . a war against the British
Raj. . . . What is our name? Ghadar. What is our work? Ghadar. Where will
ghadar break out? In India. The time will soon come when rifles and blood
will take the place of pens and ink" (Brown 1948, 299). It began in 1907
as loose party meetings among the migrant farm workers and graduate students. The Ghadar Party, initially the *Pacific Coast Hindustan Association*,
was formed in 1913 in the U.S. under the leadership of a 28-year-old Hindu
Har Dayal, with Sohan Singh Bhakna as its president. Sikh American activist
and scholar Jaideep Singh says, "the Ghadar Party . . . was a remarkable collective venture, which bridged the divisions among Sikhs, Hindus, and Muslims in the South Asian American community" (2010, 360). The "Potato
King" Jawala Singh helped found the Ghadar Party and the gurdwara in
Stockton, and "was eventually arrested and imprisoned by the British for
attempting to foment revolution in India" (Singh 2011, 1005). The mobili-
zation for a free India in the United States was a formidable task. Indicative
of the challenge to their efforts is an address President Theodore Roosevelt
made at the Methodist Episcopal Church in Washington, D.C., on January 18, 1909, where he expressed his support of British imperialism in India.
The president said,

> In India we encounter the most colossal example history affords of the success-
> ful administration by men of European blood of a thickly populated region in
> another continent. It is the greatest feat of the kind that has been performed
> since the breakup of the Roman Empire. Indeed, it is a greater feat than was
> performed under the Roman Empire. Unquestionably mistakes have been
> made; it would indicate qualities literally superhuman if so gigantic a task
> had been accomplished without mistakes. It is easy enough to point out short-
> comings; but the fact remains that the successful administration of the Indian
> Empire by the English has been one of the most notable and most admirable
> achievements of the white race during the past two centuries. On the whole it
> has been for the immeasurable benefit of the natives of India themselves. Suffer-
> ing has been caused in particular cases and at particular times to these natives;
> much more often, I believe, by well-intentioned ignorance or bad judgment
> than by any moral obliquity. But on the whole there has been a far more reso-
> lute effort to do justice, a far more resolute effort to secure fair treatment for
> the humble and the oppressed during the days of English rule in India than
> during any other period of recorded Indian history. England does not draw a
> penny from India for English purposes; she spends for India the revenues raised
> in India; and they are spent for the benefit of the Indians themselves.
> Undoubtedly India is a less pleasant place than formerly for the heads of tyran-
> nical States. There is now little or no room in it for successful freebooter chief-
> tains, for the despots who lived in gorgeous splendor while under their cruel
> rule the immense mass of their countrymen festered in sodden misery. *But the
> mass of the people have been and are far better off than ever before, and far*

better off than they would now be if English control were overthrown or with-drawn. (Roosevelt 1909, 2078–79; emphasis added)

The Ghadar movement was able to acquire weapons from Germany during World War I. On the morning of March 6, 1917, the plans for an armed rebellion against British rule was foiled when federal agents seized a large quantity of evidence with the arrest of Chandra K. Chakravarty—an organizer of the revolt—in New York for violating U.S. neutrality laws (Brown 1948, 307). In general, Americans were not publicly aware of Indian nationalism until after Pearl Harbor, when America sought Indian co-operation against Japan (Hess 1969, 72). By 1946, Washington became con-vinced that a free India would be an important ally for the United States. As a result, Congress passed the Luce-Celler Act, which allowed 200 immi-grants from India to enter each year. In 1940, the Muslim League, which was established in 1906 and worked with Indian National Congress for a free India called for not only independence, but also a separate Muslim country. The Hindu nation would keep the name "India" and the Muslim nation would be called "Pakistan." In 1947, after India and Pakistan became separate countries, the quota was divided evenly between them.

RACIAL TENSION AND RACIST ACTS

The growth of the Indian community was accompanied by resentment and discrimination. Just as the Asian immigrants did before them, Punjabi immigrants competed with white Euro-American workers in the lumber mills of the Pacific Northwest, the Western Pacific Railroad, and the grow-ing California agricultural economy. Although Punjabi immigrants had a reputation of being good workers, they were paid less than their white Euro-American counterparts. The popular press schemed with the Asiatic Exclusion League's mission to exclude Asian migration, which, combined with the economic anxiety of the loss of white jobs, resulted in the *Collier* running a headline warning of a "Hindoo Invasion" 10,000 strong, or Her-man Scheffauer's essay published in the *Forum*, "The Tide of Turbans," which reported 5,000 Indian immigrants whom he depicted as "dark, mystic race," and warned the people of the Golden State that this invasion was in its infancy. The ripe anti-Indian sentiment materialized into angry and vio-lent assaults on Indian communities throughout the Pacific Coast.

ANTI-HINDU RIOTS

White Euro-American lumberjacks saw Punjabi workers as a threat because mill owners preferred to hire at a lower wage, and for their work ethics. On September 4, 1907, the anti-immigrant sentiments erupted into violence, with people on the streets shouting "drive out the cheap labor." A mob of 500 white Euro-American lumberjacks—who were recent immigrants from Europe—forged their way to the area where Punjabi Americans rented their rooms. The Punjabi men were pulled from their rooms and beaten on the streets. They were beaten and their belongings looted. In total, the mob forced nearly 700 Indians to flee. The *Bellingham Herald* published an editorial the following day, in which the author not only condemned the mobs, but espoused racist anti-Indian sentiments, saying, "No amount of specious argument will justify the acts of the mobs." However, it would go on to express deep seeded anti-Indian sentiments, saying,

> The Hindu is not a good citizen. It would require centuries to assimilate him, and this country need not take the trouble. Our racial burdens are already heavy enough to bear. … Our cloak of brotherly love is not large enough to include him as a member of the body politics. His ways are not our ways; he is not adaptable, and will not in many generations make a good American citizen. ("Hindus Hounded from City," *Bellingham Herald*, September 5, 1907; Gallagher 2007)

Invoking a similar spirit, a letter written by Adolphus W. Mangum Jr., a soil scientist who lived in Bellingham dated September 8, 1907, says,

> These Hindos are very undesirable citizens. They are dirty and mean and will work for wages that a white man can't live on. I am not in sympathy with the laboring men who started this riot, because they ought to mob the mill men who hire these laborers rather than mob the Hindos themselves. If the mill owners did not hire them, they would not come here in such crowds. They are worse than the Japs and China-men and have caused trouble ever since they began to be numerous. The Japans and China-men have flooded this county and it begins to look like they intend to take possession of everything out here. (South Asian American Digital Archive)

The Asiatic Exclusion League blamed the Indians for the riots, citing their willingness to work for lower wages, and their "filthy and immodest habits," which "invited reprisals" (Hess 1969, 62).

Other riots against the Indian immigrants erupted in Aberdeen, Washington, on September 8, 1907; Boring, Oregon, on October 31, 1907; Everett, Washington, on November 2, 1907; Marysville, California, on January 27, 1908; and St. John, Oregon, on March 21, 1910. In each case, the white Euro-American mobs killed, injured, and robbed the "Hindoos" and drove them out of town. The public anti-immigrant sentiments were fueled, in large part, by the Asiatic Exclusion League (formerly the Japanese and Korean Exclusion League) and provided a powerful catalyst for racist policies that restricted Indian Americans from being "fully American."

The Asiatic Exclusion League was established on May 14, 1905, in San Francisco. Originally, its targets were Japanese and Korean immigrants that expanded to include immigrants from India that resulted in its renaming. The Asiatic Exclusion League's expressed mission was to foster hostile sentiment against Asians in order to exert pressure of the U.S. government to restrict Asian immigration. They were successful. According to Leonard, a 1909 federal immigration commission's investigation declared, "the Hindus are regarded as the least desirable, or, better, the most undesirable, of all the eastern Asiatic races which have come to share our soil" (1992, 24). A 1920 report to the California State Board of Control reiterated this theme, saying "The Hindu is the most undesirable immigrant in the state. His lack of personal cleanliness, his low morals, and his blind adherence to theories and teachings, so entirely repugnant to American principles make him unfit for association with American people" (1992, 24). The impact of the exclusionary policy kept the Indian community in the United States small. Prejudice coupled with xenophobia made it difficult for Indian immigrants (i.e., Punjabis) to gain admittance to the United States. According to Gary Hess, there was an increasing rejection rate of Indian applicants by the Bureau of Immigration and Naturalization. Before 1907, less than 10 percent of applicants for admission were rejected. In 1907, 28 percent were rejected (1974, 580). "Between 1908 and 1910, some 1,130 Indian arrivals were rejected" (Hess 1974, 580). Between 1911 and 1913, 50 percent or more were denied entry (Leonard 1992, 30).

Throughout 1910, the Asiatic Exclusion League targeted the removal of San Francisco commissioner of immigration Hart H. North. They claimed that North was incompetent and benefited from allowing cheap Indian laborers entry. The League and local San Francisco newspapers alleged that North allowed Indians who had communicable diseases entry via Angel Island. The League gathered a petition signed by 1,800 Californians, which they submitted to the commissioner general of immigration as well as to President William Howard Taft (Hess 1969, 62). This resulted in North's resignation at the encouragement of Washington officials, and stronger enforcement of immigration restriction at San Francisco. In 1911, some 517 Indians were admitted and 861 were rejected. In the next five years, fewer than 600 Indians were admitted, culminating on February 4, 1917, when Congress passed the Asiatic Barred Zone Act, which effectively barred immigrants from India. The act expanded the list of undesirables banned from entering the country, which included homosexuals, idiots, criminals, epileptics, insane persons, alcoholics, beggars, polygamists, anarchists, and so on. It also banned immigrants over the age of 16 who were illiterate. It included a designated "Asiatic Barred Zone," which included most of Asia and the Pacific Islands. Before this, only the Chinese were excluded.

Although President Woodrow Wilson vetoed the act in 1916, it passed Congress with an overwhelming majority the following year. A direct result of the anti-Indian policies decreased the size of the Indian communities in the United States. Between 1908 and 1920, 3,453 Indians were denied entry, mostly on the grounds that they were likely to become "public charges" (Takaki 1989, 296). Between 1911 and 1920, approximately 1,400 Indians left the United States voluntarily, and an additional 235 were deported (Hess 1974, 582). By the 1940s, the Indian population in the United States decreased to 2,405, with 60 percent residing in California.

INDIANS, NOT WHITE BY LAW

Indian eligibility for naturalization was still in question after the passage of the 1917 Asiatic Barred Zone Act. The Naturalization Act of 1790 restricted U.S. naturalization and citizenship rights to the "white race" only, which effectively excluded Chinese, Japanese, and Korean immigrants from naturalization. But, Indians were, anthropologically speaking, "Caucasian." Indian immigrants challenged the definition of "whiteness" in the courts, thereby exerting their right to be American. The Asiatic Exclusion League advocated for the deportation of the remaining Indian immigrants. However, some have already become naturalized citizens based on historic and anthropological evidence that Indians are "Aryans."

In 1923, the U.S. Supreme Court, in *United States v. Bhagat Singh Thind*, rendered a restrictive interpretation of the Naturalization Act of 1790 that declared only "free, White persons" can become naturalized citizens. Thind was born in the Punjab in 1892. By 1912, he had settled in Seattle, Washington. During World War I, he served in the U.S. Army, similar to Korean American Easurk Emsen Charr. Thind was a light-skinned, high-caste Sikh immigrant who not only served in the U.S. Army but also earned a doctorate from the University of California at Berkeley. In 1920, Thind applied for citizenship in Oregon and was challenged by the U.S. Bureau of Naturalization. Prior to Thind's attempt, Indians applying for citizenship yielded mixed results as some courts classified them as "white" while others did not. For instance, in the 1910 *United States v. Balsara* and the 1913 Ajkoy Kumar Mazumdar decisions, the courts held that Indians from India were "Caucasians" and therefore entitled to be legally considered as "white persons" eligible for citizenship under the 1790 law.

At first, Thind was successful and was granted citizenship by the federal district court in Oregon. Meanwhile, the U.S. Supreme Court heard its first racial prerequisite case, *Takao Ozawa v. United States* (1922). In the Ozawa decision, the court denied naturalization rights to Japanese immigrant Ozawa, ruling that "white" was synonymous with "Caucasian." This seemed to bode well for Thind's case because, as an Indian from India, he was technically "Aryan" and therefore "Caucasian." However, Attorney General Charles J. Bonaparte was convinced that Indians were not white and he challenged the successful naturalization of some Indian Americans. Thind's case reached the U.S. Supreme Court, and there the court conceded that Indians were "Caucasians" and that anthropologists considered them to be of the same race as white Americans, but argued that "the average man knows perfectly well that there are unmistakable and profound differences." Justice George Sutherland wrote the unanimous opinion of the court, saying:

> What we now hold is that the words "free white persons" are words of common speech, to be interpreted in accordance with the understanding of the common man, synonymous with the word "Caucasian" only as that word is popularly understood. As so understood and used, whatever may be the speculations of the ethnologist, it does not include the body of people to whom the appellee belongs. It is a matter of familiar observation and knowledge that the physical group characteristics of the Hindus render them readily distinguishable from the various groups of persons in this country commonly recognized as white. The children of English, French, German, Italian, Scandinavian, and other European parentage, quickly merge into the mass of our population and lose the distinctive hallmarks of their European origin. On the other hand, it cannot be doubted that the children born in this country of Hindu parents would retain indefinitely the clear evidence of their ancestry. It is very far from our thought to suggest the slightest question of racial superiority or inferiority. What we suggest is merely racial difference, and it is of such character and extent that the great body of our people instinctively recognize it and reject the thought of assimilation. (1923)

The *Thind* decision also led to successful efforts to denaturalize some who had previously become citizens. "Between 1923 and 1926, the naturalization certificates of nearly sixty Indians were cancelled" (Hess 1969, 69). In addition, between 1920 and 1940, some 3,000 Indian immigrants returned to India. The *Thind* decision also made California's 1913 Alien Land Law more potent, which impacted Punjabi Americans from establishing family and community.

SECOND WAVE

By 1946, Congress recognized that India would soon be independent and a major world power. The India Welfare League and the India League of America, advocates of Indian immigration and naturalization, successfully maneuvered the Luce-Celler Act through Congress, which President Harry S. Truman signed on July 2, 1946. The Luce-Celler Act allotted India an annual quota of 100, which ended nearly 30 years of exclusion; and it made it possible for Indian immigrants to become American citizens, thereby reversing the *Thind* decision. In 1957, largely with support from Anglo and Mexican American voters, the first Sikh American senator, Dalip Singh Saund, was elected to Congress representing California's Imperial Valley. Similar to many early Indian immigrants before him, Saund came to the United States from the Punjab at age 22. After he earned a doctorate in mathematics from the University of California at Berkeley in 1924, Saund broke his promise to his parents to return to India after receiving his degree and stayed in the United States to work as a foreman on an Indian American–owned farm in the Imperial Valley. Saund was involved in efforts to repeal the *Thind* decision. He applied for naturalization and received citizenship in 1949. While more educated and professional Indians began to enter America, immigration restrictions and tight quotas ensured that only small numbers of Indians entered the country prior to 1965. Between 1947 and 1965, roughly 7,000 immigrants from India, and 1,500 immigrants from Pakistan arrived in the United States. They include family members of the earlier Indian immigrants who became naturalized citizens, in addition to wives of Punjabi men who had returned to India to marry.

Large waves of migrants from India were pulled by changes to immigration quotas that passed with the 1965 Immigration Act. With this act, the quota system limiting the number of immigrants allowed into the United States was changed to allow entry for 20,000 people from each country annually. This was the first time that migrants from Asian nations had access equal to European migrants. The post-1965 wave of Indian immigrants are not rural people, instead, they come from urban areas, are highly educated professionals who migrate with their spouses and children. Nearly 40 percent of all Indian immigrants who have entered the United States in the decades after 1965 arrived on student or exchange visitor visas. In terms of ethnicity, the new Indian immigrants are much more diverse than the first wave: They come from all over India and speak many languages which reflects the 19 major vernacular languages in India. The most numerous regional groups are Gujaratis, Punjabis, and Malayalis.

REFERENCES

Ahmad, Ahrar. "Bangladeshi Immigrants." In *Multicultural America: An Encyclopedia of the Newest Americans*, edited by Ronald H. Bayor. Santa Barbara, CA: ABC-CLIO, 2011.

Anupama, Jain. *How to Be South Asian in America: Narratives of Ambivalence and Belonging*. Philadelphia: Temple University Press, 2011.

Arora, Anupama. "Mexican-Indian Marriages." In *Asian American History and Culture: An Encyclopedia*, edited by Huping Ling and Allan Austin. Armonk, NY: M. E. Sharpe, 2010.

Bald, Vivek. *Bengali Harlem and the Lost Histories of South Asian America*. Cambridge, MA: Harvard University Press, 2013.

Bowman, John Stewart, ed. *Columbia Chronologies of Asian History and Culture*, New York: Columbia University Press, 2000.

Brown, Giles T. "The Hindu Conspiracy, 1914–1917." *Pacific Historical Review* 17:3 (August 1948): 299–310.

Chan, Sucheng. *Asian Americans: An Interpretive History*. New York: Twayne, 1991.

Ciment, James. "The Indian American Experience: History and Culture." In *Asian American History and Culture: An Encyclopedia*, edited by Huping Ling and Allan Austin. Armonk, NY: M. E. Sharpe, 2010.

Daniels, Roger. *History of Indian Immigration to the United States: An Interpretative Essay*. New York: Asia Society, 1989.

Gallagher, Mary Lane. "1907 Bellingham Mob Forced East Indian Workers from Town." *The Bellingham Herald*, September 2, 2007.

Helweg, Arthur W. *Strangers in a Not-So-Strange Land: Asian Indians in America*. New York: Praeger, 1988.

Hess, Gary R. "The Forgotten Asian Americans: The East Indian Community in the United States." *Pacific Historical Review* 43:4 (November 1974): 576–96.

Hess, Gary R. "The 'Hindu' in America: Immigration and Naturalization Policies and India, 1917–1946." *Pacific Historical Review* 38:1 (February 1969): 59–79.

Hing, Bill O. *Making and Remaking Asian American through Immigration Policy 1850–1990*. Stanford, CA: Stanford University Press, 1993.

Hurwitz, Robert R. "Constitutional Law: Equal Protection of the Laws: California Anti-Miscegenation Laws Declared Unconstitutional." *California Law Review* 37:1 (March 1949): 122–29.

Ingram, Scott. *South Asian Americans*. Milwaukee, WI: World Almanac Library, 2007.

Koritala, Srirajasekhar Bobby. "A Historical Perspective of Americans of Asian Indian Origins: 1790–1997." http://www.infinityfoundation.com/mandala/h_es/h_es_korit_histical.htm (accessed June 11, 2014).

Lai, Eric, and Dennis Arguelles, eds. *The New Face of Asian Pacific America: Numbers, Diversity, and Change in the 21st Century*. San Francisco: AsianWeek, 2003.

Leonard, Karen Isaken. "Indian (Asian Indian) Immigrants." In *Multicultural America: An Encyclopedia of the Newest Americans*, edited by Ronald H. Bayor. Santa Barbara, CA: ABC-CLIO, 2011.

Leonard, Karen Isaken. *Making Ethnic Choices: California's Punjabi Mexican Americans*. Philadelphia: Temple University Press, 1992.

Leonard, Karen Isaken. *The South Asian Americans*. Westport, CT: Greenwood Press, 1997.

Lindel, Bill. "Mexican-Hindu: In Yuba City, Traces Remain of Fading Mexican-Hindu Culture." *Sacramento Bee*, November 11, 1991.

Melendy, H. Brett. *Asians in America: Filipinos, Koreans, and East Indians*. Boston: Twayne Publishers, 1977.

Menchaca, Martha. "The Anti-Miscegenation History of the American Southwest, 1837 to 1970: Transforming Racial Ideology into Law." *Cultural Dynamics* 20 (2008): 279–318.

Moore, Kathleen. "Pakistani Immigrants." In *Multicultural America: An Encyclopedia of the Newest Americans*, edited by Ronald H. Bayor. Santa Barbara, CA: ABC-CLIO, 2011.

Odo, Franklin, ed. *The Columbia Documentary History of the Asian American Experience*. New York: Columbia University Press, 2002.

Pavri, Tinaz. "Asian Indian Americans." *Multicultural America*. http://www.everyculture.com/multi/A-Br/Asian-Indian-Americans.html (accessed June 11, 2014).

Roosevelt, Theodore. *Presidential Addresses and State Papers and European Addresses, December 8, 1908, to June 7, 1910*.

Scheffauer, Herman. "The Tide of Turbans." *Forum* 43 (June 1910): 616–18.

Scott, James Brown. "Japanese and Hindu Naturalization in the United States." *American Journal of International Law* 17:2 (April 1923): 328–30.

Singh, Jaideep. "Jawala Singh (1859–1938)." In *Asian American History and Culture: An Encyclopedia*, edited by Huping Ling and Allan Austin. Armonk, NY: M. E. Sharpe, 2010.

Singh, Jaideep. "Punjabi Americans: History, People, and Culture." In *Encyclopedia of Asian American Folklore and Folklife*, edited by Jonathan H. X. Lee and Kathleen M. Nadeau. Santa Barbara, CA: ABC-CLIO, 2011.

South Asian American Digital Archive (SAADA). University of North Carolina, Chapel Hill, last modified May 3, 2013. http://www.saadigitalarchive.org/item/20110910-354 (accessed September 10, 2014).

Starr, Kevin. *Golden Dreams: California in an Age of Abundance, 1950–1963*. Oxford: Oxford University Press, 2009.

Street, Richard S. *Beasts of the Field: A Narrative History of California Farmworkers, 1769–1913*. Stanford, CA: Stanford University Press, 2004.

Takaki, Ronald T. *Strangers from a Different Shore: A History of Asian Americans*. Rev. ed. Boston: Little, Brown, 1989.

United States v. Bhagat Singh Thind (February 19, 1923).

Watts, J. F., and Fred L. Israel, eds. *Presidential Documents: the Speeches, Proclamations, and Policies that Have Shaped the Nation from Washington to Clinton*. New York: Routledge, 2000.

Watts, Tim J. "Acculturation and the Indian American Community." In *Asian American History and Culture: An Encyclopedia*, edited by Huping Ling and Allan Austin. Armonk, NY: M. E. Sharpe, 2010.

Zaki, Khalida. "Pakistanis and Pakistani Americans, 1940–Present." In *Immigrants in American History: Arrival, Adaptation, and Integration*, edited by Robert Barkan. Santa Barbara, CA: ABC-CLIO, 2013.

_____ *Chapter 5* _____

Filipinos in America

Filipino Americans can trace their ancestral origins to the archipelago known as the Philippines, located in the western Pacific Ocean as part of Southeast Asia. The earliest recorded presence of Filipinos, in what is today the United States, dates to October 18, 1587, when mariners under Spanish command landed on Morro Bay, California (Mercene 2007, 40). The earliest known Filipino settlers in America established fishing and shrimping villages in the bayous of Louisiana in 1763. These so-called "Manilamen" jumped ship to escape the harsh treatment on the Spanish galleons that sailed the Manila-Acapulco route. In 1883, Lafcadio Hearn described the community at Saint Malo, saying:

> Most of them are cinnamon-colored men; a few are glossily yellow, like that bronze into which a small proportion of gold is worked by the molder. Their features are irregular without being actually repulsive; some have the cheekbones very prominent, and the eyes of several are set slightly aslant. The hair is generally intensely black and straight, but with some individuals it is curly and browner. In Manila there are several varieties of the Malay race, and these Louisiana settlers represent more than one type. None of them appeared tall; the greater number were undersized, but all well knit, and supple as freshwater eels. Their hands and feet were small; their movements quick and easy, but sailorly likewise, as of men accustomed to walk upon rocking decks in rough weather. They speak the Spanish language; and a Malay dialect is also used among them. There is only one white man in the settlement—the ship-carpenter, whom all the Malays address as "Maestro." He has learned to speak their Oriental dialect, and has conferred upon several the sacrament of baptism according to the Catholic rite; for some of these men were not Christians at the time of their advent into Louisiana. There is but one black man in this lake village—a Portuguese negro, perhaps a Brazilian maroon. The Maestro told us

Settlement of Tagalas from Philippine Islands in swampland of southeastern Louisiana: (1) Bataille's house; (2) Farewell to St. Malo (fishing boat departing); (3) Bayou, St. Malo; (4) Oldest house in St. Malo; (5) El Maestro's house, 1883. (Library of Congress)

> that communication is still kept up with Manila, and money often sent there to aid friends in emigrating. Such emigrants usually ship as seamen on board some Spanish vessel bound for American ports, and desert at the first opportunity. It is said that the colony was founded by deserters—perhaps also desperate refugees from Spanish justice. (1883; reprinted in Bronner 2002, 57)

Hearn's ethnographic account describes a bachelor society community where houses are built on stilts, "in true Manila style," and residents lived intimately with nature. Despite the early presence of Filipinos in America, it was not until the early decades of the twentieth century that Filipino migration to the United States increased, in large part due to American colonization of the Philippines.

FACTORS OF FILIPINO MIGRATION

Substantial numbers of Filipinos arrived in the United States in three distinct waves: The first wave is from 1903 to 1935; the second wave unfolds between the 1940s and 1950s; the third wave is the post-1965 arrivals. The Philippines had been a Spanish colony since 1565. The Spanish colonial government recorded approximately 124 revolts throughout the islands between the sixteenth and nineteenth centuries (Bautista 1998, 34). By the middle of the nineteenth century, native Catholic priests began openly criticizing and defying the Spanish clergy while educated Filipino elites such as national hero Jose Rizal critiqued Spanish abuse in his writings. The accumulation of protests, resistances movements, growing nationalism, and patriotism brewing in secret societies and among the peoples resulted in the Philippine Revolution that began in August 30, 1896 (known as the Tagalog War by Spain), in which Filipinos engaged in military battle against Spanish troops. Filipino revolutionary leader and nationalist Andrés Bonifacio led the *Katipunan*, an anticolonial secret society. Internal power struggles among the revolutionaries coupled with the military superiority of the Spanish colonialists led to the defeat of the Filipino revolutionaries.

The United States intervened in the Philippines as a result of the Spanish-American War (April 12 to August 13, 1898) that ignited on February 15, 1898, when the battleship USS *Maine* exploded in Cuba's Havana Harbor killing 266 sailors (Offner 2004, 56). Filipino resistance fighters became allied with the United States, and together they defeated Spain. On May 1, 1898, Commodore George Dewey's Asiatic Squadron destroyed the Spanish fleet at Manila Bay, which undermined Spanish control over the entire colony (May 1983, 354). Exiled Filipino independence leader Emilio Aguinaldo declared Philippine independence making it Asia's first democratic government (Rodell 2005, 15). While Aguinaldo was attempting to establish an independent sovereign nation-state, President William McKinley was "becoming interested in acquiring the Philippines" (May 1983, 354–55). President McKinley interpreted the annexation of the Philippines as a "gift" from God and a moral "responsibility" of a benevolent United States, saying,

> When I next realized that the Philippines had dropped into our laps I confess I did not know what to do with them ... I thought first we would take only Manila; then Luzon; then other islands ... And one night late it came to me this way ... (1) That we could not give them back to Spain—that would be cowardly and dishonorable; (2) that we could not turn them over to France and Germany—our commercial rivals in the Orient-that would be bad business and discreditable; (3) that we not leave them to themselves—they are unfit for self-government—and they would soon have anarchy and misrule over there worse than Spain's wars; and (4) that there was nothing left for us to do but to take them all, and to educate the Filipinos, and uplift and civilize and Christianize them, and by God's grace do the very best we could by them, as our fellow-men for whom Christ also died. (1899; reprinted in Watts and Israel 2000, 193–95)

President McKinley expressed a form of "racial imperialism" that guided U.S. foreign and domestic policies with respects to people of color whom whites considered barbaric and thus incapable of self-government (Ngozi-

Brown 1997, 43–44). On December 10, 1898, Spain and the United States completed negotiations for the Treaty of Paris, formally ending the Spanish-American War (Pérez 1998, 22). The Treaty of Paris negotiations excluded Filipino representation, whereby "Spain merely transferred (at the price of twenty million dollars) its colonial power to the United States" (Yeo 2011, 37). On February 6, 1899, the U.S. Senate ratified the treaty and the United States annexed the Philippines. The United States subsequently fought a three-year war to suppress the Philippines' struggle for independence, known as the "Philippine Insurrection" or Philippine-American War of 1899–1902 (Tuason 1999). During the Spanish-American War, Theodore Roosevelt was lieutenant colonel of the Rough Rider Regiment, which he led on a charge at the battle of San Juan. In 1900, Roosevelt expressed the justification of U.S. colonization of the Philippines as a "History" of westward expansion, in accepting the nomination as vice president, saying, "To grant self-government to Luzon under Aguinaldo would be like granting self-government to an Apache reservation under some local chief" (cited in Judis 2004, 62). American forces responded to Filipino counterinsurgency with a "scorched earth policy, widespread use of torture, and using the latest military technologies, in mass killings of civilian sympathizers" (Abraham 2006, 674). The Philippine-American War resulted in millions of casualties, destruction of cities, and the territorial annexation of the Philippines. The geopolitical relationship between the United States and the Philippines set the political and economic parameters for the significant migration of Filipinos to the United States.

FIRST WAVE

After the United States acquired the Philippines from Spain in 1898, Filipinos arrived in Hawai'i and the continental United States for work and education. Two categories of Filipinos arrived during the first wave: students and laborers. In addition, indigenous Filipinos were exhibited at two world fairs. U.S. occupation of the Philippines allowed Filipinos to come, as Steffi San Buenaventura notes, with " 'ward' status without citizenship rights ... a very convenient solution to the problem of not having to assimilate a 'barbarous' people living in a distant U.S. territory in the Pacific" (1998, 7). Filipinos who journeyed to the United States from 1903 to 1935 reflect a movement of "subjugated 'nationals' who were highly motivated to pursue their expanded colonial boundaries abroad" (San Buenaventura 1998, 21).

INDIGENOUS FILIPINOS

Indigenous Filipinos—Igorots, Moros, Tinguianes, Negritos, and others—were transported to the United States as living exhibits in the world fairs

The St. Louis Exposition of 1904 displays a group of Igorot villagers from the Philippines for visitors. This highlighted American civilization in contrast to uncivilized indigenous Filipinos and provided ideological legitimacy for the colonization of the Philippines. (Corbis)

in St. Louis in 1904 and the Alaska Yukon Pacific Exposition 1908. According to the manager of the Igorot Village at the St. Louis World Fair, there were 114 "natives" consisting of Igorots and Tinguianes (Hung 1904, 36). Christopher Vaughan describes the popularity of the Igorot exhibit, saying,

> Mounted on display the fruits of the United States's recent embrace of colonial empire, the sprawling, forty-acre Philippine Reservation featured separate exhibits for tribes from throughout the archipelago's more than seven thousand islands. The 'civilized' Visayans, despite offering hourly theatrical and orchestral performances—concluding with 'The Star Spangled Banner,' sung in English by the entire village—went relatively ignored in comparison to the Igorots, whose ceremonial dances, near-nakedness, and daily consumption of dog stew captured headlines and the entertainment dollars of fairgoers. Gate receipts at the Igorot concession nearly quadrupled the total for the Visayans and tripled that of the colorful Moros. (1996, 222)

The Igorot exhibit presented a clear and sharp contrast between the civilized Americans and the savagery of the Filipinos. Perhaps for this reason, nonindigenous Filipinos have muted and silenced the experience of indigenous Filipinos, as Igorot American scholar Mark S. Leo suggests:

> [T]he Filipino American "mainstream" refers to the dominant Tagalog-speaking, Catholic, and hetero-normative Filipino American community. These people originate from various areas of the Philippines ranging from

Manila in Luzon, Cebu City in central Visayas, Ilocos Norte, and Ilocos Sur. Although Filipinos from these areas have their own distinct regional dialects, they are fluent in Tagalog and have been heavily influenced by Spanish and American colonialism. Igorots are from the mountainous region—also known as the Cordillera. The Cordillera are indigenous to the Philippines, and successfully resisted three hundred years of Spanish colonialism. As such, Igorot American identity does not conform to the mainstream historical narrative or identity of homogenous pan-Filipino America. (2011, 3–4)

Although it is beyond the scope of this present work to explore, contemporary indigenous Filipino American communities, especially among the youth, are engaged in efforts to write themselves into the historical experiences of the Filipinos in America.

PENSIONADOS

Five years after the Spanish-American War, Governor General William Howard Taft's government through the Philippine Commission passed the Pensionado Act of 1903. The goal of the act was to "educate and bind current and future Filipino leaders to the American colonial administration" (Dela Cruz and Agbayani-Siewert 2003, 46). They were welcomed as "trainees in democracy who would eventually return to their islands, carrying the message of democracy to their own peoples" (Melendy 1974, 521). Under this act, pensionados, or Filipino students, were selected to study science, mathematics, engineering, technology, law, government, business, economics, and so on at American high schools and colleges/universities and were expected to return to the Philippines upon graduation to rebuild their nation (Posadas 1996, 38). These students were sponsored by the colonial government and received fellowships with stipends (pension; hence, pensionado). By 1907, there were 180 pensionados studying across the United States (Okamura 1995, 429).

During this period, the colonial government was building the educational system in the Philippines, which under Spanish rule was limited to the elite population. After the University of the Philippines was established in 1908, the system of sending students to the United States was in large part abandoned until 1919, when the need was felt for more men and women with highly specialized training and the pensionado system was again put into practice (Marquardt 1945, 138). By 1912, 209 pensionados obtained degrees from American institutions of higher learning (Salamanca 1968, 91). The program lasted until the outbreak of World War II: 500 students arrived during the first two decades of the program (Esguerra 2011, 710).

In total, there were roughly 700 students studying in the United States during the program's tenure (Orosa 2005, 2). Mario Orosa documents his father's journey to the United States as a pensionado:

> [I]n August of 1906, my father Vicente Ylagan Orosa became a pensionado, one of only seven appointed that year. Several months short of his seventeenth birthday, he successfully hurdled the examinations, was plucked from his home town of Bauan, Batangas and went to America. ... [He spent his] first ... year at the Cincinnati Technical School in Cincinnati, Ohio (where I now live). ... He then transferred to the University of Illinois in Champaign-Urbana where he spent the next four years and earned a degree in civil engineering. ... In the US, the great earthquake of San Francisco happened in April and when Vicente's ship landed in San Francisco on September 10 like the previous batches of pensionados, he would have witnessed the devastation there. From San Francisco, my father would have traveled by train across the United States, crossing the Rockies, the plains states and the prairies of the Midwest before arriving in Cincinnati. The entire trip from Bauan to Cincinnati would have taken at least four weeks by boat and train. This trip today takes 24 hours. (2005, 2–3)

The pensionados were intelligent, as noted by W. W. Marquardt, pensionado student director from 1919 to 1923, who said, "In competition with American students they clearly proved their intellectual capacity and won far more than their share of recognition in Phi Beta Kappa and scientific honorary societies" (1945, 138). Upon their return to the Philippines, they were required to serve the government for the same number of years they spent abroad (Young 1982, 220–21). By 1910, the majority of the students who arrived in the first phase had returned to the Philippines and acquired positions with the government in various administrative, cultural, and economic areas or became university professors; and later, some became entrepreneurs (Espiritu 1995, 3–4). In addition, some took positions as teachers, doctors, lawyers, and engineers (Posadas 1996, 38).

Besides the government-sponsored pensionados, about 14,000 non-government-sponsored students, who were inspired by the success of the pensionados, journeyed to the United States between 1910 and 1938. They arrived independently and without funding from the colonial government. They too did not intend to stay in the United States, but rather to return to the Philippines to become civil servants. They worked as unskilled laborers while attending school, which made completing their educational goals nearly impossible. In addition to the demands of school and work, they faced discrimination. With the advent of the Great Depression, they abandoned their goals of education and dropped out entirely. These "proud young men, whose families had shipped them off with flags flying, they could not—would not—return home as 'failures' " (Posadas and Guyotte 1990, 27). While Filipino students traveled to the U.S. mainland, their laboring compatriots immigrated to Hawai'i as plantation workers.

FILIPINOS IN HAWAI'I

Throughout the nineteenth century, Filipino peasants, while under Spanish colonial rule, became landless sharecroppers. This situation continued under U.S. colonial rule. Poverty-stricken peasants migrated internally in the Philippines in search of food and work. Meanwhile, the plantation economies of the United States needed a source of cheap labor, which resulted from the exclusion of Chinese laborers via the Chinese Exclusion Act of 1882; Korean laborers halted when the Korean government stopped emigration in 1905 due to the mistreatment of Koreans in Hawai'i and Mexico as well as Japanese laborers via the Gentlemen's Agreement of 1908. In addition, Chinese, Japanese, and Korean plantation workers were striking or threatening to go on strike, such as the 1909 strike by Japanese plantation workers on Oahu. The Hawaiian Sugar Planters' Association (HSPA), representing 30 plantations located on the islands of Maui, Oahu, Kauai, and Hawai'i, initiated a policy and practice of employing as many different ethnic groups as they could so as to pit one group against another (cited in Sharma 1980, 95). Filipino migration to Hawai'i was largely a private HSPA undertaking, albeit with government support (Sharma 1984a, 582). In fact, they were the first to recruit labor from the Philippines (Baldoz 2011, 13). Filipino subjects, as "Asians," were located outside of the exclusion laws because they were simultaneously "nationals" or "colonial subjects" of the United States since 1898. Their unique legal status allowed them to travel freely between the Philippines and the United States, which made them attractive to the Hawaiian sugar plantation owners. Yen Le Espiritu notes, "because the Philippines was a 'ward' of the United States from 1905 to 1935, the Hawaii Sugar Planters Association . . . could rely on the assistance of American colonial officials there" (1995, 5). Beginning in 1906, and by the early 1920s, Filipinos comprised the largest segment of the plantation workforce in the islands.

The Philippine government tried to discourage HSPA from recruiting Filipino laborers because they needed the labor for their own growing sugar industry (Sharma 1984a, 582). The HSPA employed aggressive tactics and offered migrants free round-trip passage. The targeted recruitment of Filipino workers was so successful that by the mid-1920s, the HSPA stopped offering free round-trip passage as an incentive. By 1926, the HSPA stopped recruiting altogether. Espiritu says: "Hopeful migrants not only were willing to pay their own passage, they even bribed the recruiters to assure being chosen. Some educated people tried to pass themselves off as illiterates in order to circumvent HSPA policy to recruit the physically strong and the less educated, who were thought to be more likely to remain on the plantations and perform the menial work they were hired to do" (1995, 6). Thus, between 1926 and 1928, "unsolicited boatloads" of Filipino workers arrived, and by 1931, the HSPA ceased recruiting altogether (Sharma 1984a, 583).

The HSPA recruiting efforts were first concentrated in central Luzon and central Visayas; after 1915, it shifted to the Visayan Islands and then to the Ilocano region in northwestern Luzon. In a 1916 *Report of the Commissioner of Labor Statistics*, the commissioner wrote, "Plantations have to view laborers primarily as instruments of production. Their business interests require cheap, not too intelligent, docile unmarried men" (cited in Sharma 1984a, 583). The HSPA viewed Asian laborers as a mere commodity and likened them to "cattle upon the mountain ranges" or "jute bags from India" (Sharma 1980, 94–95).

The ethnic composition of the plantation laborers changed drastically with the importation of Filipino laborers. In 1902, Japanese laborers comprised 73.5 percent of the plantation workforce (Okihiro 1991, 59). By 1915, they comprised 19 percent of the plantation workforce and the Japanese 54 percent. By 1930, the Japanese laborers decreased to only 19 percent, and the Filipinos increased to 70 percent of the workforce (Sharma 1980, 97; San Buenaventura 1996, 75). By 1931, the Filipino population in Hawai'i reached its peak with more than 63,000, which represented 17.1 percent of the islands' people (Sharma 1984a, 586). Between 1906 and 1934, an estimated 118,556 *sakadas*, or contract laborers were recruited to Hawai'i: "103,513 were men, 8,952 women, and 6,091 children" (Posadas 1999, 15). Many of these early *sakadas* did not intend to settle in the United States. Instead, they planned on returning to the Philippines with their savings to buy a plot of land and establish a family, but the high cost of living and the economic exploitation they experienced made it difficult for them to save enough to realize their dream. It was also difficult for them to return to the Philippines as failures. The *sakadas* left the Philippines because they suffered severe economic displacement and dislocation that resulted from the colonial capitalists' focus on agricultural export (i.e., sugar). In addition, they were landless, were indebted to local "bid men" (*caciques*), were charged high interest rates, and had crop failure due to typhoons and periods of seasonal drought. Staying in the Philippines meant no job or food; leaving, even for low wages, was a "better" option. Although financial circumstances in Hawai'i were difficult, there were countless Filipino laborers who "collectively sent enormous sums [of

remittance] home but who were unable to save for their return passage"
(Sharma 1984a, 586).

Filipino Women in Hawai'i

Filipino workers were predominately males who were young, single,
uneducated, and poor from the rural areas of Ilocos and Visayas regions
(Tompar-Tiu and Sustento-Seneriches 1995, 8). In 1910, the sex imbalance
was most acute because there were more than 10 Filipinos for every one Fil-
ipina (Sharma 1984a, 583). The HSPA purposefully recruited unmarried
men as laborers with the expectation that they would work harder without
familial responsibilities. However, the limited number of Filipino women
and the high proportion of unmarried Filipino men led to social problems
for the plantation. To remedy the issue, the HSPA recruited more Filipino
women in the early 1920s (Sharma 1980, 95). By 1930, women comprised
16.6 percent of the Filipino population on the islands (Espiritu 1995, 6).
Due to the shortage of Filipino women in Hawai'i, they possessed higher
status in decisions regarding control over their family finances (Sharma
1980, 108).

Plantation Life and Labor

Plantation management employed close surveillance of Filipino workers
as a means to suppress subversive activities and exercised widespread political, economic, and moral control over its workforce. The HSPA utilized
"race pride" strategy to elicit more work from the competing ethnic
laborers. Plantation foremen told Filipino workers, "Work hard and be
thrifty and don't get into trouble. Don't show laziness—that would look
bad on us Filipinos" (Takaki 1990, 41). The divide-and-control policy was
effective: workers of different nationalities and ethnicities emphasized their
interests and identities, which led to interethnic tensions that at times
evolved into violent mass clashes.

The divide-and-control policy of the planters was augmented by a system
of residential segregation of ethnic groups, racial stratification, and differential pay and occupations for ethnic groups. Plantation housing was ethnically segregated into Portuguese, Spanish, Puerto Rican, Chinese, Japanese,
Filipino, and Korean camps. "The Caucasian plantation manager lived in a
spacious mansion at the top of the hill, and the other Caucasians—lunas,
office workers, and supervisors—lived along the manager's road in comfort-
able homes" (Kawakami 1993, 169). "According to one camp resident on
Maui, the plantation resembled a 'pyramid.' The manager's big house was
located on the highest slope, with the houses of the foreman tiered below
it. Farther down the slope was the Japanese camp, and at the bottom were

the Filipinos" (Takaki 1990, 42). The planters privately maintained a labor surplus, while publically lamenting a labor shortage. This effectively protected them against labor strikes (Sharma 1980, 97). Planters exercised control through a structure of paternalism, whereby workers first needed to get permission to see a doctor and a fee was deducted from their paychecks. Planter paternalism coupled the ethos of Christian charity and Western progress and civilization. Indeed, many plantations were established by missionaries (Okihiro 1991, 39). Plantation masters conceived plantations as a means to civilization; thus they upheld Christianity through parental discipline and affection, cultivating morality among its charges (Okihiro 1991, 39–40). In addition, the planters provided "free" housing that empowered them to evict anyone they deemed to be subversive. Thus, housing was used as a means of reward and punishment (Sharma 1980, 97–98).

Systematic daily control of virtually all aspects of workers' lives created a dependency among the recipients of planter benevolence that established the planter's claim to obedience while acting as a check against protest. However, more than 8,000 Japanese and Filipino laborers united in the 1920 sugar plantation strike in Hawai'i. This was a cross-ethnic cooperation between Japanese and Filipino laborers (Maeda 2009, 35). The planters "responded by evicting thousands of workers and their families from plantation housing in the midst of an influenza epidemic, and 150 died. Though workers stayed off the job for six months, the strike was largely unsuccessful" (Maeda 2009, 35). In 1924, a strike started on Oahu, which later spread to Kohala (Hawai'i) and to Kauai. Strikes were caused principally by unfair dealing and rough treatment by *lunas* and misunderstanding with plantation managements (Reinecke 1996, 123). Planters broke the 1924 Filipino strike without increasing wages by bringing in strikebreakers, imprisoning strike leaders, and evicting strikers' families from plantation housing. However, planters also instituted changes to retain and motivate the workforce: they built better plantation housing, began to provide medical care, and gave laborers annual bonuses dependent on profit (Juvik and Juvik 1999, 178). In 1946, all plantation workers finally united into "one big union," "thus signifying a measure of success in the Pilipinos' struggle to adapt to the economic conditions of plantation life" (Sharma 1980, 106).

FILIPINOS ON THE U.S. MAINLAND

Filipino laborers also resisted their oppressive conditions by leaving the plantations altogether. From the mid-1920s through the 1930s, more than 50,000 Filipinos headed for the continental United States or returned to the Philippines. One-third journeyed to the U.S. mainland from Hawai'i, "many having been blacklisted for their alleged participation in the 1924 strike" (Espiritu 1995, 8). By 1935, 58,281 workers had returned to the

Philippines, while 18,574 (many as families) moved on to the U.S. mainland (Sharma 1984a, 585–86). In addition, Filipinos who were encouraged by American teachers with tales of riches and unlimited opportunities in the United States skipped Hawai'i altogether and headed straight to San Francisco (Mabalon et al. 2008, 7). Rick Baldoz notes that by the mid-1920s, "emigration from the Philippines had gained internal momentum, fueled by a series of factors: the evolution of the transpacific imperial zone as a major political-economic hub, the steady flow of remittances from nationals working abroad, and targeted recruitment by global steamship companies eager to profit from the transpacific traffic of steerage passengers" (2011, 13). Upon arriving at San Francisco, they were swept up, piled into taxicabs, and charged $65–$75 rides to Stockton—the gathering place for Filipinos as they came to America; the same trip by bus or train cost $2 (Mabalon et al. 2008, 7; Takaki 1989, 316). Although the majority of the arriving Filipinos in the 1930 found employment in the fields of the American West, roughly 25 percent found work in hotels, homes, and restaurants as domestics, janitors, valets, drivers, gardeners, cooks, busboys, bellboys, elevator boys, dishwashers, and waiters (Gonzalez 1998, 29–30; Takaki 1989, 316–17).

Census figures indicate that the number of Filipinos in California increased in both scale and velocity during the 1920s, from 2,674 to 30,470. The influx of Filipinos filled a labor vacuum that was created in California with the passage of the Alien Land Law of 1920 and the Immigration Exclusion Act of 1924 (Christiansen 1979, 66). The Alien Land Law prohibited Japanese immigrants from leasing or owning land, which caused many Issei to give up farming. "According to a report compiled by the Japanese Consulate, there had been 995 Japanese farmers in the delta in 1920, but 575 of them left the region within three years. Issei laborers, too, had to go elsewhere, reducing their number from 750 to 400 between 1920 and 1925" (Azuma 1998, 169). The remaining Japanese farmers worked as foremen who received fixed salaries from white landlords, thereby evading the Alien Land Law. California farmers had to find other workers to perform the seasonal tasks in the fields and orchards, which was compounded by the 1924 Immigration Exclusion Act that excluded Japanese immigrants; Filipinos provided them release.

Filipino workers labored in the fields of California, Oregon, Washington, Montana, Idaho, and Colorado. Roughly 60 percent of the Filipino laborers in California worked in agriculture (Takaki 1989, 318). They moved from one place to another in search of work—Salinas, Manteca, Stockton, Lodi, Fresno, Delano, Dinuba, San Luis Obispo, Imperial, and Sacramento. They were seasonal migrants who moved around cutting spinach and picking strawberries in California; then traveled to Montana, where they topped beets; or Idaho, where they dug potatoes; or the Yakima Valley in

Washington, where they picked apples; or in Oregon, where they hoed hops (Takaki 1989, 319). The majority of the Filipino population were single men and predominately Catholic. Church officials on the West Coast became concerned with their "moral rectitude," since they were without family and relied on drinking, gambling, and dancing at halls for entertainment. In response, the archdioceses of Seattle and San Francisco created Filipino Catholic Clubs that severed as a social meeting place, but also assisted them in finding housing, jobs, and schools; provided burials; and offered money for those who wanted to return to the Philippines (Burns, Skerrett, and White 2000, 263). Moreover, Filipino immigrants established mutual assistance associations based on language and regional similarities; for example, "Ilocanos, Tagalogs, Pangasinans, and Visayans formed their own associations" as a means to maintain cultural traditions and to provide mutual aid to members (Espiritu 1995, 11).

Similar to their experience on the plantations of Hawai'i, Filipino laborers in the American West battled oppressive working conditions, low pay, and various other forms of exploitation and discrimination: Here, too, they resisted though organized labor moments. As pay and working conditions declined during the Great Depression, many Filipinos believed unions could help them. For example, in 1929, asparagus workers earned $4.14 per day. By 1934, they earned $3.30 per day (Jiobu 1988, 50). Since the American Federation of Labor (AFL) refused to organize Filipinos, believing they would take jobs from white Euro-American workers, in 1933, D. L. Marcuelo, a Filipino businessman in Stockton, California, established the Filipino Labor Union, or FLU (Bacon 2008, 209). In August 1933, the FLU called a strike against lettuce growers in the Salinas Valley demanding better working conditions and higher wages. At the time, 40 percent of the agricultural workforce was Filipino. The growers used Mexicans to break the strike. Although the strike ended when local vigilantes burned the camp to the ground and forced the strikers to flee, the FLU gained credibility with the AFL. By 1936, the AFL granted a charter to the Field Workers Union, Local 30326—a combined Filipino-Mexican organization. In 1940, the AFL chartered the Federated Agricultural Laborers Association, a completely Filipino union. In 1959, the AFL established the Agricultural Workers Organizing Committee (AWOC), with a largely Filipino union to organize grape pickers in the San Joaquin Valley. The movement was led by two Philippines-born men—Larry Itliong and Philip Vera Cruz. They worked and competed with César Chávez and his National Farm Workers Association (NFWA). Together, they mobilized enough strikers that by September 1965, they called for a strike to demand higher wages. The following year, the AWOC and NFWA merged to form the United Farm Workers (Bacon 2008, 210). In their 1969 proclamation they wrote, "Grapes must remain an unenjoyed luxury for all as long as the barest human needs and basic human rights are still luxuries for farm workers. The grapes grow sweet and heavy on the vines, but they will have to wait while we reach out first for our freedom. The time is ripe for our liberation" (Huerta 1969).

Canned Salmon on the Pacific Northwest

Besides the fields of the American West, Filipinos worked in the canneries of the Pacific Northwest and Alaska. The resource-rich environment of the Pacific Northwest needed human labor. The salmon-packing industry began in California in 1864 and from there spread northward to the Bering Sea (Newell 1988, 627). Salmon industry owners of the region had to rely on voluntary and coerced migration from labor-rich areas to fill their crews (Friday 1994, 6). In Alaska and British Columbia, Chinese laborers dominated cannery work in the 1880s and 1890s. In Alaska in 1902, Chinese workers constituted over 5,300 of the workforce of 13,800 (Newell 1988, 636). As a direct result of Chinese exclusion, the contractors began to experience a shortage of able-bodied Chinese workers. They substituted other ethnic workers, first Japanese, then Filipino, and finally Mexican (O'Bannon 1987, 562). By 1909, Japanese contract workers constituted one-third of the workforce (Newell 1988, 636). Similar to the sugar planters in Hawai'i, the canned salmon owners of Alaska employed ethnic antagonisms to divide the workers, allowing contractors and owners to exploit them ruthlessly (Friday 1994, 4). Known as "Alaskeros," the majority of Filipinos who worked in the salmon industry were mostly single men in their late teens and early 20s (Friday 1994, 194). By the 1930s, Filipinos comprised the bulk of the cannery workforce (Baldoz 2011, 13). During the Depression years of the 1930s the number of available white Euro-American workers increased. In the face of declining employment opportunities and increasing racial prejudice, the number of Filipinos migrating to the West Coast dropped sharply during this decade (Melendy 1974, 521).

Anti-Filipino Sentiments

The influx of Filipinos to the U.S. mainland during the 1920s incensed xenophobic nativist leaders who viewed the newcomers' special status as U.S. nationals as an affront to the restrictive spirit of the 1917 Asiatic Barred Zone Act (also known as the Immigration Act of 1917) and the 1924 National Origins Quota Act. Section 4 of the Philippine Bill of 1902 (also known as the Cooper Act) defined Filipinos as "citizens of the Philippine Islands and, as such, entitled to the protection of the United States." According to Rick Baldoz, Filipinos claimed "their compulsory allegiance to the United States entitled them to civic recognition from their political sovereign" and exploited "loopholes in statutory language to claim rights creating headaches for authorities" (Baldoz 2011, 14). Filipinos did not fit neatly into the preexisting racial hierarchy and social-political order, which generated a good deal of confusion for authorities tasked with enforcing a patchwork structure of racial regulations enacted at the federal, state, and local governments (Baldoz 2011, 13–14).

One example of this problem was evident in early disputes over whether Filipinos were eligible for citizenship in the United States. Clear resolution of this issue proved elusive because American naturalization law only applied to "aliens" and contained no procedure for naturalizing the newly invented class of persons known as "nationals." The U.S. Congress in 1906 did not help xenophobic nativists by allowing, under certain circumstances, persons who held allegiance to the United States to petition for citizenship. The Naturalization Act of 1906 also required immigrants to learn English in order to become naturalized citizens, which was not difficult for Filipinos since many learned English. In 1918, Congress stipulated that Filipinos (and Puerto Ricans) who served three years in the U.S. Navy, Army, Marine Corps, Coast Guard, or merchant marines could petition for citizenship.

By 1927, various groups, particularly labor organizations and so-called patriotic societies such as Native Sons and the American Legion, sought to exclude Filipinos for various economic and social reasons. Anti-Filipino legislations were thus sponsored in Congress—for example, the Welch Bill of 1928, which called for classifying Filipinos as "alien people," and the Shortridge Amendment of 1930, which limited Filipino immigration to "students, servants, attendants, merchants, government officials and their family members" (Gonzalez 1998, 30). These bills were designed to prevent Filipinos from coming to America. This was to be accomplished by the simple maneuver of changing their status from "nationals" to "aliens," thus making them subject to the provisions of the 1924 Quota Law that excluded all Asians. Unfortunately for the exclusionists, however, neither bill became law, and other solutions to the Filipino problem were explored (Christiansen 1979, 66).

In the late 1920s and early 1930s it became clear that the only effective way to exclude Filipinos would be to make the Philippines an independent sovereign nation. Among manufacturers, this was a relatively popular position, since they perceived a competition from sugar, cordage, coconut, and tobacco entering the United States from the Philippines duty free. Consequently, Congress passed the Tydings-McDuffie Act (also known as the Philippines Independence Act), which President Roosevelt signed into law on March 24, 1934. It became effective for immigration purposes on May 1, 1934. As of this date, Filipinos were considered aliens, and only 50 were allowed to enter the country annually, although Section Eight allowed Hawaiian sugar planters an exemption to import more Filipino laborers to the islands if they could demonstrate a need (Christiansen 1979, 66–67; Grant 2011, 473). In exchange for limiting Filipino migration to 50 a year, the Philippines would become an independent nation by 1946. On July 10, 1935, Congress passed the Welch Repatriation Act and financed it with $300,000 to repatriate Filipinos. The Department of Labor even charted a train leaving New York for San Francisco, making stops at Cleveland, Chicago, and St. Louis, "to deliver a trainload of Filipinos to the passenger ship *President Coolidge* for transportation to Manila" (Starr 2009, 452). In 1936, the allocation was reduced to $100,000. The majority of Filipino men residing in the United States declined the offer of aid because Section Four of the act stipulated that "no Filipino who receives the benefits of this act shall be entitled to return to the continental United States." Others declined the offer because by the late 1930s, the economy in California began to improve. The program lasted five years, and the government's goal was to lure some 45,000 Filipinos back to the Philippines, but only 2,190 Filipinos returned (Starr 2009, 452). Filipinos who stayed may have done so out of embarrassment, or the lack of opportunity in the Philippines, or concern about being able to return to the United States (Odo 2002, 234).

These legislations' aim was to decrease the size of the Filipino population to reduce employment competition in the aftermath of the Great Depression, but "just prior to independence for the new Asian republic, some 7,361 Filipinos migrated to the Territory of Hawaii" (Melendy 1974, 522). Many came at that particular time because they expected easy access to Hawaiʻi to end when the quota system went into effect following Philippine independence. Others came in response to a growing postwar need for labor on Hawaiʻi's sugar plantations. The socioeconomic conditions of the 1920s and 1930s not only transformed anti-Filipino ideology into anti-Filipino legislations, but also manifested into anti-Filipino violence.

Anti-Filipino Violence

From the late 1920s and throughout the 1930s, the Filipino population increased in size, which coupled with deepening impact of the Great Depression fueled white resentment as they viewed Filipinos was "foreigners robbing" them of their jobs (Nomura 1986–1987, 103). Fears of losing their jobs and their women to Filipinos led some whites to violence. For example, on New Year's Eve 1926, a riot erupted in Stockton, California, against Filipinos for their association with "white women" (Chacón and Davis 2006, 40). Another anti-Filipino incident organized by the American Legion unfolded in the Tulare County town of Dinuba on August 1926 (Chacón and Davis 2006, 40). Up north in Washington, on November 1927, whites drove Filipinos in the Toppenish district of the Yakima Indian Reservation "out of their houses, beat them, dumped their produce, and dragged many to freight trains leaving the Valley" (Nomura 1986–1987, 103–4). In 1928, Filipinos were driven out of Wenatchee Valley: during this anti-Filipino incident, whites stressed their concern about the relationship between the Filipinos and white women (Jamieson 1976, 211).

On October 24, 1929, a riot broke out in Exeter, California, as white workers went from ranch to ranch demanding the dismissal of all Filipino workers. Owners who did not oblige the mob's request had their property damaged (Brands 1992, 151). Three months later, a four-day riot in Watsonville led to the worst outbreak of violence. On January 19, 1930, whites attacked a hall rented by Filipino laborers for a dance in which white women were hired to be their partners; one Filipino was killed and their camp burned. In describing the events of the Watsonville anti-Filipino riot, Richard Meynell writes,

> On Wednesday, 22 January, the riot reached its peak with mobs of hundreds dragging Filipinos out of their homes, whipping and beating them, and throwing them off the Pajaro River bridge. The mobs ranged up the San Juan road, attacking Filipinos at the Storm and Detlefsen ranches; a Chinese apple-dryer that employed Filipinos was demolished, and volleys of shots were reportedly fired into a Filipino home on Ford Street. At Riberal's labor camp, twenty-two Filipinos were dragged out and beaten. This time the mob had leaders and organization—it moved "military-like" and responded to orders to attack or withdraw. The police in Watsonville, led by Sheriff Nick Sinnott, rounded up as many Filipinos as they could rescue and guarded them in the City Council's chamber. ... Early the next morning (the 23rd) bullets were fired into a bunkhouse on the Murphy ranch on the San Juan Road. Eleven Filipinos huddled in a closet to escape the fusillade. At dawn they discovered that a twelfth, Fermin Tobera, had been shot through the heart. (1998)

Howard DeWitt notes that the white mob who killed 22-year-old Tobera were not jobless farm-workers, but came from "well-to-do-families" (1979).

Shortly thereafter, on January 29, 1930, a meeting hall for the Filipino Federation of America was dynamited in Stockton, and anti-Filipino demonstrations followed in Salinas, San Jose, and San Francisco (Starr 1996, 64). H. W. Brands notes, "The summer of 1930 brought clashes between Anglos and Filipinos in several counties of northern California. A bombing in the Imperial Valley of southern California resulted in the death of one Filipino and injuries to several. Less violent demonstrations against Filipinos took place in Idaho and Utah" (1992, 151). The dual threat of Filipino men to white women and jobs is conveyed in a Yakima newspaper: "Hard-fisted, weather-beaten white ranchers from the lower Yakima Valley swore solemnly before Senator Lewis B. Schwellenbach that there soon will be bloody race riots that forever will be a blot on this State if the Federal Government does not move against Filipinos ... who unlawfully are crowding out the whites" (cited in Jamieson 1976, 211). Filipino men were thus not only an "economic danger," but a "sexual danger" as well. In exciting vigilantism and racial hatred in Pajaro Valley, California, Judge D. Rohrback emphasized a bizarre equation between miscegenation and economic displacement: "He [the Filipino] gives them silk underwear and makes them pregnant and crowds whites out of jobs in the bargain" (cited in Chacón and Davis 2006, 41). Furthermore, Rohrback also warned, "if the present state of affairs continues ... there will be 40,000 half-breeds in the State of California before ten years have passed" (cited in Chacón and Davis 2006, 41).

Filipinos and Antimiscegenation Laws

During the 1930s, state legislatures from California, Arizona, Idaho, Nevada, and other states passed statutes that would prevent interracial marriage between "white" and "Mongolian" (i.e., Asian) people. In California, Mexicans occupied a unique racial position. According to Martha Menchaca, if the phenotype of Mexicans appeared to be more than one-half white, by law they were considered to be part of the "white race," and thus forbidden from marrying Asians and blacks. Similarly, when the blood quantum of Mexicans exceeded one-eighth black, they were considered black and therefore forbidden from marry whites (2008, 303–4). California Civil Code, Section 60 thus authorized marriage clerks to interpret and determine the blood quantum of their applicants based on their physical appearance (Menchaca 2008, 304).

In 1905, Section 60 of the California Civil Code declared, "All marriages of white persons with Negroes, Mongolians, or mulattoes are illegal and void." Filipinos however, argued that they were Malay, not Mongolian. This discrepancy allowed some Filipinos to marry their white wives, while others were denied marriage licenses. Because the legislature did not specify Malays in their policy, clerks and judges had the discretion to determine their race and decide whom Filipinos could marry (Menchaca 2008, 304). The opinions of judges and state attorneys general differed on the status of Filipino-white intermarriage under Section 60—in particular, whether Filipinos were Malay or Mongolian. In 1926, California's county clerks requested California attorney general Ulysses S. Webb to determine if Filipinos were Mongolian or mixed Caucasians, because the antimiscegenation policy was not enforced uniformly (Leonard 1992; Volpp 2000). It was not until 1933 that the racial classification of Filipinos was finally determined. Salvador Roldan, a Filipino, was denied the right to marry his white fiancée when Los Angeles County clerk L. E. Lampton refused to issue a marriage license. On January 27, 1933, in the case of *Salvador Roldan v. Los Angeles*

County, the State Court of Appeals ruled that Filipino men can marry white women based on their racial classification as "Malay" because California law said nothing about "Malays" (Menchaca 2008, 305). The victory proved short-lived, as the legislature bowed to nativist pressure and passed Senate Bills 175 and 176 to amend Sections 60 and 69 of the civil code by including Malays among the nonwhite groups who could not intermarry with whites. Governor James Rolph signed these bills into law on August 21, 1933. Nevertheless, some Filipino men and their spouses circumvented the laws by traveling to states that did not have antimiscegenation laws against Malays (i.e., Filipinos). For example, the state of Washington did not have antimiscegenation laws; therefore, many of the early Filipino families in Puget Sound were interracial (Cordova and Filipino American National Historical Society, 2009, 8). Others married in Mexico.

It was not until 1948 that the California Supreme Court ruled that bans on interracial marriage were unconstitutional in the case of *Perez v. Sharp* (Hurwitz 1949). The Los Angeles County Clerk's Office denied Andrea Perez, a Mexican American, and Sylvester Davis, an African American a marriage application on that grounds that Perez looked like a "full-blooded Caucasian" (Menchaca 2008, 306). Perez and Davis sought the aid of the American Civil Liberties Union who petitioned the California Supreme Court to hear the case, bypassing the superior court level. On October 1, 1948, the California Supreme Court pronounced its decision: in the majority opinion, the court ruled that California's antimiscegenation law violated the equal protection clause of the 14th Amendment because marriage was a fundamental right (Hurwitz 1949; Menchaca 2008). Secondly, the court argued, since California's antimiscegenation law was not consistently applied, it was found to be discriminatory, and therefore, unconstitutional (Hurwitz 1949, 123). Prior to this, the rationale for upholding antimiscegenation laws was the legal precedent of "equality of application" or "separate but equal" à la *Plessy v. Ferguson* (1896). "If protecting the social welfare of whites was the basis of the statute it was illogical that they were allowed to marry people of Indian descent, yet were prohibited from marrying Asians or Blacks. *Perez* [*v. Sharp*] established the legal precedent where the 14th Amendment could be invoked in defense of a person's right to marry freely. Although, at this time it only applied to religious freedom cases, a constitutional legal precedent had been set. Likewise, it became the first ruling in U.S. history to offer the opinion that the separation of the races was a policy predicated upon ideology rather than on reliable scientific findings" (Menchaca 2008, 308). Most other states with antimiscegenation laws did not take them off their books until the U.S. Supreme Court ruled in *Loving v. Virginia* in 1967, which declared any race-based restrictions on marriage to be unconstitutional.

FILIPINOS AND THE U.S. NAVY

Immediately after the United States annexed the Philippines, it acquired Spanish military posts, including Subic Bay, and established several U.S. military bases on the islands during and after the Philippine-American War (Yeo 2011, 37). Thus, the U.S. Navy recruited Filipinos into service. In 1901, President McKinley signed an executive order that authorized the navy to enlist 500 Filipino stewards (Burdeos 2010, xii). Filipinos were the only Asian ethnic group to serve in the U.S. military without U.S. citizenship. Throughout the 1930s, 4,000 Filipinos served, but U.S. Navy policy relegated them to being stewards (mess boys who waited on officers), a position that was previously occupied by African Americans (Jiobu 1988, 50). For Filipinos without education and special skill, and no immediate relatives in America, the U.S. Navy was an opportunity for a better life (Oades 2005). A career in the U.S. Navy offered a viable alternative to poverty experienced by most Filipinos: even a steward's pay placed them among the top 25 percent of wage earners in the Philippines.

In 1918, Congress stipulated Filipinos who served in the U.S. military for three years can petition for naturalization (Reinecke 1996, 2). Eligibility for citizenship meant that Filipino immigrants can become land and home owners as early as the 1920s, while virtually all other Asians were prohibited from citizenship and thus land ownership for another 30 years. With the passage of the Tydings-McDuffie Act of 1934, Philippine independence was recognized, but there was a transition period of 10 years that would allow the United States to maintain its military bases on the islands. The act changed the legal status of Filipinos from "national" to "alien," and a quota of only 50 Filipinos were allowed to migrate to the United States. However, the U.S. Navy received a waiver to continue recruiting Filipinos even though they were now considered foreign citizens.

Even after the Philippines gained formal independence in 1946 after World War II, the U.S. military installations remained, and the 1947 Military Bases Agreement allowed the United States to leave five major bases and at least 20 minor military installations for 99 years at no cost, and to continue to recruit Filipinos for U.S. military service (Schirmer and Shalom 2000, 98). With the advent of the Korean War in the early 1950s, the U.S. Navy was allowed to enroll "up to two thousand Filipinos per calendar year for terms of four or six years" (Espiritu 1995, 15).

FILIPINOS AND WORLD WAR II (1939–1945)

In 1942, President Roosevelt signed executive orders that allowed Filipinos to enlist for military service without citizenship. This decision was based on the sheer need for manpower. In the spring of 1942, Secretary of

War Henry Stimson announced the formation of the First Filipino Battalion, made up entirely of Filipino troops and a mix of Filipino and white officers. Because of the large number of Filipinos volunteering for service, the battalion was reorganized as the First Filipino Regiment on July 13, 1942, in Salinas, California. Months later, on October 14, the Second Filipino Regiment was created, and it was activated at Fort Ord, California, on November 21, 1942. By the end of the war, about 7,000 Filipino men had volunteered for service in the U.S. Army.

World War II was an important turning point for Filipinos in America. The United States and the Philippines became allies during the war, which decreased anti-Filipino sentiments as more and more Filipinos displayed their loyalty to the United States. During the war, Filipino Americans serving in the U.S. military were granted the rights to become naturalized citizens beginning in 1943.

On July 2, 1946, Congress passed the Luce-Celler Bill (also known as the Filipino Naturalization Act and the Indian Immigration and Naturalization Act) that permitted the naturalization of all remaining Filipinos in the United States. The act granted Filipinos and Indians the right to become naturalized citizens and established a quota of 100 persons for each country.

Japanese troops guard American and Filipino prisoners in Bataan, the Philippines, following Japan's capture of the Bataan Peninsula, April 9, 1942. The prisoners were later forced to march over 60 miles from Bataan to Tarlac in what became known as the Bataan Death March. (Keystone/ Hulton Archive/Getty Images)

The act specifically granted Filipinos who arrived before 1934 the right to become naturalize citizens: 10,764 Filipinos did just that. Despite the quota, Filipinos employed other means to migrate to the United States. Filipino war brides and nurses accounted for a large number of Filipino women who emigrated after the passage of the Luce-Celler Bill. The Military War Brides Act of 1945 and the Fiancées Act of 1946 allowed for the migration of Filipinas. Approximately 118,000 spouses and children of U.S. servicemen migrated to the United States (Posadas 1999, 28). In addition, the Exchange Visitor Program (EVP) administered by the State Department in 1948 offered Filipino nurses the unique opportunity to pursue postgraduate study in American hospitals (Choy 2003).

In 1952, the McCarran-Walter Act provided family reunification to Filipinos who were U.S. citizens (native born or naturalized) even beyond the quota of 100 Filipinos who were allowed entry into the United States every year. Perhaps the major change to Filipino immigration came in 1965 with the passage of the Immigration and Nationality Act, which eliminated national origins quotas, relieved occupational shortages (specifically health care professionals), and achieved family reunification. Ten years after the passage of the 1965 Immigration and Nationality Act, more than 230,000 Filipinos immigrated to the United States, which doubled the 1960 population. In the years after the enactment of the Immigration Act of 1990, Filipino immigrants continued to come to the United States mainly for family-sponsored and employment-based categories.

REFERENCES

Abraham, Itty. "Filipinos in the US." *Economic and Political Weekly* 41:8 (February 25–March 3, 2006): 674.
Alcantara, Ruben. *Sakada: Filipino Adaptation in Hawaii.* Washington, DC: University Press of America, 1981.
Allen, James P. "Recent Immigration from the Philippines and Filipino Communities in the United States." *Geographical Review* 67:2 (April 1977): 195–208.
Andaya, Leonard Y. "From American-Filipino to Filipino-American." *Social Process in Hawaii* 37 (1996): 99–111.
Asher, Robert, and Charles Stephenson, eds. *Labor Divided: Race and Ethnicity in United States Labor Struggles, 1835–1960.* Albany: State University of New York Press, 1990.
Asian American Curriculum and Research Project. Woodring College of Education. Western Washington University. http://www.wce.wwu.edu/resources/aacr/documents.shtml (accessed June 11, 2014).
Azuma, Eiichiro. "Racial Struggle, Immigrant Nationalism, and Ethnic Identity: Japanese and Filipinos in the California Delta." *Pacific Historical Review* 67:2 (May 1998): 163–99.

Bacon, David. *Illegal People: How Globalization Creates Migration and Criminalizes Immigrants.* Boston: Beacon Press, 2008.

Baldoz, Rick. *The Third Asiatic Invasion: Empire and Migration in Filipino America, 1898–1946.* New York: New York University Press, 2011.

Barde, Robert E. *Immigration at the Golden Gate: Passenger, Ships, Exclusion, and Angel Island.* Westport, CT: Praeger, 2008.

Bautista, Veltisezar B. *The Filipino Americans: From 1763 to the Present: Their History, Culture, and Traditions.* Farmington Hills, MI: Bookhaus Publishers, 1998.

Bonacich, Edna. "Class Approaches to Ethnicity and Race." *Critical Sociology* 25:2–3 (1999): 166–94.

Bonus, Rick. *Locating Filipino Americans: Ethnicity and the Cultural Politics of Space.* Philadelphia: Temple University Press, 2000.

Borah, Eloisa G. "Filipinos in Unamuno's California Expedition of 1587." *Amerasia Journal* 21:3 (Winter 1995–1996): 175–83.

Borah, Eloisa G. *Chronology of Filipinos in America Pre-1898.* 1997–2004. http://personal.anderson.ucla.edu/eloisa.borah/chronology.pdf (accessed June 11, 2014).

Brands, H. W. *Bound to Empire: The United States and the Philippines.* Oxford: Oxford University Press, 1992.

Bronner, Simon J. ed. *Lafcadio Hearn's America: Ethnographic Sketches and Editorials.* Lexington: University Press of Kentucky, 2002.

Burdeos, Ray L. *Pinoy Stewards in the U.S. Sea Services: Seizing Marginal Opportunity.* Bloomington, IN: AuthorHouse, 2010.

Burns, Jeffery M., Ellen Skerrett, and Joseph M. White, eds. *Keeping Faith: European and Asian Catholic Immigrants.* Maryknoll, NY: Orbis Books, 2000.

Capozzola, Christopher. "Filipinas/os." In *Anti-Immigration in the United States: A Historical Encyclopedia*, edited by Kathleen R. Arnold. Santa Barbara, CA: ABC-CLIO, 2011.

Chacón, Justin A., and Mike Davis. *No One Is Illegal: Fighting Racism and State Violence on the U.S.-Mexico Border.* Photographs by Julián Cardona. Chicago: Haymarket Books, 2006.

Chan, Sucheng. *Asian Americans: An Interpretive History.* New York: Twayne, 1991.

Choy, Catherine C. *Empire of Care: Nursing and Migration in Filipino American History.* Durham, NC: Duke University Press, 2003.

Christiansen, John B. "The Split Labor Market Theory and Filipino Exclusion: 1927–1934." *Phylon* 40:1 (1979): 66–74.

Cordova, Dorothy, and Filipino American National Historical Society. *Filipinos in Puget Sound.* Charleston, SC: Arcadia Publishing, 2009.

Cruz, Adrian. "There Will Be No 'One Big Union': The Struggle for Interracial Labor Unionism in California Agriculture, 1933–1939." *Cultural Dynamics* 22:1 (2010): 29–48.

Dela Cruz, Melany, and Pauline Agbayani-Siewert. "Swimming with and against the Tide: Filipino American Demographic Changes." In *The New Face of Asian Pacific America: Numbers, Diversity and Change in the 21st Century*, edited by Eric Lai and Dennis Arguelles. San Francisco: AsianWeek, 2003.

De Los Santos, P. "*Sakada* Dreams: A Portrait of My Father." *Social Process in Hawaii* 37 (1996): 91–98.

DeWitt, Howard A. "The Filipino Labor Union: The Salinas Lettuce Strike of 1934." *Amerasia Journal* 5:2 (1978): 1–21.

DeWitt, Howard A. *Violence in the Fields: California Filipino Farm Labor Unionization during the Great Depression.* Saratoga, CA: Century Twenty One Publishing, 1980.

DeWitt, Howard A. "The Watsonville Anti-Filipino Riot of 1930: A Case Study of the Great Depression and Ethnic Conflict in California." *Southern California Quarterly* 61:3 (September 1979): 291–302.

Dunne, John G. *Delano: The Story of the California Grape Strike.* Berkeley: University of California Press, 1967.

Esguerra, Maria Paz Gutierrez. "Filipino Immigrants." In *Multicultural America: An Encyclopedia of the Newest Americans*, edited by Ronald H. Bayor. Santa Barbara, CA: ABC-CLIO, 2011.

Espina, Marina E. *Filipinos in Louisiana.* New Orleans: A. F. Laborde & Sons, 1988.

Espiritu, Yen Le. *Filipino American Lives.* Philadelphia: Temple University Press, 1995.

Espiritu, Yen Le. *Homeward Bound: Filipino American Lives across Cultures, Communities, and Countries.* Berkeley: University of California Press, 2003.

Fermin, Jose D. *1904 World's Fair: The Filipino Experience.* West Conshohocken, PA: Infinity Publishing.com, 2004.

Fredriksen, John. *Fighting Elites: A History of U.S. Special Forces.* Santa Barbara, CA: ABC-CLIO, 2012.

Friday, Chris. *Organizing Asian American Labor: The Pacific Coast Canned-Salmon Industry, 1870–1942.* Philadelphia: Temple University Press, 1994.

Fujita-Rony, Dorothy B. "1898, U.S. Militarism, and the Formation of Asian American." *Asian American Policy Review* 19 (January 1, 2010): 67–71.

Gonzalez, Joaquin L. *Philippine Labour Migration: Critical Dimensions of Public Policy.* Singapore: Institute for Southeast Asian Studies, 1998.

Grant, Larry A. "Tydings-McDuffie Act of 1934." In *Anti-Immigration in the United States: A Historical Encyclopedia*, edited by Kathleen R. Arnold. Santa Barbara, CA: ABC-CLIO, 2011.

Hamilton, Richard F. *President McKinley, War and Empire: President McKinley and America's "New Empire."* Vol. 2. New Brunswick, NJ: Transaction Publishers, 2007.

Hearn, Lafcadio. "Saint Malo: A Lacustrine Village in Louisiana." *Harper's Weekly* (March 31, 1883): 196–99.

Huerta, Dolores. "Proclamation of the Delano Grape Workers." Digital History ID 613, 1969. http://www.digitalhistory.uh.edu/disp_textbook.cfm?smtID=3&psid=613.

Hung, T. K. "The Igorot Village." In *Report of the Philippine Exposition.* St. Louis, MO: 1904.

Hurwitz, Robert R. "Constitutional Law: Equal Protection of the Laws: California Anti-Miscegenation Laws Declared Unconstitutional." *California Law Review* 37:1 (March 1949): 122–29.

Jamieson, Stuart M. *Labor Unionism in American Agriculture*. U.S. Department of Labor, Bulletin No. 836. Washington, DC: 1976.

Jiobu, Robert M. *Ethnicity and Assimilation: Blacks, Chinese, Filipinos, Japanese, Koreans, Mexicans, Vietnamese, and Whites*. Albany: State University of New York Press, 1988.

Johnson, Chalmers. *The Sorrows of Empire: Militarism, Secrecy, and the End of the Republic*, New York: Henry Holt and Company, 2004.

Judis, John B. *The Folly of Empire: What George W. Bush Could Learn from Theodore Roosevelt*. Oxford: Oxford University Press, 2004.

Juvik, James, and Sonia P. Juvik. *Atlas of Hawai'i*. 3rd ed. Honolulu: University of Hawai'i Press, 1999.

Kawakami, Barbara F. *Japanese Immigrant Clothing in Hawaii 1885–1941*. Honolulu: University of Hawai'i Press, 1993.

Leo, Mark S. "(In)Visible Within: Igorot Filipino Americans." M.A. thesis, San Francisco State University, 2011.

Leonard, Karen Isaken. *Making Ethnic Choices: California's Punjabi Mexican Americans*. Philadelphia: Temple University Press, 1992.

Lind, Andrew W. "Assimilation in Rural Hawai'i." *American Journal of Sociology* 45:2 (September 1939): 200–214.

Lind, Andrew W. "The Ghetto and the Slum." *Social Forces* 9:2 (December 1930): 206–15.

Lind, Andrew W. "Immigration to Hawai'i." *Social Process in Hawaii* 29 (1982).

Lott, Juanita Tamayo. *The Common Destiny of Multigenerational Americans: Four Generations of Filipino Americans*. Lanham, MD: Rowman & Littlefield Publishers, 2006.

Mabalon, Dawn B., Rico Reyes, Filipino American National Historical Society, and the Little Manila Foundation. *Filipinos in Stockton*. Charleston, SC: Arcadia Publishing, 2008.

Maeda, Daryl J. *Chains of Babylon: The Rise of Asian America*. Minneapolis: University of Minnesota Press, 2009.

Marquardt, W. W. "An Unparalleled Venture in Education." *Far Eastern Quarterly* 4:2 (February 1945): 135–39.

May, Glenn A. "Why the United States Won the Philippine-American War, 1899–1902." *Pacific Historical Review* 52:4 (November 1983): 353–77.

Melendy, H. Brett. *Asians in America: Filipinos, Koreans, and East Indians*. Boston: Twayne Publishers, 1977.

Melendy, H. Brett. "Filipinos in the United States." *Pacific Historical Review* 43:4 (November 1974): 520–47.

Menchaca, Martha. "The Anti-Miscegenation History of the American Southwest, 1837 to 1970: Transforming Racial Ideology into Law." *Cultural Dynamics* 20 (2008): 279–318.

Mercene, Floro L. *Manila Men in the New World: Filipino Migration to Mexico and the Americas from the Sixteenth Century*. Quezon City: University of the Philippines Press, 2007.

Merry, Sally E. "Christian Conversion and 'Racial' Labor Capacities: Constructing Racialized Identities in Hawai'i." In *Globalization under Construction:*

Governmentality, Law, and Identity, edited by Richard W. Perry and Bill Maurer. Minneapolis: University of Minnesota Press, 2003.

Meynell, Richard B. "Little Brown Brothers, Little White Girls: The Anti-Filipino Hysteria of 1930 and the Watsonville Riots." *Passport* 22 (1998). Excerpts available at http://www.modelminority.com/joomla/ (accessed June 11, 2014).

Newell, Dianne. "The Rationality of Mechanization in the Pacific Salmon-Canning Industry before the Second World War." *Business History Review* 62:4 (Winter 1988): 626–55.

Ngozi-Brown, Scot. "African-American Soldiers and Filipinos: Racial Imperialism, Jim Crow and Social Relations." *Journal of Negro History* 82:1 (Winter 1997): 42–53.

Nomura, Gail. "Within the Law: The Establishment of Filipino Leasing Rights on the Yakima Indian Reservation." *Amerasia Journal* 13:1 (1986–1987): 99–117.

Oades, Riz A. *Beyond the Mask: Untold Stories of U.S. Navy Filipinos*. National City, CA: KCS Publishers, 2005.

Odo, Franklin, ed. *The Columbia Documentary History of the Asian American Experience*. New York: Columbia University Press, 2002.

Offner, John L. "McKinley and the Spanish-American War." *Presidential Studies Quarterly* 34:1 (March 2004): 50–61.

Okamura, Jonathan Y. "Beyond Adaptationism: Immigrant Filipino Ethnicity in Hawaii." *Social Process in Hawaii* 33 (1991): 56–72.

Okamura, Jonathan Y. "Filipino Americans." In *The Asian American Encyclopedia*, edited by Franklin Ng. New York: Marshall Cavendish, 1995.

Okihiro, Gary Y. *Cane Fires: The Anti-Japanese Movement in Hawaii, 1865–1945*. Philadelphia: Temple University Press, 1991.

O'Reilly, Shauna, and Brennan O'Reilly. *Alaska Yukon Pacific Exposition*. Charleston, SC: Arcadia Publishing, 2009.

Orosa, Mario E. *The Philippine Pensionado Story*. 2005. http://www.orosa.org/The %20Philippine%20Pensionado%20Story3.pdf (accessed July 14, 2014).

Pérez, Louis A. *The War of 1898: the United States and Cuba in History and Historiography*. Chapel Hill: University of North Carolina Press, 1998.

The Philippine History Site. http://opmanong.ssc.hawaii.edu/filipino/filmig.html (accessed June 23, 2014).

Posadas, Barbara M. "At a Crossroad: Filipino American History and the Old-Timers' Generation." *Amerasia Journal* 13:1 (1986–1987): 85–97.

Posadas, Barbara M. *The Filipino Americans*. Westport, CT: Greenwood Press, 1999.

Posadas, Barbara M. "Teaching about Chicago's Filipino Americans." *OAH Magazine of History* 10:4 (Summer 1996): 38–45.

Posadas, Barbara M., and Roland L. Guyotte. "Unintentional Immigrants: Chicago's Filipino Foreign Students Become Settlers, 1900–1941." *Journal of American Ethnic History* 9:2 (Spring 1990): 26–48.

Reinecke, John E. *Filipino Piecemeal Sugar Strike of 1924–1925*. Honolulu: University of Hawai'i Press, 1996.

Rodell, Paul A. *Culture and Customs of the Philippines*. Westport, CT: Greenwood Press, 2002.

Roosevelt, Theodore. *Presidential Addresses and State Papers and European Addresses, December 8, 1908, to June 7, 1910*. Whitefish, MT: Kessinger Publishing, 2006.

Salamanca, Bonifacio S. *The Filipino Reaction to American Rule 1903–1913*. Hamden, CT: Shoe String Press, 1968.

Salyer, Lucy. "Baptism by Fire: Race, Military Service, and U.S. Citizenship Policy, 1918–1935." *Journal of American History* 91:3 (2004): 847–76.

San Buenaventura, Steffi. "The Colors of Manifest Destiny: Filipinos and the American Other(s)." *Amerasia Journal* 24:3 (1998): 1–26.

San Buenaventura, Steffi. "Hawaii's '1946 Sakada.' " *Social Process in Hawaii* 37 (1996): 74–90.

Schirmer, Daniel B., and Stephen R. Shalom, eds. *The Philippines Reader: A History of Colonialism, Neocolonialism, Dictatorship, and Resistance*. Cambridge, MA: South End Press, 2000.

Sharma, Miriam. "Labor Migration and Class Formation among the Filipinos in Hawaii, 1906–1946." In *Labor Immigration under Capitalism: Asian Workers in the United States before World War II*, edited by Lucie Cheng and Enda Bonacich. Berkeley: University of California Press, 1984a.

Sharma, Miriam. "The Philippines: A Case of Migration to Hawaii, 1906–1946." In *Labor Immigration under Capitalism: Asian Workers in the United States before World War II*, edited by Lucie Cheng and Enda Bonacich. Berkeley: University of California Press, 1984b.

Sharma, Miriam. "Pinoy in Paradise: Environment and Adaptation of Filipinos in Hawaii, 1906–1946." *Amerasia Journal* 7:2 (1980): 91–117.

Starr, Kevin. *Endangered Dreams: The Great Depression in California*. Oxford: Oxford University Press, 1996.

Starr, Kevin. *Golden Dreams: California in an Age of Abundance, 1950–1963*. Oxford: Oxford University Press, 2009.

Suri, Jeremi. *American Foreign Relations since 1898: A Documentary Reader*. Oxford: Blackwell Publishing, 2010.

Takaki, Ronald T. *Strangers from a Different Shore: A History of Asian Americans*. Rev. ed. Boston: Little, Brown, 1989.

Tiongson, Antonio, Edgardo V. Gutierrez, and Ricardo V. Gutierrez, eds. *Positively No Filipinos Allowed: Building Communities and Discourse*. Philadelphia: Temple University Press, 2006.

Tompar-Tiu, Aurora, and Juliana Sustento-Seneriches. *Depression and Other Mental Health Issues: The Filipino American Experience*. San Francisco: Jossey-Bass Publishers, 1995.

Tuason, Julie A. "The Ideology of Empire in *National Geographic* Magazine's Coverage of the Philippines, 1898–1908." *Geographical Review* 89:1 (January 1999): 34–53.

Vaughan, Christopher A. "Ogling Igorots: The Politics and Commerce of Exhibiting Cultural Otherness, 1898–1913." In *Freakery: Cultural Spectacles of the*

Extraordinary Body, edited by Rosemarie G. Thomson. New York: New York University Press, 1996.

Vergara, Benito M. *Pinoy Capital: The Filipino Nation in Daly City*. Philadelphia: Temple University Press, 2009.

Volpp, Leti. "American Mestizo: Filipinos and Antimiscegenation Laws in California." *UC Davis Law Review* 33:4 (2000): 795–835.

Westbrook, Laura. "*Mabuhay Philipino!* (Long Life!): Filipino Culture in Southeast Louisiana." Louisiana's Living Traditions, 1999. http://www. louisianafolklife.org/LT/Articles_Essays/Pilipino1.html (accessed June 11, 2014).

Yeo, Andrew. *Activists, Alliances, and Anti-U.S. Base Protests*. Cambridge: Cambridge University Press, 2011.

Young, James P. "Allies in Migration: Education and Propaganda in a Philippine Village." *Comparative Education Review* 26:2 (June 1982): 218–34.

_____ *Part II* _____

Post-1965

_____ *Chapter 6* _____

Vietnamese in America

Vietnamese for "America" is *Mỹ*. *Mỹ* is derived from the Chinese *mei gok* (*mei guo* in Mandarin), meaning "beautiful country." This translation reflects the rich and diverse history of Vietnam, which for nearly a millennium was under Chinese rule. It was during the Han dynasty (206 BCE–220 CE) that Vietnam firmly fell under Chinese rule. The collapse of the Tang dynasty (618–907 CE) in China in the early tenth century ignited a long overdue rebellion against Chinese rule in Vietnam that culminated in 938 CE when Ngo Quyen (897–944), a popular patriot, finally defeated the Chinese armies at the battle on the Bach Dang River, which concluded 1,000 years of Chinese occupation. In 939 CE, the Chinese emperor recognized Ngo Quyen as king of independent Annam (the future Vietnam). The early period of Vietnamese history witnessed repeated conflicts with China, Cambodia, Laos, and the Cham.

Vietnam's first encounter with the West occurred in 1516 when the first Portuguese sailors arrived at Danang, followed by Dominican missionaries. The French dominated Vietnam during the nineteenth century, and nearly half of the twentieth century, beginning in 1887 after defeating China in the Sino-French War (1884–1885). By 1893, France also occupied Cambodia and Laos following their victory in the Franco-Siamese War of 1893. This French holding in Southeast Asia is referred to as French Indochina. The major waves of Vietnamese migration to the United States unfolded amidst international Cold War politics, struggles for independence in former French Indochina, and U.S. involvement in the region with the aim of containing the spread of communism. The migration of Vietnamese refugees from the mid-1970s to the early 1990s occurred in tandem with refugees from Cambodia and Laos. Although the dominant image of Vietnamese Americans are as refugees fleeing war-torn Vietnam after the fall of Saigon on April 30, 1975, there is a pre-1975 population of students, some professionals, and war brides (Vu 2003, 140). There tends to be an association of Vietnamese Americans with "that" war, which translates into their perception of "helpless peasants, barbaric warriors, or cheap prostitutes" (Võ 2003, ix). Long S. Le notes, "the 'birth' of Vietnamese American experience is related to American involvement in Vietnam during the end of World War II" (2011, 1160). The result was 30 years of continuous war from 1945 to 1975, which caused great suffering and displaced millions of people. "The United States eventually resettled a total of over a million Vietnamese refugees" (UNHCR 2000, 91).

FACTORS OF VIETNAMESE MIGRATION

The pre-1975 Vietnamese migrants residing in the United States were largely comprised of students, professionals, and war brides (Vu 2003, 140). According to the U.S. Census, from 1951 to 1975, this "pre-fall" group totaled a little more than 20,000. Many of these Vietnamese students joined efforts to promote a positive public image of Vietnam as not just a site of war, but as a culturally rich and beautiful country. In addition, they criticized American foreign policy in Vietnam that turned their country upside down, leaving thousands homeless and injured. At the same time, they espoused U.S. support of the Republic of South Vietnam.

Dinh Hoa Nguyen, one of these pre-1975 students, migrated to the United States in 1948 to pursue a doctoral degree in English education (1999). Although Dinh Hoa Nguyen returned to Vietnam after he completed his degree, he returned to the United States in 1965 and settled here permanently. Another student, Long Nguyen, studied at the University of California at Berkeley while pursuing a doctoral degree in political science from 1968 to 1973. Prior to 1968, Long Nguyen was a student activist who organized protests against the Ngo Dinh Diem government (1955–1963) and the Nguyen Van Thieu government (1967–1975). As a student in the United States, Long Nguyen continued his activism and participated in anti–Vietnam War protests. In 1973, he returned to Vietnam and stayed, believing the Communist Party's proclamation that patriotism and nationalism together can lead to a coalition government that would rebuild Vietnam. He would change his position, as life conditions under communist rule were inhumane. Thus, Long Nguyen risked life and escaped successfully by boat in 1979. The experiences of Dinh Hoa Nguyen and Long Nguyen validate Vu Pham's contention that Vietnamese American history must be dated before 1975. However, they also illustrate a connection to the post-1975 refugee migration movements.

In 1930, Ho Chi Minh created the Vietnamese Communist Party, consisting of nine members. During World War II, the Japanese invaded Vietnam and forced the French out. During this time, Ho Chi Minh was a prisoner in China, and he was released with the hope that he would return to Vietnam and create a resistance force to fight against the Japanese. Ho Chi Minh returned to Vietnam in 1941 and created the Vietnam Independence Solidarity League which was better known as the Viet Minh. In 1944–1945, famine struck Vietnam, causing one million Vietnamese to starve to death (Schulzinger 1997, 18). The leader of the Viet Minh armies, Vo Nguyen Giap, led his forces against the Japanese in North Vietnamese villages and liberated tons of food. This food was then given to the peasant population, gaining the support of the people in the coming struggles. During the "August Revolution" of 1945, the Viet Minh captured power in major cities; they captured Hanoi on August 19, then Hue on August 24–25. On August 24, Emperor Bo Dai abdicated and became "Citizen Vinh Thuy" (Chan 2006, 31). On September 2, 1945, Ho Chi Minh stood before a crowd of 500,000 in the center of Hanoi and announced the birth of the Communist-run Democratic Republic of Vietnam. He started his speech by citing the United States' Declaration of Independence, and then went on to denounce the French, claiming "they have built more prisons than schools ... They have drowned our revolution in blood ... They have forced upon us alcohol and opium in order to weaken our race" (Schulzinger 1997, 19).

At the close of World War II, the Provisional Government of the French Republic restored colonial rule of French Indochina (Cambodia, Laos, and Vietnam); thus they reentered Vietnam and immediately started fighting against the Viet Minh. Communist forces battled it out with nationalist forces in the First Indochina War (December 19, 1946–August 1, 1954). The fight between Ho Chi Minh's Viet Minh forces and the newly created Vietnamese National Army, who had the support of the French and the United States, lasted eight years. The French held the cities, while the Viet Minh dominated the countryside. In order to gain support from the peasant population, the Viet Minh redistributed land previously held by the French to the peasants and began a literacy campaign. The Viet Minh forces, who were composed of only a few thousand in 1945, numbered more than 200,000 by 1950, including many guerillas and armed civilians. Also, the membership of the Indochinese Communist Party (ICP) in 1946 consisted of 20,000, while it grew to 700,000 by 1954.

The death knell for the French occurred with their embarrassing defeat against the Viet Minh at the Battle of Dien Bien Phu in May 1954: after fighting for 55 days, the besieged French garrison was captured: "eleven thousand French troops still alive and uninjured surrendered" (Chan 2006, 41). While this was unfolding, an international conference at Geneva, Switzerland (April 26–July 20, 1954), was already underway, the purpose of which was to settle issues on the Korean peninsula and in Vietnam, and to restore peace in Indochina. The meeting ended with a document known as the Geneva Accord, signed in July 1954, which temporarily spilt Vietnam into two zones at the 17th Parallel: the Democratic Republic of Vietnam in the north, governed by the Viet Minh and backed by China and the Soviet Union; and the Republic of South Vietnam, backed by the United States. The Geneva Accord stipulated that people who wished to move from north (governed by Communists) to south and vice versa could do so within a 300-day period. Between 1946 and 1948, some 55,000–70,000 ethnic Vietnamese from Cambodia and Laos fled to Thailand to escape the fighting between the French and Vietnamese Communist forces (Chan 2006, 42). According the Office of the United Nations High Commissioner for Refugees (UNHCR), with the establishment of the Communist government in the north, "more than a million people moved south in the years 1954–56" (UNHCR 2000, 80). Among them, nearly 800,000 were Roman Catholics. Conversely, those in the south who supported the communist moved north: some 130,000 were transported north by Polish and Soviet ships.

American policy toward an independent South Vietnam first took shape after the Geneva Accord. In a letter to South Vietnam's new leader, Ngo Dinh Diem, dated October 1, 1954, President Dwight D. Eisenhower explained the rationale for his support of South Vietnam: "The purpose of this offer is to assist the Government of Vietnam in developing and maintaining a strong, viable state, capable of resisting attempted subversion or aggression through military means. . . . Such a government would, I hope, be so responsive to the nationalist aspirations of its people, so enlightened in purpose and effective in performance, that it will be respected both at home and abroad and discourage any who might wish to impose a foreign ideology on your free people" (Eisenhower 1954).

THE SECOND INDOCHINA WAR

The United States entered Southeast Asia with the goal of preventing the spread of communism worldwide. American policymakers developed the "Domino Theory" as a justification for their involvement. This theory states that if South Vietnam fell to the Communists, then Laos, Cambodia, Thailand, Burma, India, and Pakistan would also fall like dominos. The Pacific Islands and even Australia could be at risk. As such, the United States pledged unlimited support in South Vietnam's fight against the northern Communists.

On August 4, 1964, in response to American surveillance along its coast, North Vietnam launched an attack against the USS *Turner Joy* and the USS *Maddox*, two American destroyers on call in the Gulf of Tonkin. The first attack occurred on August 2, when three North Vietnamese boats charged the *Maddox* and fired torpedoes at it. On August 4, the *Maddox*, now joined by the *Turner Joy*, "allegedly" attacked during a stormy night. On August 5, President Lyndon B. Johnson ordered retaliatory attacks against North Vietnam and asked Congress to pass a resolution to give him broad powers to take "all necessary measures to repel any armed attacks against the forces of the United States and to prevent further aggression" (Jones 2009, 145). Known as the Tonkin Gulf Resolution, it was passed by the Senate 88–2, and by the House of Representatives 466–0, on August 7, 1964. With this solution, the United States engaged in an undeclared war for nearly 11 years, popularly referred to as the Vietnam War (or the Second Indochina War). To date, there is no evidence that the second attack ever occurred, which many critics have argued is a conspiracy theory to escalate U.S. military actions in Southeast Asia, which had steadily increased since 1961 (Moise 1996, 226).

President Johnson first authorized an air war to destroy North Vietnam's ability to arm insurgency in South Vietnam. By 1965, the United States had 540,000 troops in Vietnam fighting against the Communists. The United States began bombing in southern Vietnam, which forced thousands of peasants from the countryside into the southern cities. Instead of helping to free the south's people of communism, the U.S. presence drove the peasants closer to the Viet Cong. In January 1968, the Viet Cong launched the Tet Offensive, during the Lunar New Year called Tet, attacking 36 out of 44 provincial capitals, 66 county seats, and many military bases for four weeks, until they were beaten back. The Tet Offensive was a defeat for the North Vietnamese and Viet Cong, whose armed units were virtually decimated. However, it was a major psychologically demoralizing defeat for the United States that fueled doubts about the war and the wisdom of continued fighting. At this point, the United States was spending $2 billion per month on the war, and the death toll of American troops continued to rise. The shift in public perception of the war was crystallized by Walter Cronkite, the avuncular CBS anchor, who exclaimed as he watched footage of the fighting, "What the hell is going on? I thought we were winning this damned war!" Confronted with a war that he could not end and win, President Lyndon B. Johnson announced he would not run for a second term. Promising an end to the war, and an honorable exit out of Vietnam, Richard M. Nixon won the presidential election of 1968.

NIXON'S VIETNAMIZATION

Upon taking office in 1969, President Richard Nixon and his advisers introduced a new strategy called Vietnamization that was aimed at ending American involvement in Vietnam without looking as if South Vietnam had been abandoned. Secretary of Defense Melvin Laird first used the term in March 1969, following a visit to South Vietnam. The Nixon administration's Vietnamization plan provided for a measured, phased withdrawal of American troops coupled with efforts to transfer all military responsibilities to South Vietnam, leaving it to take over its own defense. This would allow the United States to leave the war-torn region with its honor intact. Nixon announced his Vietnamization strategy to the American public in a nationally televised speech on November 3, 1969. He emphasized how his approach contrasted with his predecessor's strategy that relied on American troops, money, and resources. Nixon stated, "The defense of freedom is everybody's business, not just America's business. And it is particularly the responsibility of the people whose freedom is threatened ... In the previous administration, we Americanized the war in Vietnam. In this administration, we are Vietnamizing the search for peace."

In January 28, 1973, the United States negotiated a treaty with North Vietnam in Paris. During the next two months, the United States dismantled its bases, exchanged prisoners with the Communists, withdrew American combat troops, and declared the Vietnamization process complete. In his final report before leaving office that month, Secretary of Defense Laird declared the Vietnamization process completed: "As a consequence of the success of the military aspects of Vietnamization, the South Vietnamese people today, in my view, are fully capable of providing for their own in-country security against the North Vietnamese." However, on April 30, 1975, Communist troops entered the South Vietnamese capital, Saigon, and renamed it Ho Chi Minh City: South Vietnam fell to Communist forces.

FIRST WAVE OF VIETNAMESE REFUGEES

Immediately after South Vietnam fell to Communist forces, the United States worked quickly to withdraw its remaining diplomatic personnel and military advisers. Thousands of Vietnamese who had close association with the South Vietnamese regime or the American military and embassy scrambled to flee. They feared reprisals by the Communists, against whom they have been fighting. Media images of this period reveal the chaotic circumstances and environs of this period as it portrayed Vietnamese clinging to the skids of helicopters on top of the U.S. embassy compound in Saigon. Already enforced during this period was Operation New Life (April 23–November 1, 1975), which processed 111,919 Vietnamese refugees through Guam. The Indochina Migration and Refugee Assistance Act, which passed on May 23, 1975, provided $305 million for the State Department and $100 million for the Department of Health, Education, and Welfare to run Operation New Life ("Indochina Refugees" 1975). While most refugees were processed on Guam, others went through U.S. government bases in the Philippines and Wake Island in the northern Pacific Ocean.

More than 130,000 Vietnamese refugees were evacuated by air and by sea during the last few days of April 1975. This included 2,600 orphans and abandoned children who were evacuated under Operation Babylift (April 3–26, 1975). Early on, one of the airlifts ended in tragedy on April 4, 1975: sadly, nearly 150 people died in the crash, including 78 children.

This first wave consisted of refugees who were members of the social and political elites: they spoke English, were generally educated and Westernized, had political connections, and came from wealth. They included high-ranking soldiers, professionals, civic service workers, and those who had worked with American personnel or companies, ethnic Vietnamese who were educated in the United States, and individuals with family ties in the United States. The first wave consisted mainly of Roman Catholics and ethnic Vietnamese. Their resettlement was well funded in part due to America's sense of moral responsibility for the displacement of the Vietnamese refugees. However, according to Kimberly Kay Hoang, the U.S. government did not account for nearly 1.5 million "high-risk potential victims" who were former soldiers, police, and civic service workers, which included roughly 60,000 families who had been employees of the American embassy and 30,000 counterterrorist agents and many others who had worked with the CIA. They were at risk because the United States did not destroy their personnel files; as such, the Communist government captured a large portion of them and forced them into reeducation camps for 3–15 years (Hoang 2013, 1365). After their lease or escape, the reeducation camp detainees left Vietnam, either by boat, or via land to neighboring countries.

SECOND WAVE OF VIETNAMESE REFUGEES: THE "BOAT PEOPLE"

The second wave of refugees left Vietnam from 1978 to 1989. In the two years after the Communist victory, relatively few people escaped Vietnam, because the new authorities announced that certain groups of people (e.g., elected officials, employees of various counterinsurgency, religious leaders, intellectuals, military officers, the middle class, and ethnic Chinese Vietnamese) would be taken to reeducation camps located at "New Economic Zones." According to the United Nations High Commissioner for Refugees (UNHCR), more than a million people were placed in reeducation camps. There they were forced to till uncultivated land and admit to crimes against the new Communist state.

In light of these punitive measures, middle-class people and merchants, both ethnic Chinese and Vietnamese, began to escape by sea. At first, the American public did not hear much news about them because their numbers were small. The country of first asylum also wanted to keep their arrival as quiet as possible because they feared a larger exodus and influx if people in

Vietnamese refugees are rescued by the USS *Blue Ridge* in May 1984 after eight days aboard a tiny craft. Fleeing their homeland on crowded fishing boats and makeshift vessels, Vietnamese refugees became an ever-visible reminder of the Vietnam War for decades after the fall of Saigon in April 1975. (Defense Visual Information Center)

Vietnam found out that their compatriots managed to successfully escape and seek refuge. By late 1977, as the number of boat refuge-seekers increased—reaching an average of 1,500 refuge-seekers a month—Thailand, Singapore, and Malaysia, unable to accommodate refuge-seekers, began to push boats back to sea. Pressured by the international community for its moral and social responsibility for this plight, the United States responded through legislation. For example, the passage of Public Law 95-145 allowed refugees to change their status from "parolee" to "permanent resident" because it was apparent that they would not be able to return to their home countries. To counter the humanitarian crisis, President Jimmy Carter ordered the Seventh Fleet to seek vessels in distress in the South China Sea. A sizable percentage of refugees coming from Vietnam, Laos, and Cambodia were of ethnic-Chinese backgrounds, speaking either Cantonese or the Chaozhou dialects.

From 1978 to 1989, ethnic Chinese Vietnamese were persecuted amid international power struggles, increasing ethnic tensions, changing Vietnamese government policies that force Vietnamese citizenship and, by extension, military duty, and changes in economic policies. Fear of being pushed into the jungles resulted in 160,000 ethnic Chinese from all over Vietnam migrating to China's southern provinces (Chan 2006, 73–74). By the end of this exodus, nearly a quarter million Chinese Vietnamese had returned to China (Chan 2006, 74).

According to Sucheng Chan, the vast majority of boat people from southern Vietnam landed in Malaysia, while many who escaped from the north found a shorter route to Hong Kong, which eventually came to house the second-largest number of boat people. In May 1975, Hong Kong encountered its first batch of roughly 4,000 boat people, who were picked up by a Danish ship in the South China Sea. In 1976, only 191 refuge-seekers reached Hong Kong; 1,007 made it in 1997; and by 1978, nearly 9,000 arrived by small boats. Some were ethnic Chinese Vietnamese merchants who were able to utilize their contacts in Hong Kong to arrange for their passage. By spring 1979, Hong Kong housed 17,000 boat people (Chan 2006, 77). Sucheng Chan notes:

> The local people resented them tremendously because the Hong Kong government was very tough in the way it handled would-be refuge-seekers from the People's Republic of China: Hong Kong's border guards caught and deported them to the Chinese mainland without mercy. By allowing the Vietnamese boat people to stay, its critics said, the Hong Kong government was following a double standard, showing far greater leniency to the refuge-seekers from Vietnam than those from China. Members of Hong Kong's Legislative Council were also angry: They felt that Great Britain was doing nothing to relieve Hong Kong, its crown colony, of its burden, yet gave the colony no authority to deal with the situation on its own. Despite these complaints, no one foresaw that the worst was yet to come. (2006, 77)

The trafficking of refugees became a lucrative business in Vietnam and resulted in an international refugee crisis. The massive influx of new refugee-seekers placed greater and greater pressure on the limited resources in Hong Kong, which resulted in changing policies. A conference convened by UN secretary general Kurt Waldheim in Geneva on July 17–19, 1979, along with the participation of the United States, Great Britain representing Hong Kong, and ASEAN countries all agreed that something had to be done to assist the country of first asylum (e.g., Hong Kong). The Geneva Conference resulted in immediate change, although the Hong Kong government became increasingly bitter because it was shouldering 35 percent of the boat people but was only allocated 13 percent of the resettlement to countries of second asylum slots. "Between July 1979 and July 1982, more than 20 countries—led by the United States, Australia, France, and Canada —together resettled 623,800 Indochinese refugees" (UNHCR 2000, 86). The Vietnamese boat exodus continued throughout the 1980s. It is estimated that nearly 10 percent of the boat people were lost at sea, fell victims to pirate attacks, drowned, or died of dehydration.

The United States responded to the international refugee crisis by increasing its intake of refugees to 168,000 per year. Soon afterward, Congress passed the Refugee Act of 1980 as a way to facilitate the resettlement of refugees. The act, in Section 201, defines a refugee as:

> [A]ny person who is outside any country of such person's nationality or, in the case of a person having no nationality, is outside any country in which such a person last habitually resided, and who is unable or unwilling to return to, and is unable or unwilling to avail himself or herself of the protection of that country because of persecution or a well-founded fear of persecution or a well-founded fear of persecution on account of race, religion, nationality, membership in a particular racial group, or political opinion.

The Act established the Office of Refugee Resettlement within the Department of Health and Human Services to administer the domestic resettlement program. Under the resettlement program, refugees can receive cash assistance, medical assistance, and supportive services intended to ease their initial adjustment to the United States, with the goal of facilitating for their economic self-sufficiency. Henceforth, a sizable portion of Chinese Vietnamese refugees have arrived in the United States after spending time in Hong Kong or the Philippines, among other countries of first asylum. Refugees who escaped by boat were known as "boat people" and were predominately Viet Hoa, or ethnic-Chinese Vietnamese. In addition, they tended to be males, Buddhists, less wealthy, less capable in the English language, and less educated. Overall, this group of refugees were relatively young and had been urban workers in Vietnam. By the late 1980s, international willingness to accept and resettle all Vietnamese refugee-seekers was waning, and resettlement numbers were barely keeping pace with the rate of refugee arrivals in countries of first asylum. The United States accepted 44,500 Vietnamese boat refugees in 1979; 95,000 in 1980; 86,000 in 1981; 44,000 in 1982; and 20,000 each year until 1986 (Hoang 2013, 1366).

The second-wave refugees differ from the first wave in several ways. Their passage was longer, riskier, and harsher as they fled by foot through jungles to nearby seaside towns to make their final escape by boat. These boats were poorly constructed, overcrowded small fishing boats that carried upwards of 300 refuge-seekers. Their journey at sea lasted from a few days to several weeks, wherein many got sick, suffered dehydration, and fell victim to Thai pirates who pillaged their belongings and captured and raped young girls before leaving them to die. Those who attempted to flee through Cambodia were killed by the Khmer Rouge or Vietnamese soldiers. While there are no conclusive figures on the number of refuge-seekers who died, reports estimate that anywhere between 10 percent and 50 percent died in the process.

THIRD WAVE

In June 1989, a second international conference on the Indochinese refugee crisis was held in Geneva, and a new agreement was established known as the Comprehensive Plan of Action (CPA). The CPA reaffirmed some of the elements of the 1979 agreement, specifically the commitments to preserve first asylum, to decrease clandestine departures and encourage legal migration, and to resettle refugees to third countries. It also contained some new elements, such as a guarantee to institute regional refugee status determination procedures and repatriate those whose applications were rejected.

By the late 1980s, another wave of refugees consisted of individuals who came through federal government–sponsored programs, namely the Orderly Departure Program (ODP), the Humanitarian Operation Program (HOP), and the U.S. Homecoming program. The aim of these programs was to provide Vietnamese migrants an alternative to dangerous clandestine departure by boat or over land. Be that as it may, many Vietnamese migrants continue to leave by sea out of desperation and fear of persecution from the Communist government. Vietnamese Americans with U.S. citizenship can employ ODP and HOP to sponsor their family left back in Vietnam because ODP and HOP provided for family reunification. In addition, former U.S. government or company employees and former reeducation camp detainees were allowed entry under ODP and HOP. Many Vietnamese Americans who arrived with the first and second wave used their status as newly naturalized U.S. citizens or their permanent resident status to sponsor remaining family out of Vietnam.

By 1989, 165,000 Vietnamese had been admitted to the United States under the ODP. By 1997, 458,367 had been admitted (Table 6.1). Registration for ODP ended in 1994, but in 2005, the United States and Vietnam signed an agreement that allows individuals who were qualified to register, but could not do so before the program ended, an opportunity to do so. Overall, under ODP, Vietnamese refuge-seekers were resettled to over 40 countries worldwide, including a few thousand who resettled after 1997. Since the 1990s, political prisoners and their families comprise the largest categories of Vietnamese migrants to the United States. Another group that

Table 6.1   Numbers of Vietnamese Resettled under ODP Program, 1980–
1997

Country	Number of Vietnamese Resettled
United States	458,367
Canada	60,285
Australia	46,711
France	19,264
Germany	12,067
United Kingdom	4,842
Norway	3,998
Belgium	3,106
Sweden	3,079
Denmark	2,298
Other countries	9,492
Total	623,509

Sources: Compiled for the author from Courtland W. Robinson, *Terms of Refuge* (London: Zed Books, 1998) and UNHCR (Statistical Yearbooks, 1994–2012).

faced serious adjustment difficulties are the Amerasians, or "war babies"—individuals fathered by U.S. soldiers in Vietnam during the war—who came under the Homecoming Act implemented in 1989.

RESETTLEMENT AND COMMUNITY FORMATION

When considering the resettlement and community formation of Vietnamese refugees, it is important to note the iteration of migration waves that they arrived with, as funding for resettlement and general attitudes about Vietnamese refugees changed that impacts integration into American society, both positively and negatively. First-wave Vietnamese refugee resettlement and community formation unfolded in spite of a lingering consciousness of guilt among Americans for losing the war in Vietnam, which fueled humanitarian concerns and efforts to help displaced refugees. The "rescue psychology" among Americans was strong, as revealed in the generous aid the U.S. government allocated for Vietnamese refugee resettlement. The government also instituted other programs and policies that distinguished Vietnamese refugees from other immigrant groups in order to assist with their resettlement and integration into American society. Many of the first-wave refugees received help from "voluntary agencies" (VOLAGs), which provided additional resources and funding in areas such as housing, English-language classes, and employment training.

The Chinese Vietnamese refugees living in the United States today entered during the second-wave period between 1978 and 1989. Like many refugees before them, the Chinese Vietnamese refugees had to be processed and resettled in America. Upon arriving in the United States, Chinese Vietnamese refugees were first sent to four government reception centers located at Camp Pendleton, California; Fort Indiantown Gap, Pennsylvania; Fort Chaffee, Arkansas; and Eglin Air Force Base, Florida. There, they were interviewed by VOLAGs and matched with countrywide sponsors. They were initially distributed across all 50 states to minimize the negative impact of a refugee population. Despite the government's attempt to disperse the refugee population, as a result of tertiary migration from other states, California emerged as a concentrated center. In Southern California, a sizeable population of Vietnamese refugees reside in Los Angeles, Orange County, and San Diego. In Northern California, they are located in the Silicon Valley city of San Jose. Unlike the refugees who fled during the first wave, Chinese Vietnamese refugees did not benefit from America's guilty conscience; rather, they entered during a period of economic recession caused by a decline in the real estate market and high employment rates coupled with a weakened American automobile industry, which translated into "compassion fatigue." Anti-refugee Americans invoked the popular question of the day: "Why are we taking care of the refugees from Indochina, and not our own people?" (See Taggart Siegel's [1987] film, *Blue Collar and Buddha*.) Experiencing more economic and adjustment issues, some younger Vietnamese Americans joined youth gangs and engaged in criminal activities.

Economic competition among recent Vietnamese refugees and unemployed white Americans have increased racial conflict and policies. Some of the most extreme reactions occurred along the Gulf Coast states. In Texas, a conflict developed between Galveston and Corpus Christi Vietnamese shrimpers who competed with traditional Texas shrimpers. Non-Vietnamese shrimpers viewed Vietnamese shrimpers as competitors who did not respect the rules and ethics of their trade, which, coupled with the decrease in shrimp prices, resulted in anti-Vietnamese/anti-refugee violence and sentiments. Texas shrimpers and fishermen complained that Vietnamese fishermen would move in on a school of fish that another boat was already "working" on; unload their shrimp without paying the $50 "unloading license"; shrimp out of season, and use illegal fishing nets (Virgilio 1991, 61). In 1979, some Texas shrimpers accused the Vietnamese of "dirty tricks and unfair tactics" to get an edge in the shrimp market. As a result, local members of the Ku Klux Klan burned the boats of Vietnamese shrimpers and made threats on their families (Bennett 2004). Tensions reached a climax in 1979 when Vietnamese shrimpers fatally shot a Caucasian crabber, Billy Joe Aplin. For two years, Vietnamese shrimpers reported that Aplin had stolen their crab traps, threatened them, and assaulted them, but no arrest was ever made. The two Vietnamese individuals were tried for murder and acquitted based on a claim of self-defense. Similarly, in Biloxi, Mississippi, fistfights broke out between Vietnamese shrimpers and white shrimpers. The local shrimp industry printed and sold bumper stickers that read, "Save Your Shrimp Industry: Get Rid of Vietnamese, Contact Your Local Congressmen" (Arden 1981, 387).

Today, over 22 states have a "Little Saigon" business district or community. The oldest, largest, and most prominent Little Saigon is located in Orange County. The Little Saigon community originally started emerging in Westminster in 1978. The inspiration for the creation of Little Saigon first started while several businessmen were housed together at Camp Pendleton Marine Base in San Diego, where they set up shops and restaurants. Later, it was relocated to a lower-middle-class suburb of Los Angeles and quickly spread to the adjacent city of Garden Grove. Since 1978, the nucleus of Little Saigon has long been Bolsa Avenue, where early pioneer real estate developer Chinese Vietnamese Frank Jao built the highly popular Asian Garden Mall. By the mid-1980s and throughout the 1990s, Orange County's Little Saigon

Little Saigon in Orange County, California, is the oldest, largest, and most prominent Little Saigon community in the United States. It was established in the late 1970s by Chinese-Vietnamese investors and is known as the place for authentic Vietnamese cuisine, businesses, and services. (UIG via Getty Images)

became a destination secondary migration among Vietnamese immigrants who wanted to live among other Vietnamese Americans and have the cultural comforts of "home."

FIRST IMPRESSIONS

Upon arriving to America, many refugees felt ambivalent about their situation. They were also ambivalent about their experiences in Hong Kong. Overwhelmed by the new environment, they felt like fish out of water, and they struggled with survivor's guilt. Even so, for Chinese Vietnamese refugees, their dual ethnicity and ability to speak both Chinese and Vietnamese proved to be useful. Mrs. Lâm says, "The main problem coming to America was the language barrier because neither me nor my husband spoke English, which limited our job opportunities to working for our own kind who spoke either Vietnamese or Chinese." Mrs. Kim recalls,

> When I first came to the United States, I lived with my sisters in the Tenderloin [an urban district of San Francisco]. I was afraid to do anything because I did not know how to speak English well and I did not know the area. However, when I found that there were other Vietnamese in the community as well, I felt much better because whenever I was lost, I was able to ask for directions and most importantly, I was not an outcast of the community.

After securing lodging in the new environment, one of the first priorities was to find work. Many moved to neighborhoods known to have Vietnamese or Chinese immigrants. For instance, Mrs. La says, "The Tenderloin was the Vietnamese version of Chinatown. It was the center for all the Vietnamese refugees, mostly because of the cheap rent for the apartment, so we moved there." In seeking employment, Chinese Vietnamese quickly realized their inability to speak English kept them from high-paying jobs, but they felt fortunate that they could work as service workers in Chinese restaurants or sweatshops. Kevin, a second-generation Chinese-Vietnamese American, recalls his grandmother saying, "I was lucky to have work. I was an old woman, but I could still sew."

A survey conducted by Caplan, Whitmore, and Bui (1985) in the early 1980s shows that among the Southeast Asian refugees in Boston, Chicago, Houston, Seattle, and Orange County, the Chinese-Vietnamese refugee population tended to be older than the Lao and the Vietnamese, with an average age of 33 years. They were also not as proficient in English compared to other Indochinese refugees. Economically, compared to the ethnic Vietnamese, the Chinese Vietnamese refugees were less likely to be in the labor force, had a lower median monthly income, and no employment and health and retirement benefits, and were more likely to be dependent on government welfare programs. Overall, the Chinese Vietnamese were invariably at a disadvantage in terms of economic integration.

On the other hand, the Chinese Vietnamese were able to develop good relationships with other Chinese businesspeople in the United States because of common languages. Over the years, such ethnic economy has grown in size. Chinese Vietnamese now have a monopoly in the Asian grocery business, primarily because established corporations are unprepared to serve Asian customers, especially the growing, relatively affluent Asian population with a demand for Asian goods. But they are at the same time facing competition from other Asian immigrants from Thailand, Taiwan, and Hong Kong.

FROM REFUGEE TO AMERICAN BORN

There are four distinct stages in the development of Vietnamese and Chinese Vietnamese communities in America. The first stage was the wave of exiles who fled Vietnam immediately after the fall of Saigon in 1975. These exiles were primarily from middle-class backgrounds, were Catholic converts, had English proficiency, and worked with the U.S. government before Saigon fell. The communities they built tended to revolve around manufacturing in California and around fishing in the Gulf Coast (e.g., Texas, and Louisiana). The second stage included refugees who arrived between 1979 and 1982. The majority of these refugees were Chinese Vietnamese, popularly called "boat people," arriving in large numbers. They were members of the petit bourgeoisie, were rural poor of a lower socioeconomic status, and had scant or no English skills. They were scattered by resettlement, but secondary migration led them to California and Texas, to already established Vietnamese refugee communities. The third stage occurred after the 1980s. This stage was community-oriented, based on the flourishing of ethnic businesses, civic organizations, and other community social structures that were established to serve the immigrant refugee population. The fourth stage reflects the development since the 1990s, when 1.5- and second-generation Americans mature and become politically active. Their parents —refugees who fled Vietnam after 1975—began to become naturalized citizens and politically active themselves, once they acknowledged that their dream of returning to Vietnam was no longer realizable.

Similar to many immigrants before them, the first- and second-generation Chinese-Vietnamese Americans struggle to balance themselves between the forces of traditions and the new American ways, between being Chinese, Vietnamese, and American. Their parents feel this anxiety, as Mrs. Pham laments, declaring, "My first impression of America is that it is too free. Kids are raised with no traditions and moral values ... Young women are running away and getting pregnant. Boys are joining gangs and dropping out of school. America has little discipline." Both parents and children point to language barriers as the source of their intergenerational conflict and misunderstanding. Susie, a 1.5-generation Chinese-Vietnamese American who arrived when she was five years old, states, "Linguistic obstacles are by far the root of all problems in my family because it contributes to the domino effect of more problems such as changing roles within our family, stress, and anxiety about us being too American."

Another compelling example of the rift created by the language barrier between the 1.5 and second generation and their parents is evident in Nancy's statement:

> The generation gap between my mother and me are obvious. I mostly speak English. I do not know how to cook a full meal. I speak my mind whenever I feel like it. I do not know much about my Vietnamese and Chinese traditions. My mother on the other hand can whip up a meal in thirty minutes. She also holds her emotions in, instead of talking about it. It is frustrating because she expects me to know, but I can't read her mind.

For the 1.5- and second-generation Chinese-Vietnamese Americans, their development was further challenged through their encounters with racism. Hoang, a 1.5-generation Chinese-Vietnamese American, says, "I went to kindergarten like everyone else. However, the first school I went to was full of Chinese immigrants, so it felt normal, like being at home. Later, after we moved, it was different and I started hearing chants like 'Ching chong Chinaman sitting on a bench.'" Interestingly, both parents and their children are aware of the cause and source of their intergenerational conflicts. Michael, a second-generation Chinese-Vietnamese American, says, "My mother thinks differently than I do because we grew up in two different environments. I would not say that I identify with my mother's experiences, but rather understand her struggles. I have never gone through what she went through, but I get understand her struggle and for that I appreciate her sacrifice." Similarly, Barbara notes, "My mom loves her children like a lioness protecting her cubs. Although she understands that children in America have no respect for elders like the children in Vietnam. The main factors that contribute to the clash between child and parents are first and foremost, linguistic reasons and then cultural reasons." When Barbara and her mother get into arguments, she admits, laughingly, to saying, "This isn't Vietnam, Mom; get use to the American culture. . . . so just chill out."

MAINTAINING CULTURE, MAINTAINING SELF

Children who grow up in households with first-generation refugee parents expressed their childhood experiences positively, indicating that their parents have been successful in transmitting traditional values, morals, and customs to them, even though they may rebel against them. Victoria, a second-generation Chinese-Vietnamese American says, "Practicing filial piety is learning to respect and care for those around you, especially your elders. My parents taught me to respect and care for those around me, especially my elders. My parents taught me to respect and obey the older generation and to care for the parent as they get older." Conversely, Minh, a second-generation Chinese-Vietnamese American says he learned how to be an American by watching several popular American TV shows. He says,

> I didn't have my parents or anyone as a set role model but instead I had the actors and characters on TV to learn from. Everything I learnt about how to act or how to think came from TV shows and most of the time it was white character or it was the "American way." The way I dressed came from the commercials; the way I talked came from *Saved by the Bell*; the way I treated others from *Barney*; my sense of right and wrong came from *Power Rangers*; and what I know about sex, came from the media.

Many of the 1.5 and second generation said that their parents did not talk to them about important topics such as sex and birth control, and that they had to rely on their schools and friends to learn about it. They also said that much of what they learned about social values and norms was indirectly through the hierarchical nature of their family structure, which emphasized respect for the elders that included their parents and their older siblings.

DEVELOPMENT OF 1.5- AND SECOND-GENERATION CHINESE-VIETNAMESE AMERICAN IDENTITIES

Among the 1.5- and second-generation Chinese-Vietnamese Americans, the process of identity formation is complex and complicated, revealing that for them, identity is fluid, flexible, and ever changing. Justin, a second-generation Chinese-Vietnamese American, expressed a very assured identity as American, saying, "There is no question about it: I am a genuine American citizen, California-grown, and no one can touch that." While Sherwood indicates a more nuanced and sophisticated explanation of his multiple identities, saying:

> I have my own challenges growing up as a 1.5-generation Chinese-Vietnamese American. I speak Cantonese, English, and understand Vietnamese. I celebrate Chinese New Year and American New Year. I listen to Asian music and American music. My identity is very fragile and conditional in terms of my experiences. I was born Chinese Vietnamese in Saigon. I consider myself absolutely Americanized but as I grow up, clashes between the American culture and

Chinese-Vietnamese culture makes me question my identity time and time again.

Along a similar vein, expressing the difficulties of "fitting in" and "making friends," Robert, a 1.5-generationer, says, "Being a 1.5-generation Chinese-Vietnamese American, I strive to be accepted in my community as Chinese, Vietnamese, and American."

One prevailing theme that most experienced and articulated is the struggle to form and understand their identity. This is brilliantly expressed by Bao, a second-generationer who says, "My whole life has been a constant juggle of three identities and it doesn't help that it changes so drastically according to each situation such as going to Chinatown, Little Saigon, or connecting with my relatives back in Vietnam, or attending a football game. One can say having a triple identity doesn't amount to a hindrance but instead acts as a benefactor because it opens you up to more opportunities." As stated above, identity formation is a process—fluid, flexible, and changing—which is well illustrated in Tiffany's comment:

> Like most Vietnamese American teens it is difficult to meet the expectations of parents while attempting to assimilate into the American culture. When I started elementary school, my parents enrolled me in Chinese school at the same time. At this time, I thought my identity was Chinese American. Later, I realized that I was not only following Chinese traditions, but also Vietnamese culture and traditions. I not only had to assimilate to the Chinese and American cultures, but also the Vietnamese culture.

LIVING AMONG MULTIPLE WORLDS: THE POLITICS OF IDENTITY AND ASIAN AMERICAN PAN-ETHNIC IDENTITY

The post–World War II era ushered in the countercultural and civil rights movements that began to question the normative vision of American social life. The American way of life was not limited to Protestants, whites, males, heterosexuals, and middle-class households. Assimilation favored socially constructed notions of "white" identity, by excluding people with dark skin, non-European ancestries, and limited incomes—in particular Asian immigrants. The civil rights movement demanded practical changes in public policy and a transformation of American national self-identity, insisting there were manifold and legitimate alternate ways of being American. One result of this vibrant period was the creation of the homogenous taxon "Asian American"—coined by historian and activist Yuji Ichioka—which was initially used to describe the politically charged group identity in the ethnic consciousness movements of the 1960s through the 1970s.

There are discontinuities, tensions, and disadvantages between the ethnic-specific Asian identity (e.g., Chinese-Vietnamese American) and pan-ethnic

Asian American identity. The goal and mission of the ethnic consciousness movement of the civil rights era emphasized the individual community's rights and abilities of self-determination. The pan-ethnic Asian American identity, while strong in numbers and hence politically significant, depresses the interest of individual groups and, consequently, downplays an individual community's self-determination at the expense of the larger pan-ethnic Asian American community. Ironically, this in itself is a hegemonic process of homogenization that the Asian American civil rights activists protested and fought against because it denied individuals and their respective communities a means of self-determination.

REFERENCES

Aguilar-San Juan, Karin. *Little Saigons: Staying Vietnamese in America*. Minneapolis: University of Minnesota Press, 2009.

Arden, Harvey. "Troubled Odyssey of Vietnamese Fishermen: The Wanderers from Vung Tau." *National Geographic* 160:3 (1981): 378–94.

Bennett, Stephen. "The Vietnamese Shrimpers of Texas: Salvaging a Sinking Industry." In *The Scholar: St. Mary's Law Review on Minority Issues*, 6 Scholar 287 (2004).

Bounds, James. "Vietnamese in Mississippi." *Mississippi History Now: An Online Publication of the Mississippi Historical Society*. http://mshistorynow.mdah.state.ms.us/articles/372/vietnamese-in-mississippi (accessed June 10, 2014).

Burns, Jeffery M., Ellen Skerrett, and Joseph M. White, eds. *Keeping Faith: European and Asian Catholic Immigrants*. Maryknoll, NY: Orbis Book, 2000.

Caplan, Nathan, John K. Whitmore, and Quang L. Bui. *Southeast Asian Refugee Self-Sufficiency Study: Final Report*. Prepared for the Office of Refugee Resettlement, U.S. Department of Health and Human Services, 1985.

Chan, Sucheng. *Asian Americans: An Interpretive History*. New York: Twayne, 1991.

Chan, Sucheng. *The Vietnamese American 1.5 Generation: Stories of War, Revolution, Flight, and New Beginnings*. Philadelphia: Temple University Press, 2006.

Eisenhower, Dwight D. "Letter from President Eisenhower to Ngo Dinh Dien, President of the Council of Ministers of Vietnam," October 23, 1954. *Department of State Bulletin*, November 15, 1954, 735–36.

Haines, David. *Safe Haven? A History of Refugees in America*. Sterling, VA: Kumarian Press, 2010.

Hanyok, Robert J. "Skunks, Bogies, Silent Hounds, and the Flying Fish: The Gulf of Tonkin Mystery, 2–4 August 1964." *Cryptologic Quarterly*, Winter 2000–Spring 2001, 19.

Hein, Jeremy. *Ethnic Origins: The Adaptation of Cambodian and Hmong Refugees in Four American Cities*. New York: Russell Sage Foundation, 2006.

Hein, Jeremy. *From Vietnam, Laos and Cambodia: A Refugee Experience in the United States*. New York: Twayne Publishers, 1995.

Hoang, Kimberly Kay. "Vietnamese and Vietnamese Americans, 1975–Present." In *Immigrants in American History: Arrival, Adaptation, and Integration*, vol. 3, edited by Elliott R. Barkan, 1365–74. Santa Barbara, CA: ABC-CLIO, 2013.

"Indochina Refugees." Hearings before the Subcommittee on Immigration, Citizenship, and International Law of the Committee on the Judiciary House of Representatives. 94th Congress, May 5 and 7, 1975. Washington, DC: U.S. Government Printing Office, 1975.

Indochinese Housing Development Corporation. *Stories of Survival: Three Generations of Southeast Asian Americans Share Their Lives*. 10th anniversary ed. San Francisco: Indochinese Housing Development Corporation, 2001.

Jang, Lindsey, and Robert C. Winn. *Saigon, USA*. 2003. DVD.

Johnson, Chalmers. *The Sorrows of Empire: Militarism, Secrecy, and the End of the Republic*. New York: Henry Holt and Company, 2004.

Kelly, Gail. *From Vietnam to America*. Boulder, CO: Westview Press, 1977.

Jones, Howard. *Crucible of Power: A History of American Foreign Relations from 1945*. Lanham, MD: Rowman & Littlefield Publishers, 2009.

Lau, Albert, ed. *Southeast Asia and the Cold War*. New York: Routledge, 2012.

Le, Long S. "Vietnamese Americans: History, People, and Culture." In *Encyclopedia of Asian American Folklore and Folklife*, edited by Jonathan H. X. Lee and Kathleen Nadeau. Santa Barbara, CA: ABC-CLIO, 2011.

McGregor, Andrew. *Southeast Asian Development*. New York: Routledge, 2008.

Moise, Edwin E. *Tonkin Gulf and the Escalation of the Vietnam War*. Chapel Hill: University of North Carolina Press, 1996.

Nguyen, Hoa Dinh. *From the City Inside the Red River: A Cultural Memoir of Mid-Century Vietnam*. Jefferson, NC: McFarland & Company, 1999.

Nguyen, Long, with Harry Kendall. *After Saigon Fell: Daily Life under the Vietnamese Communists*. Berkeley: Institute of East Asian Studies, University of California, 1981.

Osborne, Milton. *The Mekong: Turbulent Past, Uncertain Future*. St. Leonards, Australia: Allen & Unwin, 2000.

Porter, Gareth. *Perils of Dominance: Imbalance of Power and the Road to War in Vietnam*. Berkeley: University of California Press, 2005.

Pyle, Jean Laron. "Public Policy and Local Economies: The Phenomenon of Secondary Migration." In *Southeast Asian Refugees and Immigrants in the Mill City: Changing Families, Communities, Institutions—Thirty Years Afterward*, edited by Tuyet-Lan Pho, Jeffrey N. Gerson, and Sylvia R. Cowan. Lebanon, NH: University Press of New England, 2007.

Robinson, Courtland. *Terms of Refuge*. London: Zed Books, 1998.

Schulzinger, Robert D. *A Time for War: The United States and Vietnam, 1941–1975*. Oxford: Oxford University Press, 1997.

Siegel, Taggart, and Kati Johnston. *Blue Collar and Buddha*. Collective Eye Films, 1987. DVD.

Takaki, Ronald T. *Strangers from a Different Shore: A History of Asian Americans*. Rev. ed. Boston: Little, Brown, 1989.

Trieu, Monica. *Identity Construction among Chinese-Vietnamese Americans: Being, Becoming, and Belonging.* El Paso, TX: LFB Scholarly Publishing, 2009.

United Nations High Commissioner for Refugees (UNHCR). *The State of the World's Refugees: Fifty Years of Humanitarian Action.* Oxford: Oxford University Press, 2000.

Virgilio, Joseph. "The Evacuation and Resettlement of Indochinese Refugees in Lower Southeast Texas, 1975–1980." Unpublished thesis, Lamar University–Beaumont, 1991.

Võ, Linda T. "Vietnamese American Trajectories: Dimensions of Diaspora." *Amerasia Journal* 29:1 (2003): ix–xviii.

Vu, Pham. "Antedating and Anchoring Vietnamese America: Toward a Vietnamese American Historiography." *Amerasia Journal* 29:1 (2003): 137–52.

Watts, J. F., and Fred L. Israel, eds. *Presidential Documents: The Speeches, Proclamations, and Policies that Have Shaped the Nation from Washington to Clinton.* New York: Routledge, 2000.

Westmoreland, William. "Vietnam in Perspective." In *Vietnam: Four American Perspectives: Lectures by George S. McGovern, William C. Westmoreland, Edward N. Luttwak, and Thomas J. McCormick,* edited by Patrick J. Hearden. West Lafayette, IN: Purdue University Research Foundation, 1995.

Whitmore, John K. "An Outline of Vietnamese History before French Conquest." In *The Vietnam Forum: A Review of Vietnamese Culture and Society* 8, Yale Center for International and Area Studies, Yale Southeast Asia Studies (Summer–Fall 1986): 1–9.

Zhou, Min, and Carl Bankston. *Growing Up American: How Vietnamese Children Adapt to Life in the United States.* New York: Russell Sage Foundation, 1998.

_____ *Chapter 7* _____

Cambodians and Laotians in America

According to the 2010 U.S. Census, there are approximately 256,956 Cambodians, and 233,120 self-identified Laotians (excluding Hmong) residing in the United States. The Hmong American population alone is 260,073. Together, the Laotian population is roughly 492,203, which includes the Hmong. Before the mass migration of refugees from Cambodia and Laos, following on the heels of the Vietnamese refugee flow after the fall of Saigon on April 30, 1975, there were already small numbers of Cambodian and Laotian students studying aboard in the United States.[1] This small community, especially among the Cambodians, became a central part of the refugee resettlement process, as these Cambodian "exiles" assisted the new arrivals through translation. The iterations of migration from Cambodia and Laos —as well as from Vietnam, discussed in Chapter 6—occurred from the late 1970s to the mid-1980s. This chapter introduces readers to the key macro-historical variables that influenced migration from Cambodia and Laos, which are also applicable to the Vietnamese diaspora in the United States. In addition, this chapter will provide a general overview of resettlement policies, issues, and concerns from historical and contemporary perspectives.

U.S. foreign policy following World War II, more specifically during the Cold War (1947–1989), is a primary variable that directly resulted in the proxy "Hot Wars" in Vietnam, also known as the Second Indochina War, which occurred in Vietnam, Cambodia, and Laos from 1956 to 1975. The ensuing Cold War marked an ideological battle between the Western Bloc (the United States with NATO and their allies), and the Eastern Bloc (the former Soviet Union [USSR] and its allies in the Warsaw Pact). The United States' primary objective during this period was to contain the spread of communism. As such, the United States supported the French effort to recolonize "French Indochina—Vietnam, Laos, and Cambodia" after World

War II as an important part of the worldwide effort to flight the expansion of communism. By 1954, U.S. military aid to the French topped $2 billion USD (Chan 2006, 31–33). Cambodia and Laos was dragged into the proxy war in Vietnam on the military strategy of destroying the Ho Chi Minh trail. The bombings—by land and air—in Cambodia and Laos along the Vietnam boarder proceeded in "secret" under President Richard Nixon. Jeremy Hein notes that the Cambodia-Vietnam border was bombed without congressional approval for 13 months in 1969–1970 (1995). The American military created the appearance that Cambodians and Laotians played a significant role in the coordination of the bombing raids in the border regions. A U.S. Senate refugee subcommittee concluded that the human results of the bombing were "the most pervasive reason for refugee movement. Our interviews with refugees ... largely confirm the findings of the General Accounting Office (GAO) interviewers in 1971. The GAO found that some 60 percent of the refugees interviewed cited bombardment as the principal reason for moving" (cited in Hein 1995).

CAMBODIA: FACTORS OF MIGRATION

France, like other colonial powers, drained wealth, resources, and labor from its colonies and offered very little in return. France wanted to secure trade routes with China for its silk and tea, which is why they encouraged mountain tribal people, especially the Hmong of Laos, Vietnam, and southern China, to grow opium poppies as their sole cash crop. The French then purchased all the opium that was produced. Because Cambodia's geography was not suitable for cultivating poppy, growing opium was not encouraged. France, like England, Portugal, and Holland, gained economic influence and power by trafficking opium into China, spreading addiction, and causing social and political decay. Besides opium for trade with China, France was also interested in the rubber, gems, teak, and spices that Indochina offered.

French rule in Indochina lasted almost 100 years, until 1954. French control of Cambodia was an adjunct to its control and interest in Vietnam, having incorporated Cambodia into its protectorate in 1863. By 1884, all of Vietnam was under French control, and in 1893, Laos also became a protectorate of France. Laos and Cambodia were granted greater autonomy than Vietnam, because they had fewer natural resources.

Under French rule, the Cambodian god-king held only nominal power. In 1904, for political reasons, the French backed one line of the royal family, the Sisowath line, which pushed King Norodom's heirs aside. No more than 40 years later, the French switched their support back to the Norodom line, again, for political reasons. In 1941, 19-year-old Prince Norodom Sihanouk was declared king, under the assumption that Sihanouk would be easy to

Cambodian king Norodom Sihanouk poses, May 1, 1950. Sihanouk was beloved by the people of Cambodia. (AP Photo)

manipulate and control because of his youth; however, this was not the case (Chandler 1983, 137–52).

Shortly after the young prince became king, Japan invaded and conquered Indochina, controlling the area from 1941 to 1945, through the end of World War II. Japan allowed Cambodia to be ruled by its young king, under the supervision of the Vichy French government. When Japan lost the war in 1945, it also lost control and domination of Indochina. But under the principle that Asia should be ruled by Asians, Japan urged Cambodia, Vietnam, and Laos to declare independence. France returned to its former rule, attempting to regain control of its territory in Indochina, albeit acting against a worldwide objection to colonialism. From 1945 to 1954, Sihanouk capitalized on the change in the political climate and worked skillfully to apply pressure on the French through the worldwide disfavor, in an effort to gain independence for his Royal Kingdom of Cambodia (Kampuchea). Sihanouk became prime minister of Cambodia in 1952, appointing his own cabinet, and promising to gain independence within three years. In 1953, the French gave Sihanouk control over the Cambodian armed forces, the judiciary, and foreign affairs. However, France continued to control the Cambodian economy. On November 9, 1953, Sihanouk claimed independence from France.

It should be noted that even though Sihanouk played a key role in Cambodia's struggle for independence from France after World War II, the Viet Minh (or Viet Cong) guerrilla forces, who challenged France's colonial claim over Indochina, set the stage for his success. For decades, Viet Minh forces placed both economic and military strain on France's resources. On May 7, 1954, the Viet Minh won a decisive victory over the French, after a 57-day siege that resulted in the surrender of more than 10,000 starving French troops at Diem Bien Phu. This catastrophic defeat for France shattered the remaining public support for the first French–Viet Minh Indochina war. Growing international pressure, coupled with the cost of years of guerrilla warfare, forced France to give up its colonial control and claim of Indochina. In 1954, at the Geneva Conference, Cambodia was granted full independence—along with Laos and Vietnam.

SIHANOUK AND INDEPENDENCE

Concerned that his position and power as king would be weakened after the election, Sihanouk abdicated the crown in 1955 and declared his father, Norodom Suramarit, king in his stead. Sihanouk established the People's Socialist Community (the Sangkum Reastr Niyum) and won every parliamentary seat in the election of September 1955 through legal means. For the next 15 years, Sihanouk would dominate politics in Cambodia, serving as prime minister until his father's death in 1960. Because no new king was named, Sihanouk became head of state.

In 1956, Sihanouk accepted U.S. military aid. In the early 1960s, although he feared Vietnamese communists, he was deeply concerned about Thailand and South Vietnam, who were both allies of the United States. When the South Vietnamese president, Ngo Dinh Diem, was murdered in a coup backed by the Americans, Sihanouk was shaken. Thus, he claimed the United States' CIA was masterminding a plan to overthrow him. By 1963, Sihanouk rejected the U.S. military and economic aid, and in 1965, he broke ties with Washington and sided with North Vietnam, the Viet Minh, and Communist China (Clymer 2004, 107–27). Sihanouk granted the North Vietnamese army use of Cambodian territory in their fight against South Vietnamese forces and the United States.

As the Vietnam War escalated, Sihanouk was concerned that hostilities would spill over into Cambodia. So in June 1969, he restored relations with Washington. However, his ability to balance relationships between the right and left, and among the United States, North Vietnam, and China, soon became precarious. Internally, support for his policies and his tolerance of the Viet Minh occupation of Cambodia's borders diminished. People from within his own government, the urban elite, and the military began to voice their opposition. Working under the principle of "search and destroy," the U.S. military secretly began to bomb the Cambodian countryside in March 1969. The clandestine bombing targeted the Ho Chi Minh trail that ran through Laos and Cambodia. The bombing destroyed villages, created countless refugees, and also pushed Viet Minh forces deeper into Cambodia. General Lon Nol claimed that there were as many as 40,000 Viet Minh soldiers on Cambodian soil. The bombing killed thousands of civilians and left hundreds of thousands homeless and refugees.

Because of the turmoil caused by U.S. military intervention, Cambodia's economy was stagnant by 1970; this, coupled with famine from an unsuccessful harvest, created unrest and discontent among the peasants. However, the majority of Cambodian peasants still considered Sihanouk a modern-day god-king. By comparison to the tragic events to come under the Khmer Rouge, many Cambodians today consider Sihanouk's era to have been the "golden age" (Chandler 1983, 190). Others blame his totalitarian rule as the cause of many of Cambodia's problems: an immature political system, intolerance of pluralism, and a lack of national debate. During Sihanouk's March 18, 1970, trip to France, General Lon Nol—albeit reluctantly, but with support from the United States—led a bloodless coup d'état that ousted Sihanouk (Becker 1986, 114). In April 1970, Lon Nol abolished the monarchy and established the Khmer Republic. Days later, Sihanouk established a government in exile, the National United Front of Kampuchea, seeking support from his old enemy—the Khmer Rouge. This move surprised many, because for years, Sihanouk had denounced and suppressed their activities, and had even derisively dubbed them "Khmer Rouge" (Red Khmer). Little did he know that he was laying the foundation for the Khmer Rouge victory that would come five years later.

THE LON NOL ERA

The newly formed Khmer Republic had many problems that required immediate attention: bankruptcy, a collapsing economy, famine, internal corruption, a Communist-backed civil war, Vietnamese aggression, U.S. retaliation, and an inability to control its own fate in its neighbor's escalating war. To make matters worse, many villagers and peasants did not support the new republic because their loyalty lay with the royal family and their ousted prince Sihanouk. The Khmer Republic maintained control for five terrible years, in large measure due to the economic and military aid from the United States and Thailand, who both feared a Communist takeover of the region.

From the beginning, the Lon Nol regime declared its neutrality in the region, while trying to maintain an anti-Communist campaign, which

Lon Nol was prime minister at the time of the overthrow of Norodom Sihanouk in March 1970 and went on to become president of the short-lived Khmer Republic (1972–1975) prior to the takeover by the Khmer Rouge. (AP Photo)

garnered support from the United States. Lacking support from the peasants, riots broke out in protest of his administration. In response, Lon Nol accused them of being inspired by the Viet Minh, legitimating his brutal suppression of them. Without foresight, Lon Nol was driving the peasants to join the Khmer Rouge, who, until that time, had numbered only a few hundred. Lon Nol also utilized the Cambodian fear of the Vietnamese by branding all Vietnamese within Cambodia members of the Viet Minh, demonstrating the Khmer Republic's hatred of the Vietnamese and Communists.

In June 1974, the United States withdrew its forces from Cambodia, reducing the Khmer Republic's control to only larger towns and cities, and only half the countryside. It was inconceivable that the Khmer Republic, backed by the United States, would lose to the Khmer Rouge, as it did on the morning of April 17, 1975. Two weeks before the fall of Saigon, roughly at the beginning of the Cambodian New Year, the Khmer Rouge entered

Phnom Penh as victors, with wide popular support and an increase in territorial control. Many of the Khmer Rouge cadres and soldiers were under the age of 15. That year would become Year Zero, ushering in a new phase of Cambodian history by eliminating its past cultures and traditions. Year Zero was a new start, a new beginning, marking a complete revolution of what it means to be Khmer, revolutionizing Khmer life with the hopes of making Cambodia a self-sufficient nation.

KHMER ROUGE

The Khmer Rouge regime, Democratic Kampuchea (DK), lasted from April 1975 until January 1979. It would become one of the most radical and brutal periods in world history (Etcheson 2005, 4). Under the leadership of a Paris-educated schoolteacher, Pol Pot (formerly Saloth Sar), and Chinese-Khmer Khieu Samphan (president of DK from 1976 to 1979), the Khmer Rouge attempted to transform Cambodian society into a Maoist peasant agrarian cooperative. Since 1903, the Khmer Rouge worked to gain peasant support—unsuccessfully. However, after Lon Nol ousted their prince, Sihanouk joined forces with the Khmer Rouge, eliciting support from the peasantry. Although Sihanouk hoped to use the Khmer Rouge to regain his power and kingdom, he became its pawn, instead giving the Khmer Rouge legitimacy and increasing peasant support.

Immediately after the Khmer Rouge swept into power, currency was abolished and postal services were suspended. Convincing people that the Americans were about to bomb the cities, the cities were abandoned, and the borders were closed. Urban dwellers, merchants, ethnic Chinese and ethnic Vietnamese Cambodians, along with other elites, were executed or sent to labor and reeducation camps (Chandler 1999). Survivors report that during this period, people who wore glasses were executed because they represented intellectuals, beautiful Cambodian women were forced to marry malformed Khmer Rouge veterans, and there were no dogs in the countryside because hungry Cambodians ate them due to the shortage of food (Becker 1986, 162). What followed was four years of starvation and slavery. The total number of casualties of the Khmer Rouge genocide remains a topic of debate: Vietnamese sources claim three million deaths, while others estimate one to two million deaths. Historians have called it the "Cambodian Holocaust," a pogrom of ethnic cleansing and societal reform that continues to haunt many survivors and their descendants (Chandler 1999).

The Khmer Rouge state of Democratic Kampuchea was toppled on December 25, 1978, after Vietnamese forces entered Phnom Penh to address the Khmer Rouge murder of hundreds of ethnic Vietnamese along the Vietnam-Cambodia border region. This, however, did not mean freedom for the people of Cambodia; instead, it set the stage for two decades of war in Cambodia. Cambodia was "liberated" from the Khmer Rouge's pogrom, but tens of thousands of Cambodians continued to endure Khmer Rouge terror. The Khmer Rouge established military camps at the Thai border, where they forced refugees into the camps and subjected them to systematic violations of their human rights. The Vietnamese finally withdrew from Cambodia in 1989, leaving their client regime, the People's Republic of Kampuchea, to fend for itself against the Khmer Rouge and their allies. For several decades, the Khmer Rouge haunted the Cambodian landscape and people through war crimes and crimes against humanity. Thus, since 1975, the stage was set for the massive global movement of Cambodian refugees, the remaking of Cambodia as a modern nation-state, and the formation of Cambodian Americans and their communities.

LAOS: FACTORS OF MIGRATION

Contemporary Laos has its roots in the ancient Lao Kingdom of Lan Xang, established in the fourteenth century under King Fa Ngum. For 600 years, Lan Xang, "The Kingdom of a Million Elephants," had political, cultural, and social influences reaching into present-day Thailand as well as over all of modern-day Laos. After centuries of gradual decline, Laos came under the domination of the Court of Siam from the late eighteenth century after separating into the three separate kingdoms of Luang Phrabang, Vientiane, and Champassak (Bowman 2000, 456–58). In 1827, the king of Vientiane, Chao Anouvong, led a war against Siam to reclaim autonomy for Laos, but his failure sustained the gradual decline. In the late nineteenth century, Luang Phrabang became a French protectorate under the Franco-Siamese Treaty of 1893, and the rest of Laos came under the direct rule of France (Lee 1970). Laos is the only landlocked country in Southeast Asia and is bordered by China, Vietnam, Cambodia, Thailand, and Burma (Myanmar).

Major rebellion against the French colonialists did not begin until after World War II. Japan, which began having influence over Laos in 1941, finally took full control of the country from the French in March 1944. In 1945, the Luang Phrabang prince, Chao Phetsarath, declared Laos an independent kingdom and formed a group known as the Lao Issara, or "Free Lao" (Goldstein 1973, 68). Free Lao strongly opposed French occupation on nationalist, not communist, grounds, while some people supported the French because they thought Laos was not ready for complete independence. Chao Phetsarath's half brother, Chao Souphanouvong, called for armed resistance and sought support from the Viet Minh, an anti-French nationalist/Communist movement led by Ho Chi Minh. Chao Souphanouvong's political group later became the Communist Pathet Lao "Lao Nation."

In the 1960s and 1970s, a "Secret War" raged between the U.S.-backed Royal Lao government and the Pathet Lao, a Communist, nationalist political movement closely associated with the North Vietnamese Communist movement (Johnson 2004, 134). Known as the American Central Intelligence Agency's "Secret War" against the Pathet Lao, the war resulted in a massive bombing campaign in Laos (Osornprasop 2012, 186–88). During the early years of the war (the mid-1960s), young Hmong males were used for reconnaissance, but as the war became protracted, Hmong involvement grew to the point where the Hmong were active fighters—fighting against the Pathet Lao Communist forces (Fredriksen 2012, 191–92).

Between 1962 and 1973, the United States dropped as much as five million tons of cluster bombs on Laos in defiance of the 1962 Geneva Accord that recognized Laos as a neutral zone (Porter 2005, 49–53). The North Vietnamese also blatantly violated the 1962 Geneva Accord (Westmoreland 1995, 39–44). The devastating campaign of 580,000 bombing missions was the equivalent of a planeload of bombs every eight minutes, 24 hours a day, for nine years. By 1973, an estimated 200,000 people lost their lives in the conflict, whether they were in combat or were combatants, not civilians, killed in bombing, and nearly twice as many were wounded.

By 1975, when the Pathet Lao gained control of the country after violating the 1973 peace agreement, which resulted in the establishment of a coalition government in Laos, Laos was rife with internal ethnic strife and had gained the distinction of being the most heavily bombed country in history. Individuals who served in the Royal Lao Army served the U.S. military—such as the Hmong—or who were considered a threat to the new Pathet Lao government were subsequently held in the Lao gulag "reeducation" labor camps called "seminars" in rural Laos (McGregor 2008, 84). Some remained in these camps for well over a decade. Many died from malnutrition, disease, sickness, and mistreatment. Those who were fortunate enough to survive were left with various forms of long-lasting trauma. Some survivors have written vivid accounts of their experiences living in reeducation camps, which illustrate a dark period in Lao history.

As a result of the "Secret War," hundreds of thousands of Laotian refugees, about 10 percent of the population at the time, fled their homeland between 1975 and the early 1990s, many of them immigrating to the United States. The majority of Laotian and Hmong refugees who fled Laos spent time in refugee camps in Thailand and the Philippines before settling in countries such as Argentina, Australia, Canada, China, France, French Guiana, Japan, New Zealand, and the United States. These camps held the promise of escape from war, but more often delivered a reality of poverty and violence. Some camps were also organizing bases for insurgent groups fighting against the Lao communists.

REFUGEES FROM CAMBODIA AND LAOS

The passage of the Indochina Migration and Refugee Assistance Act of 1975 allowed for Southeast Asians who had been closely associated with the U.S. military in Vietnam, Laos, and Cambodia to receive passage to the United States. Later on, the Refugee Act of 1980, sponsored by Senator Edward M. Kennedy and signed into law by President Jimmy Carter, admitted more Southeast Asian refugees—in particular, the "boat people" from Vietnam (many were ethnic Chinese Vietnamese), Khmer Rouge survivors from Cambodia, and multiethnic Laotian refugees of Laos.

In 1979, Vietnam invaded Cambodia and ended Khmer Rouge rule. However, the Khmer Rouge's pogrom had claimed the lives of between 1.5 million and 3 million Cambodians—about one-third of the entire population. Over 100,000 Cambodians fled to the Thai border following the fall of the Khmer Rouge. Refugee camps were established by the United Nations, and over the next decade, Cambodians were allowed to resettle in other countries, primarily the United States.

The first wave of Cambodian migrants to the United States included the fortunate 4,600 Cambodians who managed to flee the country just before the 1975 Khmer Rouge takeover, and who were comprised mainly of former government officials and those with associations to the United States. As such, the composition of the first wave reflected an educated, urbanized, and middle-class refugee population (Mortland 2010: 78).

The second wave took place following the fall of the Khmer Rouge in 1979. The majority of these refugees were from the rural areas of Cambodia, where there was less access to formal education. Many in this wave were also ethnic Chinese Cambodians who survived the genocide (Haines 2010, 17). By 1990, 147,708 Cambodian refugees had resettled in the United States. The United States normalized its relations with Cambodia in 1991, but it was following the United Nations–supervised elections in May 1993, that diplomatic relations with the United States was fully reestablished with an embassy (Thayer 2012, 97). Since then, efforts by Cambodian Americans to sponsor relatives left behind in Cambodia have resulted in some new immigrants to the United States. A small number of Cambodian immigrants have also arrived as spouses of Cambodian American and other U.S. citizens, adopted children, and arrived on their own on tourist, student, business, or missionary visas. Since 2000, "visa marriages" among Cambodians and Cambodian Americans have also been common (Thompson 2013).

Between 1975 and 1979, approximately 22,000 Laotian refugees arrived in the United States. The majority of these earlier refugees were relatives of Laotians who were employed by the U.S. Information Service, the U.S. Agency for International Development, or the U.S. embassy in Vientiane.

Between 1979 and 1981, 105,477 refugees arrived in the United States. Additionally, between 1986 and 1989, 52,864 Laotian refugees arrived in the United States. Unlike the first waves, they were mainly farmers and villagers who were not as educated or as ready for life in an urban setting. Laotian refugees continued to immigrate to the United States from the 1980s to the early 1990s, albeit in small numbers.

Because the Hmong had become targets in their own land, they began to migrate out of Laos, across the Mekong River into Thailand. For many years, Hmong leaders and their often fragmented families were kept in refugee camps in northern Thailand. In the camps, some families had to wait for years before they were granted permission to resettle in another country. Unlike the 150,000 Vietnamese who were immediately evacuated in April 1975, as "allowed by the United States under the 'parole' power of the U.S. Attorney General" (Chan 1994, 49), Hmong refugees did not receive that same privilege. During this period, only 3,000 Hmong refugees were granted asylum under the Refugee Assistance Act of 1975. Nevertheless, the Refugee Act of 1980 eventually opened the door for all refugees. By the mid-1990s, Hmong refugees had resettled in France, Canada, Australia, and other countries, with roughly 90 percent of them relocated to the United States (see Table 7.1). Then in 2004, 15,000 Hmong refugees from Wat Tham Krabok Temple in Thailand were relocated to the United States. Ban Vinai was the largest of the camps that held Hmong refugees. At Ban Vinai, the water was often bad, food was scarce, and the living conditions were crowded (Long 1993). By the early 1980s, Hmong families who could demonstrate their participation in the war were obtaining immigration status to the United States. In the years that followed, many Hmong refugees made their way to the United States.

ADJUSTING TO LIFE IN AMERICA

Most Cambodians, Laotians, and Hmong arrived in the United States as refugees who had experienced the trauma of war, genocide, and poor living conditions in refugee camps. Refugee resettlement was enabled by the passage of the federal Refugee Act of 1980, which included a domestic policy of refugee assistance through the Office of Refugee Resettlement (ORR). This included assistance with housing, English courses, job training, health care, and financial support. Unfortunately, the federal resettlement program was uneven and unsystematic. By the early 1980s, the decline of the auto industry and ensuing economic recession resulted in systematic underfunding for refugee resettlement. Cuts in federal spending-cum-funding therefore covered only a fraction of the cost faced by states, counties, cities, and institutions responsible for assisting with refugee resettlement. "Voluntary

Table 7.1 Indo-Chinese Refugee Resettlement, 1975–1997

Country	Vietnamese	Laotians	Cambodians	Total Resettled	Notes
United States	883,317	251,334 (Includes Hmong and other highlanders)	152,748	1,287,399	
Vietnam			320,000	320,000	Includes 150,000 Cambodians and 170,000 ethnic Chinese and ethnic Vietnamese who fled the Khmer Rouge.
China	263,000			263,000	Nearly all ethnic Chinese.
Canada	163,415	17,274	21,489	202,178	
Australia	157,863	10,239	17,605	185,700	
France	46,348	34,236	38,598	119,182	
Germany	28,916	1,706	998	31,620	
United Kingdom	24,267	346	381	24,994	
New Zealand	6,099	1,350	5,995	13,344	
Netherlands	11,546	33	523	12,102	
Japan	8,231	1,273	1,223	10,727	
Norway	10,066	2	178	10,246	
Malaysia			10,000	10,000	Cambodian Muslims
Switzerland	7,304	593	1,717	9,614	
Sweden	9,099	26	214	9,339	
Denmark	7,007	12	51	7,070	
Belgium	5,158	989	896	7,043	
Other countries	10,343	4,694	8,268	25,605	
Grand Total	1,642,179	324,107	580,884	2,547,170	

Sources: Compiled for the author from Courtland W. Robinson, *Terms of Refuge* (London: Zed Books, 1998) and UNHCR (Statistical Yearbooks, 1994–2012).

Southeast Asian refugees (mostly Laotian) waiting to be processed (circa 1980) after arriving on a Flying Tigers charter flight used to shuttle refugees into the United States by the International Organization for Migration (primarily from camps in Thailand and the Philippines). Refugees landed at Travis, Oakland, or San Francisco International Airport (SFO) and were then bussed to Hamilton Transit Center overnight before proceeding to their sponsors throughout the United States. (Laurie Reemsnyder)

agencies" (VOLAGs), such as churches and other charitable organizations, were also involved in the sponsorship, resettlement, and support of Cambodian, Laotian, Hmong, and Vietnamese refugees. These civil society groups were strongest during the early period, 1975 to the mid-1980s, as "compassion fatigue" slowly impacted this aspect of resettlement resources for the refugee populations.

The ORR attempted to spread Cambodian, Hmong, and Laotian refugees in cities and towns across the United States so as not to overburden the institutions and resources of any single area. This policy of dispersal proved to be ineffective and slowed the pace of integration into American society, as resettling them together, in strong communities, would have provided the refugee population cultural, moral, and social support through networks, cultural familiarity, and ability to collectively experience displacement and replacement together. However, secondary migration resulted in Long Beach, California, making it a Cambodian destination. Long Beach had a small yet established prewar Cambodian community, which assisted in the resettlement of new arrivals. As more and more Cambodians moved into Long Beach, it became a destination for those seeking to reunite with long-lost family members, relatives, and friends. Moreover, Southern California's weather and generous welfare assistance programs made Long Beach the place to be. Unlike the Cambodians, Laotian refugees live in geographically diverse communities. The largest concentration lives in California, in particular Sacramento, San Diego, and the San Francisco Bay Area. Other sizable communities live in Texas, Washington, Minnesota, Wisconsin, Illinois, Georgia, Texas, North Carolina, and Oregon. The Hmong communities are largest in California, Minnesota, and Wisconsin.

STORIES OF SURVIVAL

A Cambodian American recalls her passage to America, and her initial impressions. She says,

> One of my sisters had gotten to America and she sponsored us to come to America too, but first we had to go to another camp in the Philippines. Then we moved to San Francisco, to the Tenderloin, but my mom and dad could not stay there because it was too crowded and my mom got upset because she saw homeless people and was sick all the time. So we moved to Stockton. When I got there I went directly to high school. It was very difficult because I did not know English. (Indochinese Housing Development Corporation 2001, 31–32)

A similar narrative is expressed by a Laotian female who stayed in refugee camps in Thailand and the Philippines before arriving in California in 1981:

> When we got to America they sent us to live in Ukiah. It's four hours from San Francisco, up North. And the people that sponsored us were called Ten Thousand Buddhist temple. They were I think a Chinese Buddhist Temple. They were the people that sponsor us to come to the U.S. So we went there and we stayed there for three months ... They had like maybe two or three hundred refugees, also living there at the same time. (Indochinese Housing Development Corporation 2001, 60)

In her memoir, Kao Kalia Yang describes her experiences in the refugee camp as a child:

> Ban Vinai refugee camp was a dirty place. Dust particles flew high in the hot wind. Young women held pieces of cloth over their noses when they walked in the noon sun to pick rations for their families in a patch of designated ground. The cotton prints of their tube skirts swooshed in the air. Young men

narrowed their eyes and breathed through their noses, drawing the dirt in, eye-
ing the groups of women ... Little boys and girls ran around as they did in every
other part of the world where there is little to do and many people to look after
them. The dust went into my throat, got into my nostrils. When I blew my nose
on the inside corner of my shirt ... I saw black dirt on the fabric. Somehow the
dust turned black inside my nose when in the air it looked orange ... I couldn't
ask an adult why and how the dust changed its color inside my nose. Ban Vinai
refugee camp was a place where kids kept secrets and adults stayed inside themselves. (Yang 2008, 55)

Cambodian, Laotian, and Hmong refugees faced a wide range of challenges as they adjusted to life in the United States. These challenges included
problems of lingering postwar trauma; schools that were ill equipped to
meet the unique cultural, academic, and linguistic needs of Cambodian and
Laotian refugee students; lack of needed social services; gang involvement
and conflicts with other ethnic minority gangs; early marriage; and welfare
dependency. For Cambodian Americans, the issue of forced deportations
of nonnaturalized citizens has remained a current critical issue. On
March 22, 2002, Cambodia and the United States entered into a repatriation
agreement. The agreement broadly established that Cambodia would fully

Mien grandmother carrying baby waiting to be processed at Travis AFB
circa 1979. (Laurie Reemsnyder)

cooperate in the repatriation of their own nationals from the United States. The Cambodian American community, and some 1,400 young men and women who had been ordered deported to Cambodia, for the first time faced the prospect of the forced return of family members to the country that they had fled just three decades earlier.

Changes in immigration laws in 1996 greatly impacted the Cambodian American community. Making matters worse was the terrorist attack on September 11, 2001, which made the U.S. government leery of all noncitizens. Before 1996, judges had discretion in deportation cases; after 1996, the policy was draconian, and judges no longer had discretion. Cambodian refugees who maintained their permanent alien status and did not become naturalized citizens were particularly at risk. Many refugees did not become naturalized citizens because of English-as-a-Second-Language issues. Younger Cambodian Americans who committed petty crimes while teenagers were targets of the new policy. Immigration reform made deportation mandatory for all legal permanent residents who were sentenced to a year or more for "aggravated felonies," "moral turpitude," or use of controlled substances. Judges had no discretion in individual cases and could not consider his/her prison experience, rehabilitation, attitude, behavior, ties to family, and length of time living in the United States.

NOTE

1. In this chapter, the use of the term "Laotian" refers to someone who comes from Laos. The word "Laotian" is problematic and not generally accepted by scholars or people with the diverse communities. Khamchong Luangpraseut differentiate "Lao" as referring to members of the Lao ethnic group, while "Laotian" refers to anyone who comes from Laos. Luangpraseut's classification is contested for being "Lao-centric." As such, most people from different non-Lao ethnic groups prefer to be called by their own groups' ethnic group names, like Hmong, Iu Mien, Khmu, Tai Dam, Tai Lue, and so on. However, some will clarify by saying they come from Laos, or are "Laotian" when speaking to people who are unfamiliar with Laos and its diverse ethnic and cultural groups. The present government in Laos officially recognizes 49 ethnic groups and many more subgroups in Laos. Before 1975, 68 ethnic groups were recognized. The Lao, Tai Dam and Tai Lue speak languages in the Tai-Kadai linguistic family, the Hmong and Iu Mien speak languages in the Hmong-Iu Mien linguistic family, the Khmu language is in the Mon-Khmer linguistic family, and the Lahu and Akha speak languages in the Tibeto-Burman linguistic family. It is generally recognized that the native peoples of Laos all speak languages and dialects within these four language groups. Many Lao Isan people from Northeast Thailand, a territory once linked to the Lao Lan Xang Kingdom, also live in the United States.

REFERENCES

Becker, Elizabeth. *When the War Was Over: Cambodia and the Khmer Rouge Revolution.* New York: PublicAffairs, 1986.

Bowman, John Stewart, ed. *Columbia Chronologies of Asian History and Culture.* New York: Columbia University Press, 2000.

Caplan, Nathan, John K. Whitmore, and Quang L. Bui. *Southeast Asian Refugee Self-Sufficiency Study: Final Report.* Prepared for the Office of Refugee Resettlement, U.S. Department of Health and Human Services, 1985.

Chan, Sucheng. *Asian Americans: An Interpretive History.* New York: Twayne, 1991.

Chan, Sucheng. *Hmong Means Free: Life in Laos and America.* Philadelphia: Temple University Press, 1994.

Chan, Sucheng. *Survivors: Cambodian Refugees in the United States.* Champaign: University of Illinois Press, 2004.

Chan, Sucheng. *The Vietnamese American 1.5 Generation: Stories of War, Revolution, Flight, and New Beginnings.* Philadelphia: Temple University Press, 2006.

Chandler, David. *A History of Cambodia.* Boulder, CO: Westview Press, 1983.

Chandler, David. *Voices from S-21: Terror and History in Pol Pot's Secret Prison.* Berkeley: University of California Press, 1999.

Chhim, Sun-him. "Introduction to Cambodian Culture." Multifunctional Resource Center, San Diego State University, 1989.

Clymer, Kenton. *The United States and Cambodia, 1870–1969: From Curiosity to Confrontation.* New York: RoutledgeCurzon, 2004.

Etcheson, Craig. *After the Killing Fields: Lessons from the Cambodian Genocide.* Lubbock: Texas Tech University Press, 2005.

Evans, Grant. *The Politics of Ritual and Remembrance: Laos since 1975.* Honolulu: University of Hawai'i Press, 1998.

Fredriksen, John. *Fighting Elites: A History of U.S. Special Forces.* Santa Barbara, CA: ABC-CLIO, 2012.

Goldstein, Martin. *American Policy towards Laos.* Cranbury, NJ: Associated University Presses, 1973.

Grabias, David, and Nicole Newnham, directors. *Sentenced Home.* IMDbPro, 2006. DVD.

Haines, David. *Safe Haven? A History of Refugees in America.* Sterling, VA: Kumarian Press, 2010.

Hein, Jeremy. *Ethnic Origins: The Adaptation of Cambodian and Hmong Refugees in Four American Cities.* New York: Russell Sage Foundation, 2006.

Hein, Jeremy. *From Vietnam, Laos and Cambodia: A Refugee Experience in the United States.* New York: Twayne Publishers, 1995.

"Indochina Refugees." Hearings before the Subcommittee on Immigration, Citizenship, and International Law of the Committee on the Judiciary House of Representatives. 94th Congress, May 5 and 7, 1975. Washington, DC: U.S. Government Printing Office, 1975.

Indochinese Housing Development Corporation. *Stories of Survival: Three Generations of Southeast Asian Americans Share Their Lives.* 10th anniversary ed. San Francisco: Indochinese Housing Development Corporation, 2001.

Johnson, Chalmers. *The Sorrows of Empire: Militarism, Secrecy, and the End of the Republic.* New York: Henry Holt and Company, 2004.

Jones, Howard. *Crucible of Power: A History of American Foreign Relations from 1945.* Lanham, MD: Rowman & Littlefield Publishers, 2009.

Lai, Eric, and Dennis Arguelles, eds. *The New Face of Asian Pacific America: Numbers, Diversity, and Change in the 21st Century.* San Francisco: AsianWeek, 2003.

Lau, Albert, ed. *Southeast Asia and the Cold War.* New York: Routledge, 2012.

Lee, Chae-Jin. *Communist China's Policy toward Laos: A Case Study, 1945–67.* Lawrence: Center for East Asian Studies, University of Kansas, 1970.

Lee, Jonathan H. X., ed. *Cambodian American Experiences: Histories, Communities, Cultures, and Identities.* Dubuque, IA: Kendall and Hunt Publishing Company, 2010.

Livo, Norma, and Dia Cha. *Folk Stories of the Hmong: Peoples of Laos, Thailand, and Vietnam.* Westport, CT: Libraries Unlimited, 1991.

Long, Lynellyn. *Ban Vinai: The Refugee Camp.* New York: Columbia University Press, 1993.

Luangpraseut, Khamchong. *Laos Culturally Speaking.* San Diego, CA: San Diego State University, Multifunctional Resource Center, 1987.

McGregor, Andrew. *Southeast Asian Development.* New York: Routledge, 2008.

McLellan, Janet. *Cambodian Refugees in Ontario: Resettlement, Religion, and Identity.* Toronto: University of Toronto Press, 2009.

Model, David. *State of Darkness: US Complicity in Genocides since 1945.* Bloomington, IN: AuthorHouse, 2008.

Mortland, Carol. "Cambodian Resettlement in America." In *Cambodian American Experiences: Histories, Communities, Cultures, and Identities,* edited by Jonathan H. X. Lee. Dubuque, IA: Kendall and Hunt Publishing Company, 2010.

Needham, Susan, and Karen Quintiliani. *Cambodians in Long Beach (Images of America).* Mount Pleasant, SC: Arcadia Publishing, 2008.

Ngaosyvathn, Mayoury, and Pheuiphanh Ngaosyvathn. *Paths to Conflagration: Fifty Years of Diplomacy and Warfare in Laos, Thailand, and Vietnam, 1778–1828.* Ithaca, NY: Cornell University, Southeast Asia Program Publications, 1998.

Odo, Franklin, ed. *The Columbia Documentary History of the Asian American Experience.* New York: Columbia University Press, 2002.

Osborne, Milton. *The Mekong: Turbulent Past, Uncertain Future.* St. Leonards, Australia: Allen & Unwin, 2000.

Osornprasop, Sutayut. "Thailand and the Secret War in Laos, 1960–74." In *Southeast Asia and the Cold War,* edited by Albert Lau. New York: Routledge, 2012.

Porter, Gareth. *Perils of Dominance: Imbalance of Power and the Road to War in Vietnam.* Berkeley: University of California Press, 2005.

Pyle, Jean Laron. "Public Policy and Local Economies: The Phenomenon of Secondary Migration." In *Southeast Asian Refugees and Immigrants in the Mill City: Changing Families, Communities, Institutions—Thirty Years Afterward*, edited by Tuyet-Lan Pho, Jeffrey N. Gerson, and Sylvia R. Cowan. Lebanon, NH: University Press of New England, 2007.

Qiu, Lian. "First International Lao New Year Festival." *AsianWeek*, April 3, 2009.

Quincy, Keith. *Hmong: History of a People*. Cheney: Eastern Washington University Press, 1988.

Scripter, Sami, and Sheng Yang. *Cooking from the Heart: The Hmong Kitchen in America*. Minneapolis: University of Minnesota Press, 2009.

Sen, Srila. "The Lao in the United States since Migration." PhD diss., University of Illinois at Urbana-Champaign, 1987.

Shawcross, William. *Quality of Mercy: Cambodia, Holocaust, and Modern Conscience*. New York: Simon and Schuster, 1984.

Siegel, Taggart, and Kati Johnston. *Blue Collar and Buddha*. Collective Eye Films, 1987. DVD.

Streed, Sarah. *Leaving the House of Ghosts: Cambodian Refugees in the American Midwest*. Jefferson, NC: McFarland & Company, 2002.

Stuart-Fox, Martin. *A History of Laos*. Cambridge: Cambridge University Press, 1997.

Su, Christine. "Southeast Asians and Southeast Asian Americans, 1940–Present." In *Immigrants in American History: Arrival, Adaption, and Integration*, edited by Elliott Barkan, 1295–314. Santa Barbara, CA: ABC-CLIO, 2013.

Takaki, Ronald T. *Strangers from a Different Shore: A History of Asian Americans*. Rev. ed. Boston: Little, Brown, 1989.

Thayer, Carlyle. "Cambodia–United States Relations." In *Cambodia: Progress and Challenges Since 1991*, edited by Pou Sothirak, Geoff Wade, and Mark Hong. Singapore: Institute of Southeast Asian Studies, 2012.

Thompson, Nathan. "Doing Your Duty—Visa Marriage in the Provinces." *Phnom Penh Post*, September 13, 2013. http://www.phnompenhpost.com/7days/doing-your-duty-%E2%80%93-visa-marriage-provinces (accessed June 8, 2014).

United Nations High Commissioner for Refugees (UNHCR). *The State of the World's Refugees: Fifty Years of Humanitarian Action*. Oxford: Oxford University Press, 2000.

Virgilio, Joseph. "The Evacuation and Resettlement of Indochinese Refugees in Lower Southeast Texas, 1975–1980." Unpublished thesis, Lamar University–Beaumont, 1991.

Watts, J. F., and Fred L. Israel, eds. *Presidential Documents: The Speeches, Proclamations, and Policies that Have Shaped the Nation from Washington to Clinton*. New York: Routledge, 2000.

Welaratna, Usha. *Beyond the Killing Fields: Voices of Nine Cambodian Survivors in America*. Stanford, CA: Stanford University Press, 1993.

Westmoreland, William. "Vietnam in Perspective." In *Vietnam: Four American Perspectives: Lectures by George S. McGovern, William C. Westmoreland,*

Edward N. Luttwak, and Thomas J. McCormick, edited by Patrick J. Hearden. West Lafayette, IN: Purdue University Research Foundation, 1995.

Whitmore, John K. "An Outline of Vietnamese History before French Conquest." In *The Vietnam Forum: A Review of Vietnamese Culture and Society*. Yale Center for International and Area Studies, Yale Southeast Asia Studies (Summer–Fall 1986): 1–9.

Willmott, William. *The Chinese in Cambodia*. Vancouver, BC, Canada: University of British Columbia, 1976.

Yang, Kao Kalia. *The Latehomecomer: A Hmong Family Memoir*. Minneapolis, MN: Coffee House Press, 2008.

Yeo, Andrew. *Activists, Alliances, and Anti-U.S. Base Protests*. Cambridge: Cambridge University Press, 2011.

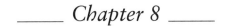

Chapter 8

New Asians in America

Thus far, we have examined the histories of early Asian immigrants to the United States: Chinese, Japanese, Korean, Indian, and Filipinos. We have also examined post–Vietnam War refugees from Cambodia, Laos, and Vietnam. However, Asian American communities are diverse, in country and region of origin, languages, religions, and cultures. There is a dearth of scholarship on many "new" or "emerging" Asian American communities whose population size are smaller, and whose length of time in the United States is shorter. While it is beyond the scope of this book, and this chapter to cover all Asian American communities and their histories in the United States, I wish to highlight some communities for our consideration.

Among Southeast Asian Americans, the common interlocutors are post–Vietnam War refugees. However, just as Asia is diverse, Southeast Asia, as a category, is inherently diverse. Although non–Vietnam War refugee Southeast Asian migrants contemporaneously arrived in the United States, they have received less attention.

FACTORS OF BURMESE MIGRATION AND RESETTLEMENT

According to the 2010 U.S. Census, there are 91,085 Burmese Americans who self-identify as "Burmese alone." Additionally, 9,115 identified as Burmese with one or more other ethnicity or racial identity, which makes the total Burmese American population 100,200. However, this total might not represent the actual population size because many ethnic groups who come from Burma (present-day Myanmar) might not identify as "Burmese," but rather with their ethnic-specific reference. Approximately 70 percent of Burma's 50 million in population are comprised of "ethnic Burman." But, there are more than 160 ethnic groups in Burma; for example, Shan, Karen,

Karenni, Kachin, Chin, Rohingya, and so on. Burma was colonized by Britain since 1886 following three Anglo-Burmese Wars (1882–1885) and, for a short period from 1942 to 1945, by Japan.

Since the end of colonialism, Burma has struggled with civil unrest. On March 2, 1962, a Burmese general named Ne Win seized control of the government and instituted military rule. After Ne Win's takeover, he nationalized all private enterprise and shut down the universities that resulted in a flight of middle-class and upper-class Anglo-Burmese, who were culturally mixed of British and Burmese. Many of them spoke English and practiced Christianity. In addition, there were ethnic Burmans, Indians, and Chinese, and who were students, professionals, and doctors. The migration of this cohort coincided with the elimination of quotas for migrants from Asia with the passage of the 1965 Immigration and Nationality Act. More migrants from Burma arrived after the August 8, 1988 (known in Burmese as *shiq ley lone*, or "four eights," 8/8/88), uprising to protest Ne Win's rule and advocate democracy. The Ne Win regime responded by killing many protestors, after which it installed a military junta that resulted in a flight of political refugees from Burma. The refugees fled to refugee camps in Thailand along the Burma-Thai border. Many of them resettled in Fort Wayne, Indiana; Los Angeles and San Francisco, California; New York City; and Washington, D.C. From 1977 to 2000, 25,229 Burmese migrated to the United States. This figure does not include Burmese migrants who arrived to the United States via other countries, such as Chinese-Burmese going through Taiwan, or Indian-Burmese going through India and Nepal.

After the terrorist attack in New York City on September 11, 2001, the USA Patriot Act prevented any of the Burmese on the Thai or Bangladeshi borders from entering the United States as refugees from 2001 to 2005. The act excluded refugee status to anyone who had provided "material support" to any known or suspected terrorists. As a result, many Burmese refugees were eliminated from immigrating as refugees because they provided water, food, and sometimes housing to guerrilla fighters. Additionally, the Patriot Act defined the Karen as "terrorists" and banned them from even applying for refugee status. In 2005, the United States offered to resettle Burmese refugees residing along the Burma-Thai border. In 2006, the State Department waived the part of the Patriot Act that prevented 9,300 ethnic Karen from entering the United States because of their association with rebels who wanted democracy in Burma. It also lifted restrictions on material support for the Karen, Chin, and Karenni. Besides the area of Fort Wayne, other areas such as St. Paul, Minnesota, and Utica, New York, are also home to large Karen and Chin populations. From 2006 to 2009, more than 50,000 Burmese refugees were admitted.

Similar to the post–Vietnam War refugees, the resettlement of Burmese refugees relied on support by nongovernmental organizations, VOLAGs, such as Catholic Charities, and other religious organizations. For example, in the Fort Wayne area, refugees are placed in the care of Catholic Charities, which receives about $425 or so to provide housing, furniture, food, and job placement assistance. Unfortunately, the lessons of poorly funded resettlement programs did not inform the resettlement of refugees from Burma. As a result, Burmese refugees struggle to integrate and adapt to their new life in America, as illustrated in the documentary *Nickel City Smiler: From the Jungle to the Streets*, which chronicles a refugee's flight out of Burma and new life in Buffalo, New York. In *Nickel City Smiler*, Smiler Greely says, limited resettlement resources and programs make it impossible for him to become middle-class Americans. Christine Su notes that less sizable populations of ethnic Chin refugees reside in Spokane, Washington, and Atlanta, Georgia; their resettlement was assisted by various churches, such as the Baptist, Catholic, Church of the Nazarene, and Pentecostal groups (2013, 1300).

FACTORS OF INDONESIAN MIGRATION AND RESETTLEMENT

Prior to the 1950s, there were few Indonesian migrants living in the United States. Beginning in the 1950s, small numbers of Indonesian migrants arrived as students. The International Cooperation Administration (ICA; since 1961, it is known as the United States Agency for International Development, or USAID) administered scholarships to medical faculty at the University of Indonesia in 1953 to study at the University of California at Berkeley. In 1956, the ICA funded the teaching staff of the Bandung Institute of Technology to study at the University of Kentucky. Between the late 1950s and early 1960s, roughly 60,000 Indos, or Dutch Indonesians who are people of mixed Dutch and Indonesian heritages, arrived in the United States as refugees following the Indonesian National Revolution (1945–1949). Dahlia Gratia Setiyawan notes that this group of Indonesians primarily resettled in South California, with sponsorship and assistance from VOLAGs (2011, 517).

In the 1960s, various political and ethnic conflicts erupted in Indonesia, which sent several thousand Indonesians, the majority of whom were Chinese Indonesian, to flee to the United States. Between the 1970s and early 1990s, small groups of Indonesians, such as the Batak of Sumatra, Minahasans of Sulawesi, and several thousand Tionghoa families, immigrated to and resettled in the United States. However, the highest concentration of Indonesians migrated to the United States between 1997 and 2001, and they included Indonesians from major urban centers such as Jakarta and Surabaya, and smaller rural villages such as Malang in East Java, and Manado in North Sulawesi; and sizable Tionghoa, Javanese, and Minahasans groups in addition to smaller numbers of other ethnic groups, such as the Acehnese (Setiyawan 2011, 518). Indonesians were fleeing interethnic and religious violence that erupted during the transition from the Suharto regime when tensions between Muslims and Christians, and Tionghoa and ethnic Indonesians were acute. Yet, others left for job opportunities as a result of the 1997 Asian Financial Crisis, and educational reasons. As such, many entered the United States with a tourist visa and worked as day laborers. Among them, some were successful in applying for asylum and changing their status to permanent resident, and eventually become naturalized citizens. However, the majority remained undocumented, or *imigran gelap* (illegal aliens).

Following the 2004 tsunami in Indonesia, many refugees from Aceh came to the United States. The recent Acehnese immigrants joined the earlier asylum-seekers who resettled in the United States in the late 1990s: the majority is located on the East Coast. According to the 2010 U.S. Census, there are approximately 63,383 self-identified Indonesian Americans. However, an additional 31,887 individuals identified as Indonesian mixed with one or more ethnic and racial groups. The total estimated population is 95,270. The majority of Indonesian Americans reside in large urban centers, such as Los Angeles, San Francisco, Houston, New York, and Chicago.

FACTORS OF THAI MIGRATION AND RESETTLEMENT

Unlike refugees from Southeast Asians who entered the United States seeking asylum as a consequence of the Vietnam War, Thais generally did not come to America in search of political freedom. Thai migration to the United States was virtually nonexistent before 1960. Interactions with U.S. armed forces in Thailand during the Vietnam War is one primary factor of migration because Thais became more aware of the opportunity for migration to the United States. By the 1970s, roughly 5,000 Thais had immigrated to America. The Thai migrants during this period consisted of professionals, especially medical doctors and nurses, and business entrepreneurs. During this period, the migrants were either ethnic Thai or Chinese Thai, and the gender ratio was three women to every man. These included Thai wives of U.S. military personnel and civilians: many of them were ethnic Lao or Thai Isaan, because the military bases were located in the northeastern Isaan region. According to Megan Ratner, the 1980 U.S. Census recorded concentrations of Thai near military installations, especially Air Force bases, in certain U.S. locales (2014). The passage of the 1987 American Homecoming Act allowed for mixed-heritage Thai-American children born of U.S. military personnel to immigrate to the United States, usually with their Thai family members.

The passage of the 1965 Immigration and Nationality Act allowed for increased immigration from Asia, so Thais with the economic resources to do so took advantage of the educational and employment opportunities in the United States. The 1965 act also established a preference for skilled labor. For example, a shortage of nurses in the United States made it possible for skilled Thai nurse-migrants to enter to work and live. In the late 1960s, the American government provided Thai nurse-migrants Green Cards as soon as they landed on American soil.

The 2010 U.S. Census estimates that there are 237,583 Thai Americans who identify as Thai or Thai mixed with one or more ethnic and racial groups. The first wave of Thai migration in the United States occurred between 1969 and 1972, when 10,093 Thais arrived. Since 1972, 3,000–5,000 have entered the United States annually. Between the 1980s and 1990s, roughly 100,000 Thais entered the United States. Similar to the Indonesians, they came to escape the collapsing economy in Thailand, which has continued to struggle. Many of them arrived as undocumented immigrants who entered on tourist or student visas, and work in low-paying and low-skill jobs. Many end up working within the ethnic Thai economy as cooks, servers, and dishwashers in Thai restaurants, often being paid below the minimum wage. Even so, they send remittance to Thailand to assist their families back home. Those who entered with student visas prior to 1984, and overstayed their visas, were given the opportunity to petition to change their status to permanent resident. As a permanent resident, they can eventually apply to become a naturalized citizen. However, after the passage of the Immigration Reform and Control Act of 1984, this path toward legalization became impossible. According to Jenjira Yahirun, marriage migration continues to be a primary method of immigration for Thai women, because the large sex tourism industry in Thailand, a legacy of the Vietnam War, soon became a popular venue for Western men seeking Thai wives (2011, 2105).

In 1999, the Los Angeles City Council designated a stretch along Hollywood Boulevard "Thai Town." This reflects the high concentration of Thai Americans who reside in Southern California. Many first-generation Thai Americans are small business owners: gas stations, beauty parlors, travel agencies, grocery stores, and the popular Thai restaurants. A sign of Thai American community formation is the establishment of *wats*, or Buddhist temples. "Today 105 *wats* can be found scattered throughout North America in 32 states, including six temples in Canada" (Perreria 2011, 1110). Nearly 30 percent of the temples are located in California (http://www.dharmanet.org).

The development of Thai Buddhism in America unfolded in two phases. Initially it was a top-down formation spearheaded by royal, ecclesial, and

civil authorities in Thailand who, in the mid-1950s and 1960s, sought to
expand Thai Buddhism beyond its geographical and national borders (Perreria 2011, 1110). During that period, Thailand envisioned itself as a "world
center of Buddhism." As such, it funded the development of the first transnational Thai temples under royal patronage in India in 1959 with the construction of Wat Thai Buddha-Gaya, and then in the United Kingdom in
1965 with Wat Buddhapadipa. There were also plans to construct a Thai
temple in New York's Staten Island, but the plan was aborted due to
complications.

Simultaneously, a group of Thai immigrants and American-born Buddhists successfully formed the Buddhist Study Center in New York as a
legal entity in 1965 (Perreria 2011, 1110). This event, followed by the
1972 establishment of the first and largest Thai temple in Los Angeles,
foreshadowed a new bottom-up, lay-centered approach to the institution-
alization of Thai Buddhism in the United States. "In June 1971 a mission
of Thai monks led by Ven. Phra Dhammakosacharn arrived in Los
Angeles, and lay people began to raise funds to purchase land. In 1972,
land was donated and construction began on a main hall, a two-story
Thai-style building that was completed and dedicated in 1979" (Cadge
2005, 27). The bottom-up approach maintained close links with Thai roy-
alty and high-ranking civil servants, but was financed and led by the growing Thai immigrant population in America. Wendy Cadge notes, "Buddha
images for the shrine hall and two sets of scriptures were carried to the
United States by monks and lay people from Thailand, and in 1979 His
Majesty the King and Her Majesty the Queen of Thailand presided over
the casting of the principal Buddha image for the temple at Wat Po (officially called Wat Phra Chetuphon, or the Monastery of the Reclining Buddha) in Thailand" (2005, 27). Throughout the 1970s, Thai immigrants
established Thai temples in several metropolitan areas: Washington, D.C.,
Chicago, Denver, and San Francisco. This expansion necessitated the formation of the Council of Thai Bhikkhus in 1977, who acted as liaisons
for the missionary monks coming from Thailand to serve the growing
community (Cadge 2005, 27).

Because the majority of Thais in Thailand, America, and within the Thai
diaspora are mainly Buddhist, Buddhist rituals and beliefs are key to being
Thai in America. In Buddhist custom, people can go to a temple any day to
offer food to the monk(s), as a part of religious practice called *thumbun*, literally meaning making merit. Buddhist monks (and nuns) are the most serious Buddhist learners and practitioners, providing a role model of Buddhism
for common people. In addition to conducting Buddhist rituals, monks are
supposed to lead and teach the way of Buddhism. Although there are some
Thai-American-born monks, the majority of monks in the United States are

invited from Thailand. Currently, there are more than 482 Thai monks in 105 temples across America.

Todd LeRoy Perreria provides five reasons why Thai contribution to Asian American and American culture is "significant" given their relatively small population size and short immigration history:

1. The long history of cordial relations between Thailand and the United States provides an important framework for considering the context in which Thais migrated to America.
2. The diverse demographics of Thais, spread out across the United States. Thais have never been forced to live or work in isolated inner-city ghettos.
3. The majority of Thais immigrated to the United States after passage of the 1965 Immigration Reform Act. Antidiscrimination and affirmative-action measures help to create a cultural climate more tolerant of ethnic diversity.
4. The incorporation of Thai heritage and traditions to mainstream American via interracial marriages, cuisines, and popularity of Buddhism in America.
5. Thais have demonstrated a high degree of civic engagement and willingness to share and celebrate their culture with non-Thais (Perreria 2004, 2008, 2011).

FACTORS OF MONGOLIAN MIGRATION AND RESETTLEMENT

A few Mongolians resided in the United States prior to World War II, and they were mainly academics. In 1949, Dilowa Gegeen Khutukhtu, a Khalkh Mongol and "living Buddha," entered the United States as a political refugee via India. From 1951 to 1952, roughly 1,000 Kalmyks, or Western Mongolians, were admitted into the United States. The Kalmyks are ethnic Mongols whose homeland of Kalmykia is located in Russia, near the western shores of the Caspian Sea. Some 2,000 Kalmyks left their homeland as refugees following the Russian Revolution in 1917. The Kalmyks escaped from Russia by way of the Black Sea. After landing in Turkey, they journeyed to Yugoslavia and Bulgaria, and some traveled as far as Czechoslovakia and France. In 1945, after the surrender of Germany, Kalmyk refugees went through hard times in Europe.

In August 31, 1951, the U.S. Congress granted Kalmyks permission to immigrate to the United States as Europeans. Between December 1951 and March 1952, 571 Kalmyks arrived in the United States (Tsend 2014). Additional family members and individuals migrated to the United States afterward. They resettled in New Jersey and established Buddhist temples. After this period, small numbers of Mongolians migrated to the United States. The fall of Communism in Mongolia in the early 1990s, following the collapse of the Soviet Union in 1991, made it possible for Mongolians to migrate. Many went to China, whose economy was booming for employment opportunities, and a few hundred Mongolian migrants a year made

Job placement steps are outlined to Sodman Dalantinow, one of the Kalmuks (or Kalmyks), of Mongolian origin, coming to the Philadelphia area to live, by state employment counselor Ruth Griffin, left, while Dalantinow's wife and two small daughters listen. Dalantinow is one of 600 Kalmuks, the first ever, to be brought to the United States. They are coming here from displaced persons camps in Germany, as the United States is the only country that would permit their immigration. Philadelphia, 1952. (AP Photo/WMW)

their way to the United States. Besides Kalmyks, small numbers of Mongolians from Inner Mongolia, China, Taiwan, and India also arrived in the United States during the 1950s and 1960s. Many of them were scholars and Buddhist monks seeking political asylum (Kohn 2011, 812). Since the 1990s, the primary purpose for immigrating is to improve economic and educational opportunities. As of 2000, the U.S. Census estimates there were roughly 3,500 Mongolian Americans residing in the United States. By 2010, that number increased to 18,344.

Early Mongolian migrants resettled on the East Coast around Baltimore, Maryland, and New York City and then relocated to the other cities. Kalmyk Mongol immigrants settled in Lakewood and Freewood Acres, New Jersey, and in Philadelphia, Pennsylvania (Henochowicz 2011, 823). The International Refugee Organization furnished a special grant to several civil society groups, notably the Tolstoy Foundation and the Church World

Service, on behalf of the Kalmyk Mongolians, to cooperatively work together to help them locate new homes and resettle. Recent Mongolian immigrants settle in communities in San Francisco, Los Angeles, as well as traditional East Coast communities in New York, Washington, D.C., Philadelphia, and New Jersey, as well as in Chicago.

FACTORS OF NEPALI MIGRATION AND RESETTLEMENT

Significant Nepali migration to the United States occurred in the early 1950s when Nepal's borders were open to the outside world; before this, Nepal maintained relative isolation. In 1975, 56 Nepali immigrants arrived to the United States. The number of migrants from Nepal remained below 100 per year through 1996 (Miller 2014).

A gradual increase in Nepali migrants to the United States since the 1990s is primarily due to the introduction of the Diversity Immigration (DV) lottery, or Green Card lottery that awards up to 50,000 permanent resident visas annually to persons from countries with low rates of immigration to the United States (Greer 2011, 851). The diversity lottery was established through the 1990 Immigration and Nationality Act and conducted under the terms of Section 203(c). In 1998, 226 Nepali were winners of the DV-1999 lottery, and 593 won in the DV-2010 lottery. The 2000 U.S. Census estimates that 11,715 Nepali Americans were residing in the United States. By 2010, the U.S. Census reported an increase of the overall population to, 51,907 self-identified Nepali Americans, or 59,490 Nepali Americans who are mixed with one or more ethnic and racial groups. Significant communities of Nepali Americans exist in large metropolitan areas such as New York, Boston, Chicago, Denver, Dallas, Portland, Gainesville, and St. Paul. Sizable numbers also live in various cities of California.

FACTORS OF BHUTANESE MIGRATION AND RESETTLEMENT

Bhutanese Hindus of ethnic Nepali origin have resided in Bhutan for generations: they are estimated to be one-sixth of the population of Bhutan and are also known as Lhotshampas, or "People of the South" (Laenkholm 2007, 59). In 1989, the government of Bhutan implemented a series of nationalist regulations to suppress Lhotshampa culture, restrict the Nepali language, and tighten citizenship requirements under a policy called "One nation, One people" (Evans 2010, 26). Since then, a small trickle of them have fled to Nepal. In September and October 1990, Lhotshampas engaged in civil protest of new state policy imposed by the government that severely curtailed the cultural and religious liberties of Bhutanese people of Nepali ethnicity. In the aftermath of this peaceful demonstration, they were deprived of their Bhutanese citizenship, arbitrarily arrested, and detained

(Ridderbos 2007, 1). By the 1990s, Bhutanese refugee flight became an international refugee crisis. Hence, by the early 1990s, resettlement programs were initiated, and over 60,000 refugees resided at United Nations High Commission for Refugees (UNHCR)-organized refugee camps in Morang and Jhapa districts of eastern Nepal (Chase 2012; Singh 1992). UNHCR's primary duty is protecting and supporting refugees during their time of displacement while working toward one of three durable solutions: (1) voluntary repatriation to their country of origin; (2) local integration in their county of asylum; or (3) resettlement in a third country that agrees to offer residency status (UNHCR 2011). If attempts toward repatriation and local integration fail, third-country resettlement may be pursued, in which case the UNHCR begins working to relocate refugees through a number of partnerships with countries that operate their own national resettlement programs. Under such an arrangement, the United States has admitted over three million refugees since 1975, more than all other receiving countries combined, mostly through the U.S. Refugee Admissions Program (USRAP) (U.S. Department of State 2013).

For nearly two decades, an estimated 100,800 to 130,000 Nepali-speaking Bhutanese refugees remained in seven refugee camps (Goldhap and Thimphu 2009, 50). While in the refugee camps, they are entirely dependent upon the international community for their survival because they are restricted from any income-generating activities. In 2000, Nepal and Bhutan reached a repatriation agreement, but as of this writing, none had yet been allowed to return. In October 2006, the United States announced its willingness to resettle up to 60,000 refugees (Ridderbos 2007, 1). In 2007, UNHCR worked with the International Organization for Migration (IOM) to resettle Bhutanese refugees to third countries. By 2013, "[t]he United States of America [had] accepted the largest numbers (66,134), followed by Canada (5,376), Australia (4,190), New Zealand (747), Denmark (746), Norway (546), the Netherlands (326) and the United Kingdom (317)" ("100,000 Milestone for Bhutanese Refugee Resettlement" 2014). As of 2014, more 8,000 refugees remain in camps awaiting resettlement ("75,000th Bhutanese Refugee off to US for Resettlement" 2014). One community of approximately 600 Bhutanese refugees lives in Burlington, Vermont (Chase 2012, 47), another vibrant community resides in the San Francisco Bay Area (Jeung, Jeung, Subba, and Gurung 2012); and a third lives in Pittsburgh, Pennsylvania (Smith 2013).

FACTORS OF TIBETAN MIGRATION AND RESETTLEMENT

Similar to the Mongolians and Nepali who share their Buddhist faith, Tibetan migration to the United States is relatively recent. Few high-status Tibetans and living lamas, or living Buddhas, arrived in the United States before World War II to teach at American universities. The Tibetan diaspora takes shape in 1949 when the People's Republic of China invaded Tibet and, after defeating the small Tibetan army, seized control of the remote high-plateau civilization nested in the Himalayas (Katsiaficas 2013, 106). The 14th Dalai Lama, Tenzin Gyatso, remained in Tibet for approximately 10 years after the Chinese invasion (Sherab 2011, 1134). In 1959, the Tibetans rebelled against the Chinese, but were defeated by the People's Liberation Army, killing more than 87,000 Tibetans (Shakya 1999, 45). On March 17, 1959, the Dalai Lama, members of his government, and roughly 80,000 Tibetans fled to India (Shakya 1999, 42–45). They sought political asylum in India, Nepal, and Bhutan and announced the formation of a Tibetan government-in-exile (Katsiaficas 2013, 112–14). Since 1959, 54 refugee settlements have been established in India, Nepal, and Bhutan. It is estimated that more than 1.2 million Tibetans have died as a result of the Chinese invasion and occupation of Tibet (Katsiaficas 2013, 113).

In 1959, 1961, and 1965, the United Nations passed three resolutions on Tibet expressing concern over human rights violations (Shakya 1999, 52–90). The global Tibetan diaspora consider this government-in-exile, based in Dharamsala, India, to be the singular legitimate government of Tibet and its people. It is estimated that well over 120,000 Tibetans were living in exile by the late 1990s, including some 5,000 living outside of the Indian subcontinent (Miller 2014). Currently, large numbers of Tibetans continue to flee their country in order to escape Chinese occupation, persecution, internal displacement, and forced assimilation to the Sino-cultural world. Many of these exiles depend on the United Nations High Commission for Refugees (UNHCR), foreign nongovernmental organizations, VOLAGs, and the governments of India, Nepal, and Bhutan for assistance.

The exodus of Tibetans in 1949 was fueled by the Chinese occupation of Tibet: though the majority resettled in neighboring India, some made their way to the United States as political refugees. According to the 1990 U.S. Census, there were 2,185 Tibetans residing in the United States (Miller 2014). There might have been earlier Tibetans (as well as Mongolians and Nepali immigrants) before 1949, but since they were classified as "Other Asian" by the U.S. Immigration Bureau, it is not possible to ascertain the exact figure. Most, if not all, Tibetan Americans have entered the United States as refugees. The Refugee Act of 1980 makes it possible for individuals to enter the United States as refugees if there are humanitarian concerns. Arrangement for their transportation to the United States are usually organized through the International Organization for Migration, which also facilitated the resettlement of post–Vietnam War Cambodian, Laotian, and Vietnamese refugees from 1975 to the 1990s. The Immigration and Naturalization Service admits the refugees officially to the United States at the point of entry, and relies on support by VOLAGs to assist the new arrival with housing, schooling, and employment. As part of the Immigration Act of 1990, 1,000 displaced Tibetans were given special immigrant visas and have since resettled throughout the United States (Miller 2014). Tibetans, classified as "citizens" of China, were not eligible to participate in the 1998 DV-99 diversity lottery (Miller 2014).

While 40 percent of the Tibetan American population resides in Southern California, many communities have been established in other urban centers such as New York City; Washington, D.C.; Seattle, Washington; and Portland, Oregon. Tibetan Americans have formed strong communities in Northern California as well, primarily in Berkeley. In 2014, the Tibetan Association of Northern California (TANC) purchased property and established a center in Richmond. TANC says, "It belongs to each and every Tibetan. It is your home and our home. We want to turn it into a roaring place of activities of all things Tibetan" (TANC 2014). TANC estimates that there are 2,000 Tibetans residing in the San Francisco Bay Area.

FACTORS OF PAKISTANI MIGRATION AND RESETTLEMENT

Pakistan as a nation-state was created in 1947. However, Muslims from India, in the region that is now Pakistan, arrived with the first wave of Hindu and Sikh immigrants who worked as agricultural laborers and as miners in California, Oregon, and Washington. Today, Pakistani immigrants make up the second-largest group of South Asians, following Indians, and the second-largest Muslim community, following Iranian Americans, in the United States. The experiences of early Pakistani immigrants in the United States mirror the experiences of Punjabi Sikhs and Hindus who arrived in large wave in the early twentieth century. In 1907, some 2,000 Indians, which include Muslims who are most likely from today's Pakistan, worked alongside Sikhs, Hindus, Chinese, Japanese, and Korean laborers. They worked on the Western Pacific railway in California, and afterward, they moved into agricultural work. Like other Indians, they became targets of the Asiatic Exclusion League that was organized in 1907 to advocate the expulsion and exclusion of Asian workers. Due to antimiscegenation laws, immigration exclusion, and the nonexistent Muslim women immigration, early Pakistani men married Mexican women to establish families. It was only in 1947 that the U.S. Congress passed a bill allowing naturalization for Indians. According to reports from the Immigration and Naturalization Service, between 1947 and 1965, there were 2,500 Pakistani immigrants who entered the United States: the majority entered on student visas. They remained in the United States upon graduation.

The 1965 Immigration Act ended national quotas, and it is after this that Pakistani immigrants, from the newly formed nation-state has steadily grown in the United States. Unlike the earlier immigrants, the post-1965 Pakistani immigrants were urban, well educated, and professional. Many of them had come from cities such as Karachi, Rawalpindi, and Lahore, and were familiar with Western culture and ways of living. However, the dependents and relatives that they have since sponsored for permanent residence in the United States in the years after 1965 have tended to be characterized by lower levels of education. It is during this period that a distinct Pakistani community in America takes shape. The 1990 U.S. Census shows 100,000 Pakistani Americans residing in the United States. By 2005 the Pakistani population doubled to 210,000. The 2010 U.S. Census reveals more dramatic growth with 363,699 self-identified Pakistani, and 409,163 who identified as Pakistani or mixed with one or more ethnic and racial groups. New York City is home to the largest concentration of

Pakistani immigrant Sobia Akbar waits with her family to receive U.S. citizenship certificates for her children at the U.S. Citizenship and Immigration Services (USCIS) district office on January 29, 2013, in New York City. Some 118,000 immigrants applied for U.S. citizenship, and 2,500 children received citizenship certificates in the New York City district in 2012. Although minors of naturalized immigrants usually receive U.S. citizenship, they must go through a process at the USCIS in order to receive legal certificates. (John Moore/Getty Images)

Pakistani Americans: the 2010 U.S. Census indicates that 194,000 Pakistani live there, primarily in the boroughs of Queens and Brooklyn.

As Muslims, Pakistani Americans face unique challenges. Rabia Kamal notes that in 2000, the U.S. Census added a new racial category, "Middle Eastern," and people of Pakistani descent have been included in this category because of their shared religious faith: Islam (2011, 956). Furthermore, Pakistani Americans, although they share cultural practices and history with Indians, are partial to identifying with Pakistan, not India. "This is due to a history of antagonism between the two nations in the post-colonial Subcontinent" (Kamal 2011, 956).

2010 AND ONWARD

According to the 2010 U.S. Census (Table 8.1), 17.3 million people, or 5.6 percent of all people in the United States, identity as "Asian alone" or "Asian in combination with one or more other races." Since 2000, the Asian American population grew at a faster rate compared with all other ethnic and racial groups in the country. This demographic trend, in large measure, is a byproduct of changes in immigration policies since the end of Second World War, which ushered in the counter-cultural movements that began to question the normative perception and conception of American social life and brought with it a reevaluation of the expectation that immigrants would assimilate into mainstream society.

The civil rights movements of the 1960s and 1970s did not merely express dissatisfaction with racial and prejudicial beliefs and public policies, but it also revealed a deep-seated quandary with the principle of assimilation. To the extent that the American way of life was normatively white and middle-class, it was unfeasible for various segments of the population to ever become completely "American." The imagined consensus promoted by those who favored assimilation could only be sustained by excluding people with dark skin, non-European ancestries, and limited incomes—in particular Asian immigrants. The civil rights movement not only insisted on sensible changes in public policies, it also demanded a transformation and reconstitution of American national self-identity; it insisted that America recognize and reconstitute itself to be a pluralistic society, and that there were manifold and legitimate alternative ways of being American. This produced the pluralistic attitude of American life, one that resembled a "salad bar" indicating that Americans and American life are multifarious culturally, religiously, linguistically, ethnically, politically, sexually, socially, economically, and nationally. Between 1882 and 1965, exclusionist ideologies gave way to the melting pot attitude, which then gave way, starting in the 1980s, to the ideology of cultural pluralism which continues to dominate public discourse surrounding issues of multiculturalism and diversity.

Table 8.1 Asian Population by Number of Detailed Groups

Detailed Group	Asian alone		Asian in combination with one or more races		Detailed Asian group alone or in any combination
	One detailed Asian group reported	Two or more detailed Asian groups reported	One detailed Asian group reported	Two or more detailed Asian groups reported	
Total	14,327,580	346,672	2,429,530	217,074	17,320,856
Asian Indian	2,843,391	75,416	240,547	23,709	3,183,063
Bangladeshi	128,792	13,288	4,364	856	147,300
Bhutanese	15,290	3,524	442	183	19,439
Burmese	91,085	4,451	4,077	587	100,200
Cambodian	231,616	23,881	18,229	2,941	276,667
Chinese	3,347,229	188,153	334,144	140,588	4,010,114
Chinese, except Taiwanese	3,137,061	185,289	317,344	140,038	3,779,732
Taiwanese	196,691	2,501	15,781	468	215,441
Filipino	2,555,923	94,050	645,970	120,897	3,416,840
Hmong	247,595	4,728	7,392	358	260,073
Indonesian	63,383	6,713	22,425	2,749	95,270
Iwo Jiman	1	1	7	3	12
Japanese	763,325	78,499	368,094	94,368	1,304,286
Korean	1,423,784	39,690	216,288	27,060	1,706,822
Laotian	191,200	18,446	19,733	2,751	232,130
Malaysian	16,138	5,730	3,214	1,097	26,179
Maldivian	98	4	25	–	127

(continued)

Table 8.1 (Continued)

| Detailed Group | Asian alone | | Asian in combination with one or more races | | Detailed Asian group alone or in any combination |
	One detailed Asian group reported	Two or more detailed Asian groups reported	One detailed Asian group reported	Two or more detailed Asian groups reported	
Mongolian	14,366	772	2,779	427	18,344
Nepalese	51,907	5,302	1,941	340	59,490
Okinawan	2,753	2,928	3,093	2,552	11,326
Pakistani	363,699	19,295	24,184	1,985	409,163
Singaporean	3,418	1,151	645	133	5,347
Sri Lankan	38,596	2,860	3,607	318	45,381
Thai	166,620	16,252	48,620	6,091	237,583
Vietnamese	1,548,449	84,268	93,058	11,658	1,737,433
Other Asian, not specified	218,922	19,410	366,652	18,777	623,761

Source: 2010 U.S. Census, http://www.census.gov/

The Asian American experience in the United States continues to grow, not only in terms of population size, but in terms of regional, linguistic, religious, and cultural diversity. Asians were in the United States. They continued to be here, and will continued to come to the United States. As such, Asian Americans, from the first wave to the next wave, will continue to reshape and redefine the American mosaic.

REFERENCES

Bahrampour, Tara. "Mongolians Meld Old, New in Making Arlington Home." *Washington Post*, July 3, 2006.

Cadge, Wendy. *Heartwood: The First Generation of Theravada Buddhism in America*. Chicago: University of Chicago Press, 2005.

Cadge, Wendy, and Sidhorn Sangdhanoo. "Thai Buddhism in America: An Historical and Contemporary Overview." *Contemporary Buddhism* 6:1 (May 2005): 7–35.

Chase, Liana. "Psychosocial Resilience among Resettled Bhutanese Refugees in the US." *Forced Migration Review* 40 (2012): 47.

Cheah, Joseph. "The Function of Ethnicity in the Adaptation of Burmese Religious Practices." In *Emerging Voices: Experiences of Underrepresented Asian Americans*, edited by Huping Ling. New Brunswick, NJ: Rutgers University Press, 2008.

Dharma Net: Worldwide Net of Study, Practice, and Action. http://www.dharmanet.org/ (accessed September 10, 2014).

Evans, Rosalind. "The Perils of Being a Borderland People: On the Lhotshampas of Bhutan." *Contemporary South Asia* 18:1 (2010): 25–42.

Goldhap and Thimphu. "Bhutanese Refugees in Nepal: Point of No Return, Going West Rather Than Home." *Economist* 390:8614 (January 15, 2009): 50.

Greer, Marsha. "Nepali Americans: History, People, Culture." In *Encyclopedia of Asian American Folklore and Folklife*, edited by Jonathan H. X. Lee and Kathleen Nadeau, 851–54. Santa Barbara, CA: ABC-CLIO, 2011.

Haines, David. *Safe Haven? A History of Refugees in America*. Sterling, VA: Kumarian Press, 2010.

Henochowicz, Anne. "Mongolian American Family and Community." In *Encyclopedia of Asian American Folklore and Folklife*, edited by Jonathan H. X. Lee and Kathleen Nadeau, 822–23. Santa Barbara, CA: ABC-CLIO, 2011.

Hutt, Michael. *Unbecoming Citizens: Culture, Nationhood, and the Flight of Refugees from Bhutan*. Oxford: Oxford University Press, 2005.

International Organization for Migration. *Cultural Profile: The Bhutanese Refugees in Nepal: A Tool for Settlement Workers and Sponsors*. Damak, Nepal: IOM, 2008.

Jeung, Joan, Russell Jeung, Jiwan Subba, and Bina Gurung. *Needs and Aspirations of Bhutanese Refugees in Northern California*. Alameda: Bhutanese Community in California, 2012.

Kamal, Rabia. "Pakistani Americans: History, People, and Culture." In *Encyclopedia of Asian American Folklore and Folklife*, edited by Jonathan H. X. Lee and Kathleen Nadeau, 955–60. Santa Barbara, CA: ABC-CLIO, 2011.

Katsiaficas, George. *Asia's Unknown Uprisings, Volume 2: People Power in the Philippines, Burma, Tibet, China, Taiwan, Bangladesh, Nepal, Thailand, and Indonesia, 1947–2009*. Oakland, CA: PM Press, 2013.

Kohn, Michael. "Mongolian Americans: History, People, and Culture." In *Encyclopedia of Asian American Folklore and Folklife*, edited by Jonathan H. X. Lee and Kathleen Nadeau, 811–16. Santa Barbara, CA: ABC-CLIO, 2011.

Laenkholm, Christer. "Resettlement of Bhutanese Refugees." *Forced Migration Review* 29 (December 2007): 59–60.

Miller, Olivia. "Nepalese Americans." In *Countries and Their Cultures*. 2014. http://www.everyculture.com/multi/Le-Pa/Nepalese-Americans.html (accessed August 26, 2014).

"100,000 Milestone for Bhutanese Refugee Resettlement." *Himalayan Times*, April 26, 2014. http://www.thehimalayantimes.com/ (accessed July 15, 2014).

Perreria, Todd LeRoy. "The Gender of Practice: Some Findings among Thai Buddhist Women in Northern California." In *Emerging Voices: Experiences of Underrepresented Asian Americans*, edited by Huping Ling, 160–82. New Brunswick, NJ: Rutgers University Press, 2008.

Perreria, Todd LeRoy. "Sasana Sakon and the New Asian American: Intermarriage and Identity at a Thai Buddhist Temple in Silicon Valley." In *Asian American Religions: The Making and Remaking of Borders and Boundaries*, edited by Tony Carnes and Fenggang Yang, 313–37. New York: New York University Press, 2004.

Perreria, Todd LeRoy. "Thai Americans: Religion." In *Encyclopedia of Asian American Folklore and Folklife*, edited by Jonathan H. X. Lee and Kathleen Nadeau, 1109–12. Santa Barbara, CA: ABC-CLIO, 2011.

Ratner, Megan. "Thai Americans." In *Countries and Their Cultures*. 2014. http://www.everyculture.com/multi/Sr-Z/Thai-Americans.html (accessed June 18, 2014).

Ridderbos, Katinka. *Last Hope: The Need for Durable Solutions for Bhutanese Refugees in Nepal and India*. Human Rights Watch 19: 7C (May 2007).

Rogers, Robert. "Work at Richmond Tibetan Center Speeds Up Ahead of Dalai Lama Visit." *Contra Costa Times*, February 12, 2014.

Rubel, Paula. *The Kalmyk Mongols: A Study in Continuity and Change*. Bloomington: Indiana University Press, 1967.

Setiyawan, Dahlia. "Indonesian Americans: History, People, and Culture." In *Encyclopedia of Asian American Folklore and Folklife*, edited by Jonathan H. X. Lee and Kathleen Nadeau, 515–20. Santa Barbara, CA: ABC-CLIO, 2011.

"75,000th Bhutanese Refugee off to US for Resettlement." *Himalayan Times*, April 8, 2014. http://www.thehimalayantimes.com/ (accessed July 15, 2014).

Shakya, Tsering. *The Dragon in the Land of Snows: A History of Modern Tibet since 1947*. New York: Columbia University Press, 1999.

Sherab, Tenzin. "Dalai Lama (1935–)." In *Encyclopedia of Asian American Folklore and Folklife*, edited by Jonathan H. X. Lee and Kathleen Nadeau, 1133–34. Santa Barbara, CA: ABC-CLIO, 2011.

Singh, Kedar. "Stir in Shangri-La: Indian Help Sought over Bhutanese Refugees." *Far Eastern Economic Review* 155 (July 23, 1992): 29.

Smith, Andrew. "Conceptualizing Integration: Resettlement Experiences of Bhutanese Refugees in Pittsburgh, PA." MA thesis, Duquesne University, 2013.

Su, Christine. "Southeast Asians and Southeast Asian Americans, 1940–Present." In *Immigrants in American History: Arrival, Adaption, and Integration*, edited by Elliott Barkan, 1295–314. Santa Barbara, CA: ABC-CLIO, 2013.

Tibetan Association of Northern California (TANC). http://www.tanc.org/ (accessed June 19, 2014).

Tsend, Baatar. "Mongolian Americans." In *Countries and Their Cultures*. http://www.everyculture.com/multi/Le-Pa/Mongolian-Americans.html (accessed July 14, 2014).

United Nations High Commissioner for Refugees (UNHCR). *The State of the World's Refugees: Fifty Years of Humanitarian Action*. Oxford: Oxford University Press, 2000.

United Nations High Commissioner for Refugees (UNHCR). *Resettlement Handbook*. Geneva: UNHCR, 2011.

United Nations Refugee Convention, Article 1A (2). *United Nations Convention Relating to the Status of Refugees* (CRSR), 1951.

U.S. Department of State. "Refugee Admissions." Bureau of Population, Refugees and Migration, 2013. http://www.state.gov/j/prm/ra/ (accessed July 15, 2014).

Yahirun, Jenjira. "Thai Immigrants." In *Multicultural America: An Encyclopedia of the Newest Americans*, edited by Ronald H. Bayor, 2097–133. Santa Barbara, CA: ABC-CLIO, 2011.

Bibliography

Abelmann, Nancy, and John Lie. *Blue Dreams: Korean Americans and the Los Angeles Riots*. Cambridge, MA: Harvard University Press, 1997.

Abraham, Itty. "Filipinos in the US." *Economic and Political Weekly* 41: 8 (February 25–March 3, 2006): 674.

Aguilar-San Juan, Karin. *Little Saigons: Staying Vietnamese in America*. Minneapolis: University of Minnesota Press, 2009.

Ahmad, Ahrar. "Bangladeshi Immigrants." In *Multicultural America: An Encyclopedia of the Newest Americans*, edited by Ronald H. Bayor. Santa Barbara, CA: ABC-CLIO, 2011.

Alcantara, Ruben. *Sakada: Filipino Adaptation in Hawaii*. Washington, DC: University Press of America, 1981.

Allen, James P. "Recent Immigration from the Philippines and Filipino Communities in the United States." *Geographical Review* 67:2 (April 1977): 195–208.

Andaya, Leonard Y. "From American-Filipino to Filipino-American." *Social Process in Hawaii* 37 (1996): 99–111.

Anupama, Jain. *How to Be South Asian in America: Narratives of Ambivalence and Belonging*. Philadelphia: Temple University Press, 2011.

Arden, Harvey. "Troubled Odyssey of Vietnamese Fishermen: The Wanderers from Vung Tau." *National Geographic* 160:3 (1981): 378–94.

Arora, Anupama. "Mexican-Indian Marriages." In *Asian American History and Culture: An Encyclopedia*, edited by Huping Ling and Allan Austin. Armonk, NY: M. E. Sharpe, 2010.

Asher, Robert, and Charles Stephenson, eds. *Labor Divided: Race and Ethnicity in United States Labor Struggles, 1835–1960*. Albany: State University of New York Press, 1990.

Asian American Curriculum and Research Project. Woodring College of Education. Western Washington University. http://www.wce.wwu.edu/resources/aacr/documents.shtml (accessed June 11, 2014).

Azuma, Eiichiro. "Racial Struggle, Immigrant Nationalism, and Ethnic Identity: Japanese and Filipinos in the California Delta." *Pacific Historical Review* 67:2 (May 1998): 163–99.

Bacon, David. *Illegal People: How Globalization Creates Migration and Criminalizes Immigrants*. Boston: Beacon Press, 2008.

Bahrampour, Tara. "Mongolians Meld Old, New in Making Arlington Home." *Washington Post*, July 3, 2006.

Bald, Vivek. *Bengali Harlem and the Lost Histories of South Asian America*. Cambridge, MA: Harvard University Press, 2013.

Baldoz, Rick. *The Third Asiatic Invasion: Empire and Migration in Filipino America, 1898–1946*. New York: New York University Press, 2011.

Barde, Robert E. *Immigration at the Golden Gate: Passenger, Ships, Exclusion, and Angel Island*. Westport, CT: Praeger, 2008.

Bautista, Veltisezar B. *The Filipino Americans: From 1763 to the Present: Their History, Culture, and Traditions*. Farmington Hills, MI: Bookhaus Publishers, 1998.

Becker, Elizabeth. *When the War Was Over: Cambodia and the Khmer Rouge Revolution*. New York: Public Affairs, 1986.

Bennett, Stephen. "The Vietnamese Shrimpers of Texas: Salvaging a Sinking Industry." In *Scholar: St. Mary's Law Review on Minority Issues* 6 (2004).

Bishop, Janine. "Adopted." In *East to America: Korean American Life Stories*, edited by Elaine Kim and Eui-Young Yu. New York: New Press, 1996.

Bonacich, Edna. "Class Approaches to Ethnicity and Race." *Critical Sociology* 25:2–3 (1999): 166–94.

Bonus, Rick. *Locating Filipino Americans: Ethnicity and the Cultural Politics of Space*. Philadelphia: Temple University Press, 2000.

Borah, Eloisa G. *Chronology of Filipinos in America Pre-1898*. 1997–2004. http://personal.anderson.ucla.edu/eloisa.borah/chronology.pdf (accessed June 11, 2014).

Borah, Eloisa G. "Filipinos in Unamuno's California Expedition of 1587." *Amerasia Journal* 21:3 (Winter 1995–1996): 175–83.

Bounds, James. "Vietnamese in Mississippi." *Mississippi History Now: An Online Publication of the Mississippi Historical Society*. http://mshistorynow.mdah.state.ms.us/articles/372/vietnamese-in-mississippi (accessed June 10, 2014).

Bowman, John Stewart, ed. *Columbia Chronologies of Asian History and Culture*. New York: Columbia University Press, 2000.

Brands, H. W. *Bound to Empire: The United States and the Philippines*. Oxford: Oxford University Press, 1992.

Bronner, Simon J., ed. *Lafcadio Hearn's America: Ethnographic Sketches and Editorials*. Lexington: University Press of Kentucky, 2002.

Brown, Giles T. "The Hindu Conspiracy, 1914–1917." *Pacific Historical Review* 17:3 (August 1948): 299–310.

Burdeos, Ray L. *Pinoy Stewards in the U.S. Sea Services: Seizing Marginal Opportunity*. Bloomington, IN: AuthorHouse, 2010.

Burgan, Michael. *The Japanese American Internment: Civil Liberties Denied*. Minneapolis, MN: Compass Point Books, 2007.

Burns, Jeffery M., Ellen Skerrett, and Joseph M. White, eds. *Keeping Faith: European and Asian Catholic Immigrants*. Maryknoll, NY: Orbis Books, 2000.

Cadge, Wendy. *Heartwood: The First Generation of Theravada Buddhism in America*. Chicago: University of Chicago Press, 2005.

Cadge, Wendy, and Sidhorn Sangdhanoo. "Thai Buddhism in America: An Historical and Contemporary Overview." *Contemporary Buddhism* 6:1 (May 2005): 7–35.

California Supreme Court. *Reports of Cases Determined in the Supreme Court of the State of California*. Volume 20. San Francisco: Bancroft-Whitney Company, 1906.

Caplan, Nathan, John K. Whitmore, and Quang L. Bui. *Southeast Asian Refugee Self-Sufficiency Study: Final Report*. Prepared for the Office of Refugee Resettlement, U.S. Department of Health and Human Services, 1985.

Capozzola, Christopher. "Filipinas/os." In *Anti-Immigration in the United States: A Historical Encyclopedia*, edited by Kathleen R. Arnold. Santa Barbara, CA: ABC-CLIO, 2011.

Chacón, Justin A., and Mike Davis. *No One Is Illegal: Fighting Racism and State Violence on the U.S.-Mexico Border*. Photographs by Julián Cardona. Chicago: Haymarket Books, 2006.

Chan, Sucheng. *Asian Americans: An Interpretive History*. New York: Twayne, 1991.

Chan, Sucheng. "Introduction." In *Quiet Odyssey: A Pioneer Korean Woman in America*, by Mary Paik Lee. Seattle: University of Washington Press, 1990.

Chan, Sucheng. *Hmong Means Free: Life in Laos and America*. Philadelphia: Temple University Press, 1994.

Chan, Sucheng. *Survivors: Cambodian Refugees in the United States*. Champaign: University of Illinois Press, 2004.

Chan, Sucheng. *The Vietnamese American 1.5 Generation: Stories of War, Revolution, Flight, and New Beginnings*. Philadelphia: Temple University Press, 2006.

Chandler, David. *A History of Cambodia*. Boulder, CO: Westview Press, 1983.

Chandler, David. *Voices from S-21: Terror and History in Pol Pot's Secret Prison*, Berkeley: University of California Press, 1991.

Chang, Iris. *The Chinese in America*. New York: Penguin, 2004.

Chang, Roberta, with Wayne Patterson. *The Koreans in Hawai'i: A Pictorial History 1903–2003*. Honolulu: University of Hawai'i Press, 2003.

Charr, Easurk Emsen. *The Golden Mountain: The Autobiography of a Korean Immigrant 1895–1960*. Edited and with an Introduction by Wayne Patterson. 2nd ed. Urbana: University of Illinois Press, 1996.

Chase, Liana. "Psychosocial Resilience among Resettled Bhutanese Refugees in the US." *Forced Migration Review* 40 (2012): 47.

Cheah, Joseph. "The Function of Ethnicity in the Adaptation of Burmese Religious Practices." In *Emerging Voices: Experiences of Underrepresented Asian Americans*, edited by Huping Ling. New Brunswick, NJ: Rutgers University Press, 2008.

Chee, Maria W. L. *Taiwanese American Transnational Families: Women and Kin Work.* London: Routledge, 2005.

Chen, Jack. *The Chinese of America: From the Beginnings to the Present.* San Francisco: Harper & Row, 1980.

Chhim, Sun-him. "Introduction to Cambodian Culture." San Diego, CA: Multifunctional Resource Center, San Diego State University, 1989.

Chin, Frank. *Born in the USA: A Story of Japanese America, 1889–1947.* Lanham, MD: Rowman & Littlefield Publishers, 2002.

Chinn, Thomas, H. Mark Lai, and Philip Choy, eds. *A History of the Chinese in California: A Syllabus.* San Francisco: Chinese Historical Society of America, 1969.

Cho, Grace. *Haunting the Korean Diaspora: Shame Secrecy, and the Forgotten War.* Minneapolis: University of Minnesota Press, 2008.

Ch'oe, Yong-ho. "The Early Korean Immigration: An Overview." In *From the Land of Hibiscus: Koreans in Hawai'i, 1903–1950,* edited by Yong-ho Ch'oe. Honolulu: University of Hawai'i Press, 2007.

Choi, Anne Soon. " 'Are They Koreaned Enough?' Generation and the Korean Independence Movement before World War II." *Amerasia Journal* 29:3 (2003–2004): 55–77.

Choi, Anne Soon. " 'Hawai'i Has Been My America:' Generation, Gender, and Korean Immigrant Experience in Hawai'i before World War II." *American Studies* 45:3 (Fall 2004): 139–55.

Choy, Bong Youn. *Koreans in America.* Washington, DC: Burnham Inc. Publishing, 1979.

Choy, Catherine C. *Empire of Care: Nursing and Migration in Filipino American History.* Durham, NC: Duke University Press, 2003.

Choy, Philip. *Canton Footprints: Sacramento's Chinese Legacy.* Sacramento, CA: Chinese American Council of Sacramento, 2007.

Choy, Philip. *San Francisco Chinatown: A Guide to Its History and Architecture.* San Francisco: City Lights Books, 2012.

Christiansen, John B. "The Split Labor Market Theory and Filipino Exclusion: 1927–1934." *Phylon* 40:1 (1979): 66–74.

Chung, Sue Fawn. *In Pursuit of Gold: Chinese American Miners and Merchants in the American West.* Champaign: University of Illinois Press, 2011.

Chung, Sue Fawn, and Priscilla Wegars, eds. *Chinese American Death Rituals: Respecting the Ancestors.* New York: AltaMira Press, 2005.

Ciment, James. "The Indian American Experience: History and Culture." In *Asian American History and Culture: An Encyclopedia,* edited by Huping Ling and Allan Austin. Armonk, NY: M. E. Sharpe, 2010.

Clymer, Kenton. *The United States and Cambodia, 1870–1969: From Curiosity to Confrontation.* New York: RoutledgeCurzon, 2004.

Coombs, F. Alan. "Congressional Opinion and War Relocation, 1943." In *Japanese Americans: From Relocation to Redress,* edited by Roger Daniels, Sandra Taylor, Harry Kitano, and Leonard Arrington. Seattle: University of Washington Press, 1992.

Cordova, Dorothy, and Filipino American National Historical Society. *Filipinos in Puget Sound.* Charleston, SC: Arcadia Publishing, 2009.

Cruz, Adrian. "There Will Be No 'One Big Union': The Struggle for Interracial Labor Unionism in California Agriculture, 1933–1939." *Cultural Dynamics* 22:1 (2010): 29–48.

Danico, Mary Yu. *The 1.5 Generation: Becoming Korean American in Hawai'i.* Honolulu: University of Hawai'i Press, 2004.

Daniels, Roger. *Asian America: Chinese and Japanese in the United States since 1850.* Seattle: University of Washington Press, 1988.

Daniels, Roger. *History of Indian Immigration to the United States: An Interpretative Essay.* New York: Asia Society, 1989.

Daniels, Roger. *Prisoners without Trial: Japanese Americans in World War II.* New York: Hill and Wang, 2004.

Daniels, Roger, Sandra Taylor, Harry Kitano, and Leonard Arrington, eds. *Japanese Americans: From Relocation to Redress.* Seattle: University of Washington Press, 1992.

Dela Cruz, Melany, and Pauline Agbayani-Siewert. "Swimming with and against the Tide: Filipino American Demographic Changes." In *The New Face of Asian Pacific America: Numbers, Diversity and Change in the 21st Century*, edited by Eric Lai and Dennis Arguelles. San Francisco: AsianWeek, 2003.

De Los Santos, P. "*Sakada* Dreams: A Portrait of My Father." *Social Process in Hawaii* 37 (1996): 91–98.

DeWitt, Howard A. "The Filipino Labor Union: The Salinas Lettuce Strike of 1934." *Amerasia Journal* 5:2 (1978): 1–21.

DeWitt, Howard A. *Violence in the Fields: California Filipino Farm Labor Unionization during the Great Depression.* Saratoga, CA: Century Twenty One Publishing, 1980.

DeWitt, Howard A. "The Watsonville Anti-Filipino Riot of 1930: A Case Study of the Great Depression and Ethnic Conflict in California." *Southern California Quarterly* 61:3 (September 1979): 291–302.

Dharma Net: Worldwide Net of Study, Practice, and Action. http://www.dharmanet.org/ (accessed September 10, 2014).

Dickinson, Frederick R. "Japanese Empire." In *Encyclopedia of the Age of Imperialism, 1800–1914*, edited by Carl C. Hodge. Westport, CT: Greenwood Press, 2008.

Dickinson, Frederick R. *War and National Reinvention: Japan in the Great War, 1914–1919.* Cambridge, MA: Harvard University Press, 1999.

Djun Kil Kim. *The History of Korea.* Westport, CT: Greenwood Press, 2005.

Dunne, John G. *Delano: The Story of the California Grape Strike.* Berkeley: University of California Press, 1967.

Easton, Stanley, and Lucien Ellington. "Japanese Americans." *Multicultural America*, 2011. http://www.everyculture.com/multi/Ha-La/Japanese-Americans.html (accessed June 11, 2014).

Echenberg, Myron. *Plague Ports: The Global Urban Impact of Bubonic Plague, 1894–1901.* New York: New York University Press, 2007.

Eisenhower, Dwight D. "Letter from President Eisenhower to Ngo Dinh Dien, President of the Council of Ministers of Vietnam" October 23, 1954. *Department of State Bulletin* (November 15, 1954): 735–36.

Esguerra, Maria Paz Gutierrez. "Filipino Immigrants." In *Multicultural America: An Encyclopedia of the Newest Americans*, edited by Ronald H. Bayor. Santa Barbara, CA: ABC-CLIO, 2011.

Espina, Marina E. *Filipinos in Louisiana*. New Orleans, LA: A. F. Laborde & Sons, 1988.

Espiritu, Yen Le. *Filipino American Lives*. Philadelphia: Temple University Press, 1995.

Espiritu, Yen Le. *Homeward Bound: Filipino American Lives across Cultures, Communities, and Countries*. Berkeley: University of California Press, 2003.

Estate of Tetsubumi Yano. Supreme Court of California. Sac. No. 3191. https://casetext.com/case/estate-of-tetsubumi-yano#.VBCLN2O_6pQ (accessed September 10, 2014).

Etcheson, Craig. *After the Killing Fields: Lessons from the Cambodian Genocide*. Lubbock: Texas Tech University Press, 2005.

Eui-Young Yu, Peter Choe, and Sang Il Han. "Korean Population in the United States, 2000, Demographic Characteristics and Socio-Economic Status." *International Journal of Korean Studies* 6:1 (Spring–Summer 2002): 71–107.

Evans, Grant. *The Politics of Ritual and Remembrance: Laos since 1975*. Honolulu: University of Hawai'i Press, 1998.

Evans, Rosalind. "The Perils of Being a Borderland People: On the Lhotshampas of Bhutan." *Contemporary South Asia* 18:1 (2010): 25–42.

Fermin, Jose D. *1904 World's Fair: The Filipino Experience*. West Conshohocken, PA: Infinity Publishing.com, 2004.

Fredriksen, John. *Fighting Elites: A History of U.S. Special Forces*. Santa Barbara, CA: ABC-CLIO, 2012.

Friday, Chris. *Organizing Asian American Labor: The Pacific Coast Canned-Salmon Industry, 1870–1942*. Philadelphia: Temple University Press, 1994.

Friends of Burma, Inc. http://friendsofburma.org/ (accessed June 18, 2014).

Fryer, Heather. "The Japanese American Experience: History and Culture." In *Asian American History and Culture: An Encyclopedia*, edited by Huping Ling and Allan Austin. Armonk, NY: M. E. Sharpe, 2010.

Fuchs, Lawrence H. *The American Kaleidoscope: Race, Ethnicity, and the Civic Culture*. Middletown, CT: Wesleyan University Press, 1990.

Fujita-Rony, Dorothy B. "1898, U.S. Militarism, and the Formation of Asian American." *Asian American Policy Review* 19 (January 1, 2010): 67–71.

Gallagher, Mary Lane. "1907 Bellingham Mob Forced East Indian Workers from Town." *Bellingham Herald*, September 2, 2007.

Gardiner, C. Harvey. *Pawns in a Triangle of Hate: The Peruvian Japanese and the United States*. Seattle: University of Washington Press, 1981.

Gesensway, Deborah, and Mindy Roseman. *Beyond Words: Images from America's Concentration Camps*. Ithaca, NY: Cornell University Press, 1988.

Goldhap and Thimphu. "Bhutanese Refugees in Nepal: Point of No Return, Going West Rather Than Home." *Economist* 390:8614 (January 15, 2009): 50.

Goldstein, Martin. *American Policy towards Laos*. Cranbury, NJ: Associated University Presses, 1973.

Gonzalez, Joaquin L. *Philippine Labour Migration: Critical Dimensions of Public Policy*. Singapore: Institute for Southeast Asian Studies, 1998.

Grabias, David, and Nicole Newnham, directors. *Sentenced Home*. IMDbPro, 2006. DVD.

Grace, Stephen. *It Happened in Denver: From the Pikes Peak Gold Rush to the Great Airport Gamble, Twenty-Five Events That Shaped the History of the Mile-High City*. Guilford, CT: Morris Book Publishing, 2007.

Grant, Larry A. "Tydings-McDuffie Act of 1934." In *Anti-Immigration in the United States: A Historical Encyclopedia*, edited by Kathleen R. Arnold. Santa Barbara, CA: ABC-CLIO, 2011.

Greer, Marsha. "Nepali Americans: History, People, Culture." In *Encyclopedia of Asian American Folklore and Folklife*, edited by Jonathan H. X. Lee and Kathleen Nadeau, 851–54. Santa Barbara, CA: ABC-CLIO, 2011.

Gwak, S. Sonya. *Be(com)ing Korean in the United States: Exploring Ethnic Identity Formation through Cultural Practices*. Amherst, NY: Cambria Press, 2008.

Haines, David. *Safe Haven? A History of Refugees in America*. Sterling, VA: Kumarian Press, 2010.

Hamilton, Richard F. *President McKinley, War and Empire: President McKinley and America's "New Empire."* Vol. 2. New Brunswick, NJ: Transaction Publishers, 2007.

Haney López, Ian. *White by Law: The Legal Construction of Race*. New York: New York University Press, 1996.

Hanyok, Robert J. "Skunks, Bogies, Silent Hounds, and the Flying Fish: The Gulf of Tonkin Mystery, 2–4 August 1964." *Cryptologic Quarterly*, Winter 2000–Spring 2001, 19.

Harth, Erica. *Last Witnesses: Reflections on the Wartime Incarceration of Japanese Americans*. New York: Palgrave Macmillan, 2001.

Hawaii Nikkei History Editorial Board, compiler. *Japanese Eyes, American Heart: Personal Reflections of Hawaii's World War II Nisei Soldiers*. Honolulu, HI: Tendai Educational Foundation, 1998.

Hayashi, Brian Masaru. *Democratizing the Enemy: The Japanese American Internment*. Princeton, NJ: Princeton University Press, 2004.

Hearn, Lafcadio. "Saint Malo: A Lacustrine Village in Louisiana." *Harper's Weekly*, March 31, 1883, 196–99.

Hein, Jeremy. *Ethnic Origins: The Adaptation of Cambodian and Hmong Refugees in Four American Cities*. New York: Russell Sage Foundation, 2006.

Hein, Jeremy. *From Vietnam, Laos and Cambodia: A Refugee Experience in the United States*. New York: Twayne Publishers, 1995.

Helweg, Arthur W. *Strangers in a Not-So-Strange Land: Asian Indians in America*. New York: Praeger, 1988.

Henochowicz, Anne. "Mongolian American Family and Community." In *Encyclopedia of Asian American Folklore and Folklife*, edited by Jonathan H. X. Lee and Kathleen Nadeau, 822–23. Santa Barbara, CA: ABC-CLIO, 2011.

Hess, Gary R. "The Forgotten Asian Americans: The East Indian Community in the United States." *Pacific Historical Review* 43:4 (November 1974): 576–96.

Hess, Gary R. "The 'Hindu' in America: Immigration and Naturalization Policies and India, 1917–1946." *Pacific Historical Review* 38:1 (February 1969): 59–79.

Hing, Bill O. *Making and Remaking Asian American through Immigration Policy 1850–1990.* Stanford, CA: Stanford University Press, 1993.

Hoang, Kimberly K. "Vietnamese and Vietnamese Americans, 1975–Present." In *Immigrants in American History: Arrival, Adaptation, and Integration,* edited by Elliott R. Barkan, vol. 3, 1365–74. Santa Barbara, CA: ABC-CLIO, 2013.

Hood, Philip H. *The Impossible Land: Story and Place in California's Imperial Valley.* Albuquerque: University of New Mexico Press, 2008.

Houchins, Lee, and Chang-su Houchins. "The Korean Experience in America, 1903–1924." *Pacific Historical Review* 43:4 (November 1974): 548–75.

Hsu, Madeline Y. "Exporting Homosociality: Culture and Community in Chinatown America, 1882–1943." In *Cities in Motion: Interior, Coast, and Diaspora in Transnational China,* edited by David Strand, Sherman Cochran, and Wen-Hsin Yeh. Berkeley, CA: Institute of East Asian Studies, 2007.

Huang, Shaoxiong. "Opium and Warlordism." In *Modern China and Opium: A Reader,* edited by Alan Baumler. Ann Arbor: University of Michigan Press, 2001.

Huerta, Dolores. "Proclamation of the Delano Grape Workers." Digital History ID 613, 1969. http://www.digitalhistory.uh.edu/disp_textbook.cfm?smtID=3&psid=613.

Hung, T. K. "The Igorot Village." In *Report of the Philippine Exposition.* St. Louis, MO: 1904.

Hurh, Won Moo. *The Korean Americans.* Westport, CT: Greenwood Press, 1998.

Hurh, Won Moo. "Korean Immigrants." In *Multicultural America: An Encyclopedia of the Newest Americans,* edited by Ronald H. Bayor. Santa Barbara, CA: ABC-CLIO, 2011.

Hurh, Won Moo, and Kwang Chung Kim. *Korean Immigrants in America: A Structural Analysis of Ethnic Confinement and Adhesive Adaptation.* Cranbury, NJ: Fairleigh Dickinson University Press, 1984.

Hurwitz, Robert R. "Constitutional Law: Equal Protection of the Laws: California Anti-Miscegenation Laws Declared Unconstitutional." *California Law Review* 37:1 (March 1949): 122–29.

Hutt, Michael. *Unbecoming Citizens: Culture, Nationhood, and the Flight of Refugees from Bhutan.* Oxford: Oxford University Press, 2005.

Hyun, John K. *A Condensed History of the Kungminhoe: The Korean National Association (1903–1945).* Seoul: Korean Cultural Research Center, Korea University, 1986.

Ichioka, Yuji. *The Issei: The World of the First Generation Japanese Immigrants, 1885–1924.* New York: Free Press, 1988.

Inada, Fusao, ed. *Only What We Could Carry: The Japanese American Internment Experience.* Berkeley, CA: Heyday Books, 2000.

"Indochina Refugees." Hearings before the Subcommittee on Immigration, Citizenship, and International Law of the Committee on the Judiciary House of Representatives. 94th Congress, May 5 and 7, 1975. Washington, DC: U.S. Government Printing Office, 1975.

Indochinese Housing Development Corporation. *Stories of Survival: Three Generations of Southeast Asian Americans Share Their Lives.* 10th anniversary ed. San Francisco: Indochinese Housing Development Corporation, 2001.

Ingram, Scott. *South Asian Americans.* Milwaukee, WI: World Almanac Library, 2007.

International Organization for Migration. *Cultural Profile, the Bhutanese Refugees in Nepal: A Tool for Settlement Workers and Sponsors.* Damak, Nepal: IOM, 2008.

Ion, A. Hamish. *The Cross and the Rising Sun: The British Protestant Missionary Movement in Japan, Korea, and Taiwan, 1865–1945.* Vol. 2. Waterloo, Ontario, Canada: Wilfrid Laurier University Press, 1993.

Jamieson, Stuart M. *Labor Unionism in American Agriculture.* U.S. Department of Labor, Bulletin No. 836, Washington, D.C., 1976.

Jang, Lindsey, and Robert C. Winn. *Saigon, USA.* 2003. DVD.

Jeffers, H. Paul. *Command of Honor: General Lucian Truscott's Path to Victory in World War II.* New York: Penguin Books, 2008.

Jeung, Joan, Russell Jeung, Jiwan Subba, and Bina Gurung. *Needs and Aspirations of Bhutanese Refugees in Northern California.* Alameda: Bhutanese Community in California, 2012.

Jiobu, Robert M. *Ethnicity and Assimilation: Blacks, Chinese, Filipinos, Japanese, Koreans, Mexicans, Vietnamese, and Whites.* Albany: State University of New York Press, 1988.

Jo, Sunny. "The Making of KAD Nation." In *Outsiders Within,* edited by Jane Jeong Trenka, Julia Chinyere Oparah, and Sun Yung Shin. Cambridge, MA: Southend Press, 2006.

Johnson, Chalmers. *The Sorrows of Empire: Militarism, Secrecy, and the End of the Republic.* New York: Henry Holt and Company, 2004.

Jones, Howard. *Crucible of Power: A History of American Foreign Relations from 1945.* Lanham, MD: Rowman & Littlefield Publishers, 2009.

Judis, John B. *The Folly of Empire: What George W. Bush Could Learn from Theodore Roosevelt.* Oxford: Oxford University Press, 2004.

Jung, Moon-Ho. *Coolies and Cane: Race, Labor, and Sugar in the Age of Emancipation.* Baltimore: Johns Hopkins University Press, 2006.

Juvik, James, and Sonia P. Juvik. *Atlas of Hawai'i.* 3rd ed. Honolulu: University of Hawai'i Press, 1999.

Kamal, Rabia. "Pakistani Americans: History, People, and Culture." In *Encyclopedia of Asian American Folklore and Folklife,* edited by Jonathan H. X. Lee and Kathleen Nadeau, 955–60. Santa Barbara, CA: ABC-CLIO, 2011.

Kang, K. Connie. *Home Was the Land of Morning Calm: A Saga of a Korean-American Family.* Cambridge, MA: Da Capo Press, 1995.

Kang, S. Steve. *Unveiling the Socioculturally Constructed Multivoiced Self: Themes of Self Construction and Self Integration in the Narratives of Second-*

Generation Korean American Young Adults. Lanham, MD: University Press of America, 2002.

Katsiaficas, George. *Asia's Unknown Uprisings, Volume 2: People Power in the Philippines, Burma, Tibet, China, Taiwan, Bangladesh, Nepal, Thailand, and Indonesia, 1947–2009*. Oakland, CA: PM Press, 2013.

Kawakami, Barbara F. *Japanese Immigrant Clothing in Hawaii 1885–1941*. Honolulu: University of Hawai'i Press, 1993.

Keim, Barry, and Robert A. Muller. *Hurricanes of the Gulf of Mexico*. Baton Rouge: Louisiana State University Press, 2009.

Kelly, Gail. *From Vietnam to America*. Boulder, CO: Westview Press, 1977.

Kim, Do-Hyung, and Yong-ho Ch'oe. "The March First Movement of 1919 and Koreans in Hawai'i." In *From the Land of Hibiscus: Koreans in Hawai'i, 1903–1950*, edited by Yong-ho Ch'oe. Honolulu: University of Hawai'i Press, 2007.

Kim, Elaine H., and Eui-Young Yu, eds. *East to America: Korean American Life Stories*. New York: New Press, 1996.

Kim, Eleana. "Korean Adoptees Role in the United States." In *Korean-Americans: Past, Present, and Future*, edited by Ilpyong Kim. Elizabeth, NJ: Hollym International Corp., 2004.

Kim, Han-Kyo. "The Korean Independence Movement in the United States: Syngman Rhee, An Ch'ang-Ho, and Pak Yong-Man." In *Korean-Americans: Past, Present, and Future*, edited by Ilpyong Kim. Elizabeth, NJ: Hollym International Corp., 2004.

Kim, Ilpyong J., ed. *Korean-Americans: Past, Present, and Future*. Elizabeth, NJ: Hollym International Corp., 2004.

Kim, Lili M. "Korean Independence Movement in Hawai'i and the Continental United States." In *Major Problems in Asian American History: Documents and Essays*, edited by Lon Kurashige and Alice Yang Murray. Boston: Houghton Mifflin Company, 2003.

Kim, Lili M. "The Pursuit of Imperfect Justice: The Predicament of Koreans and Korean Americans on the Homefront during World War II." PhD diss., University of Rochester, 2001.

Kim, Richard S. *The Quest for Statehood: Korean Immigrant Nationalism and U.S. Sovereignty, 1905–1945*. Oxford: Oxford University Press, 2011.

Kim, Warrant Y. *Koreans in America*. Seoul: P. Chin Chai Printing Co., 1971.

Kimball, Richard, and Barney Noel. *Native Sons of the Golden West*. Charleston, SC: Arcadia, 2005.

Kingston, Maxine Hong. *China Men*. New York: Vintage Books, 1980.

Kohn, Michael. "Mongolian Americans: History, People, and Culture." In *Encyclopedia of Asian American Folklore and Folklife*, edited by Jonathan H. X. Lee and Kathleen Nadeau, 811–16. Santa Barbara, CA: ABC-CLIO, 2011.

Koltyk, Jo Ann. *New Pioneers in the Heartland*. Boston: Allyn and Bacon, 1998.

Koritala, Srirajasekhar Bobby. *A Historical Perspective of Americans of Asian Indian Origins: 1790–1997*. http://www.infinityfoundation.com/mandala/h_es/h_es_korit_histical.htm (accessed June 11, 2014).

Kurashige, Lon. *Japanese American Celebration and Conflict: A History of Ethnic Identity and Festival, 1934–1990*. Berkeley: University of California Press, 2002.

Kwok, D. W. Y. "By History Remembered." In *Sailing for the Sun: The Chinese in Hawaii 1789–1989*, edited by Arlene Lum, 10–25. Honolulu: Hawaii National Bank, 1988.

Kwon, Brenda L. *Beyond Ke'eaumoku: Koreans, Nationalism, and Local Culture in Hawai'i*. New York: Garland Publishing, 1999.

Kwon, Hyeyong, and Chanhaeng Lee. *Korean American History*. Los Angeles: Korean Education Center in Los Angeles, 2009.

Kwong, Peter. *Chinatown, New York: Labor and Politics, 1930–1950*. New York: Monthly Review Press, 1979.

Kwong, Peter. *The New Chinatown*. New York: Hill and Wang, 1996.

Kwong, Peter, and Dusanka Miscevic. *Chinese America: The Untold Story of America's Oldest New Community*. New York: New Press, 2007.

Laenkholm, Christer. "Resettlement of Bhutanese Refugees." *Forced Migration Review* 29 (December 2007): 59–60.

Lai, Eric, and Dennis Arguelles, eds. *The New Face of Asian Pacific America: Numbers, Diversity, and Change in the 21st Century*. San Francisco: AsianWeek, 2003.

Lai, Him Mark. "Historical Development of the Chinese Consolidated Benevolent Association/Huiguan System." *Chinese America: History and Perspectives* (1987): 13–51.

Lau, Albert, ed. *Southeast Asia and the Cold War*. New York: Routledge, 2012.

Le, Long S. "Vietnamese Americans: History, People, and Culture." In *Encyclopedia of Asian American Folklore and Folklife*, edited by Jonathan H. X. Lee and Kathleen Nadeau. Santa Barbara, CA: ABC-CLIO, 2011.

Lee, Anthony. *Picturing Chinatown: Art and Orientalism in San Francisco*. Berkeley: University of California Press, 2001.

Lee, Chae-Jin. *Communist China's Policy toward Laos: A Case Study, 1945–67*. Lawrence: Center for East Asian Studies, University of Kansas, 1970.

Lee, Erika. *At America's Gates: Chinese Immigration during the Exclusion Era, 1882–1943*. Chapel Hill: University of North Carolina Press, 2003.

Lee, Erika, and Judy Yung. *Angel Island: Immigrant Gateway to America*. Oxford: Oxford University Press, 2010.

Lee, Hyun Ah. "Korean Women in America: Gender-Role Attitude and Depression." PhD diss., University of Illinois at Urbana-Champaign, 2001.

Lee, Jonathan H. X. "Chinese Immigrants." In *Multicultural America: An Encyclopedia of the Newest Americans*, edited by Ronald H. Bayor. Santa Barbara, CA: ABC-CLIO, 2011.

Lee, Jonathan H. X., ed. *Cambodian American Experiences: Histories, Communities, Cultures, and Identities*. Dubuque, IA: Kendall and Hunt Publishing Company, 2010.

Lee, Murray. *In Search of Gold Mountain: A History of the Chinese in San Diego, California*. Virginia Beach, VA: The Donning Company Publishers, 2011.

Lee, Richard M., Hyung Chol Yoo, and Sara Roberts. "The Coming of Age of Korean Adoptees: Ethnic Identity Development and Psychological Adjustment." In *Korean-Americans: Past, Present, and Future*, edited by Ilpyong Kim. Elizabeth, NJ: Hollym International Corp., 2004.

Lee, Yur-Bok. "Korean-American Diplomatic Relations, 1882–1905." In *One Hundred Years of Korean-American Relations, 1882–1982*, edited by Yur-Bok Lee and Wayne Patterson. Tuscaloosa: University of Alabama Press, 1986.

Lee, Yur-Bok, and Wayne Patterson, eds. *One Hundred Years of Korean-American Relations, 1882–1982*. Tuscaloosa: University of Alabama Press, 1986.

Leo, Mark S. "(In)Visible Within: Igorot Filipino Americans." MA thesis, San Francisco State University, 2011.

Leonard, Karen Isaken. "Indian (Asian Indian) Immigrants." In *Multicultural America: An Encyclopedia of the Newest Americans*, edited by Ronald H. Bayor. Santa Barbara, CA: ABC-CLIO, 2011.

Leonard, Karen Isaken. *Making Ethnic Choices: California's Punjabi Mexican Americans*. Philadelphia: Temple University Press, 1992.

Leonard, Karen Isaken. *The South Asian Americans*. Westport, CT: Greenwood Press, 1997.

Lind, Andrew W. "Assimilation in Rural Hawaii." *American Journal of Sociology* 45:2 (September 1939): 200–214.

Lind, Andrew W. "The Ghetto and the Slum." *Social Forces* 9:2 (December 1930): 206–15.

Lind, Andrew W. "Immigration to Hawaii." *Social Process in Hawaii* 29 (1982).

Lindel, Bill. "Mexican-Hindu: In Yuba City, Traces Remain of Fading Mexican-Hindu Culture." *Sacramento Bee*, November 11, 1991.

Livo, Norma, and Dia Cha. *Folk Stories of the Hmong: Peoples of Laos, Thailand, and Vietnam*. Westport, CT: Libraries Unlimited, 1991.

Loewenstein, Louis K. *Streets of San Francisco: The Origins of Street and Place Names*. Illustrated by Penny deMoss. San Francisco: Lexikos, 1984.

Long, Lynellyn. *Ban Vinai: The Refugee Camp*. New York: Columbia University Press, 1993.

Lott, Juanita Tamayo. *The Common Destiny of Multigenerational Americans: Four Generations of Filipino Americans*. Lanham, MD: Rowman & Littlefield Publishers, 2006.

Luangpraseut, Khamchong. *Laos Culturally Speaking*. San Diego, CA: San Diego State University, Multifunctional Resource Center, 1987.

Lum, Arlene, ed. *Sailing for the Sun: The Chinese in Hawaii 1789–1989*. Honolulu: Hawaii National Bank, 1988.

Lydon, Sandy. *Chinese Gold: The Chinese in the Monterey Bay Region*. Aptos, CA: Capitola Book Company, 1985.

Mabalon, Dawn B. Rico Reyes, Filipino American National Historical Society, and the Little Manila Foundation. *Filipinos in Stockton*. Charleston, SC: Arcadia Publishing, 2008.

Maeda, Daryl J. *Chains of Babylon: The Rise of Asian America*. Minneapolis: University of Minnesota Press, 2009.

Marquardt, W. W. "An Unparalleled Venture in Education." *Far Eastern Quarterly* 4:2 (February 1945): 135–39.

Matray, James I. *Korea Divided: The 38th Parallel and the Demilitarized Zone.* New York: Chelsea House Publishers, 2005.

May, Glenn A. "Why the United States Won the Philippine-American War, 1899–1902." *Pacific Historical Review* 52:4 (November 1983): 353–77.

McGregor, Andrew. *Southeast Asian Development.* New York: Routledge, 2008.

McLellan, Janet. *Cambodian Refugees in Ontario: Resettlement, Religion, and Identity.* Toronto: University of Toronto Press, 2009.

Melendy, H. Brett. *Asians in America: Filipinos, Koreans, and East Indians.* Boston: Twayne Publishers, 1977.

Melendy, H. Brett. "Filipinos in the United States." *Pacific Historical Review* 43:4 (November 1974): 520–47.

Menchaca, Martha. "The Anti-Miscegenation History of the American Southwest, 1837 to 1970: Transforming Racial Ideology into Law." *Cultural Dynamics* 20 (2008): 279–318.

Mercene, Floro L. *Manila Men in the New World: Filipino Migration to Mexico and the Americas from the Sixteenth Century.* Quezon City: University of the Philippines Press, 2007.

Merry, Sally E. "Christian Conversion and 'Racial' Labor Capacities: Constructing Racialized Identities in Hawai'i." In *Globalization under Construction: Governmentality, Law, and Identity*, edited by Richard W. Perry and Bill Maurer. Minneapolis: University of Minnesota Press, 2003.

Meynell, Richard B. "Little Brown Brothers, Little White Girls: The Anti-Filipino Hysteria of 1930 and the Watsonville Riots." *Passport* 22 (1998). Excerpts available at http://www.modelminority.com/joomla/ (accessed June 11, 2014).

Miller, Olivia. "Nepalese Americans." In *Countries and Their Cultures.* 2014. http://www.everyculture.com/multi/Le-Pa/Nepalese-Americans.html (accessed August 26, 2014).

Min, Pyong Gap. "Korean Americans." In *Asian Americans: Contemporary Trends and Issues*, edited by Pyong Gap Min. Thousand Oaks, CA: Pine Forge Press, 2006.

Mitchell, Don. *The Lie of the Land: Migrant Workers and the California Landscape.* Minneapolis: University of Minnesota Press, 2003.

Model, David. *State of Darkness: US Complicity in Genocides since 1945.* Bloomington, IN: AuthorHouse, 2008.

Moise, Edwin E. *Tonkin Gulf and the Escalation of the Vietnam War.* Chapel Hill: University of North Carolina Press, 1996.

Moon, Hyung June. "The Korean Immigrant in America: The Quest for Identity in the Formative Years." PhD diss., University of Nevada at Reno, 1976.

Moore, Kathleen. "Pakistani Immigrants." In *Multicultural America: An Encyclopedia of the Newest Americans*, edited by Ronald H. Bayor. Santa Barbara, CA: ABC-CLIO, 2011.

Mortland, Carol. "Cambodian Resettlement in America." In *Cambodian American Experiences: Histories, Communities, Cultures, and Identities*, edited by

Jonathan H. X. Lee. Dubuque, IA: Kendall and Hunt Publishing Company, 2010.

Murchie, Scott, and Brett Williams, directors. *Nickel City Smiler: From the Jungle to the Streets*. Chance Encounter Productions, 2010. DVD.

Nakasone, Ronald, ed. *Okinawan Diaspora*. Honolulu: University of Hawai'i Press, 2002.

Nash, Robert. "The Chinese Shrimp Fishery in California." PhD diss., University of California, Los Angeles, 1973.

Needham, Susan, and Karen Quintiliani. *Cambodians in Long Beach (Images of America)*. Mount Pleasant, SC: Arcadia Publishing, 2008.

Newell, Dianne. "The Rationality of Mechanization in the Pacific Salmon-Canning Industry before the Second World War." *Business History Review* 62:4 (Winter 1988): 626–55.

Ngai, Mae M. *Impossible Subjects: Illegal Aliens and the Making of Modern America*. Princeton, NJ: Princeton University Press, 2003.

Ngaosyvathn, Mayoury, and Pheuiphanh Ngaosyvathn. *Paths to Conflagration: Fifty Years of Diplomacy and Warfare in Laos, Thailand, and Vietnam, 1778–1828*. Ithaca, NY: Cornell University Southeast Asia Program Publications, 1998.

Ngozi-Brown, Scot. "African-American Soldiers and Filipinos: Racial Imperialism, Jim Crow and Social Relations." *Journal of Negro History* 82:1 (Winter 1997): 42–53.

Nguyen, Hoa Dinh. *From the City Inside the Red River: A Cultural Memoir of Mid-Century Vietnam*. Jefferson, NC: McFarland & Company, 1999.

Nguyen, Long, with Harry Kendall. *After Saigon Fell: Daily Life under the Vietnamese Communists*. Berkeley: Institute of East Asian Studies, University of California, 1981.

Nomura, Gail. "Within the Law: The Establishment of Filipino Leasing Rights on the Yakima Indian Reservation." *Amerasia Journal* 13:1 (1986–1987): 99–117.

Nordyke, Eleanor, and Richard K. C. Lee. "The Chinese in Hawai'i: A Historical and Demographic Perspective." *Hawaiian Journal of History* 23 (1989): 196–216.

Oades, Riz A. *Beyond the Mask: Untold Stories of U.S. Navy Filipinos*. National City, CA: KCS Publishers, 2005.

O'Bannon, Patrick W. "Waves of Change: Mechanization in the Pacific Coast Canned-Salmon Industry, 1864–1914." *Technology and Culture* 28:3 (July 1987): 558–77.

Odo, Franklin, ed. *The Columbia Documentary History of the Asian American Experience*. New York: Columbia University Press, 2002.

Offner, John L. "McKinley and the Spanish-American War." *Presidential Studies Quarterly* 34:1 (March 2004): 50–61.

Okada, John. *No-No Boy*. Seattle: University of Washington Press, 1976.

Okamura, Jonathan Y. "Beyond Adaptationism: Immigrant Filipino Ethnicity in Hawaii." *Social Process in Hawaii* 33 (1991): 56–72.

Okamura, Jonathan Y. "Filipino Americans." In *The Asian American Encyclopedia*, edited by Franklin Ng. New York: Marshall Cavendish, 1995.

Okihiro, Gary Y. *Cane Fires: The Anti-Japanese Movement in Hawaii, 1865–1945.* Philadelphia: Temple University Press, 1991.

Okihiro, Gary Y. *Island World: A History of Hawai'i and the United States.* Berkeley: University of California Press, 2008.

Okihiro, Gary Y. *Pineapple Culture: A History of the Tropical and Temperate Zones.* Berkeley: University of California Press, 2009.

Okihiro, Gary Y., and David Drummond. "The Concentration Camps and Japanese Economic Losses in California Agriculture, 1900–1942." In *Japanese Americans: From Relocation to Redress*, edited by Roger Daniels, Sandra Taylor, Harry Kitano, and Leonard Arrington. Seattle: University of Washington Press, 1992.

Omi, Michael, and Howard Winant. *Racial Formation in the United States.* 3rd ed. London: Routledge, 2015.

O'Reilly, Shauna, and Brennan O'Reilly. *Alaska Yukon Pacific Exposition.* Charleston, SC: Arcadia Publishing, 2009.

Orosa, Mario E. *The Philippine Pensionado Story.* 2005. http://www.orosa.org/The %20Philippine%20Pensionado%20Story3.pdf (accessed July 14, 2014).

Osborne, Milton. *The Mekong: Turbulent Past, Uncertain Future.* St. Leonards, Australia: Allen & Unwin, 2000.

Osornprasop, Sutayut. "Thailand and the Secret War in Laos, 1960–74." In *Southeast Asia and the Cold War*, edited by Albert Lau. New York: Routledge, 2012.

Pan, Erica Y. Z. *The Impact of the 1906 Earthquake on San Francisco's Chinatown.* San Francisco: Peter Lang, 1995.

Park, Kyeyoung. *The Korean American Dream: Immigrants and Small Business in New York City.* Ithaca, NY: Cornell University Press, 1997.

Patterson, Wayne. *The Ilse: First-Generation Korean Immigrants in Hawai'i, 1903–1973.* Honolulu: University of Hawai'i Press, 2000.

Patterson, Wayne. *The Korean Frontier in America: Immigration to Hawaii, 1896–1910.* Honolulu: University of Hawai'i Press, 1988.

Patterson, Wayne, and Hilary Conroy. "Duality and Dominance: A Century of Korean-American Relations." In *One Hundred Years of Korean-American Relations, 1882–1982*, edited by Yur-Bok Lee and Wayne Patterson. Tuscaloosa: University of Alabama Press, 1986.

Pavri, Tinaz. "Asian Indian Americans." In *Countries and Their Cultures.* 2014. http://www.everyculture.com/multi/A-Br/Asian-Indian-Americans.html (accessed June 11, 2014).

Pérez, Louis A. *The War of 1898: The United States and Cuba in History and Historiography.* Chapel Hill: University of North Carolina Press, 1998.

Perreria, Todd LeRoy. "The Gender of Practice: Some Findings among Thai Buddhist Women in Northern California." In *Emerging Voices: Experiences of Underrepresented Asian Americans*, edited by Huping Ling, 160–82. New Brunswick, NJ: Rutgers University Press, 2008.

Perreria, Todd LeRoy. "Sasana Sakon and the New Asian American: Intermarriage and Identity at a Thai Buddhist Temple in Silicon Valley." In *Asian American Religions: The Making and Remaking of Borders and Boundaries*, edited by

Tony Carnes and Fenggang Yang, 313–37. New York: New York University Press, 2004.

Perreria, Todd LeRoy. "Thai Americans: Religion." In *Encyclopedia of Asian American Folklore and Folklife*, edited by Jonathan H. X. Lee and Kathleen Nadeau, 1109–12. Santa Barbara, CA: ABC-CLIO, 2011.

Pfaelzer, Jean. *Driven Out: The Forgotten War against Chinese Americans*. Berkeley: University of California Press, 2007.

The Philippine History Site. http://opmanong.ssc.hawaii.edu/filipino/filmig.html (accessed June 23, 2014).

Porter, Gareth. *Perils of Dominance: Imbalance of Power and the Road to War in Vietnam*. Berkeley: University of California Press, 2005.

Posadas, Barbara M. "At a Crossroad: Filipino American History and the Old-Timers' Generation." *Amerasia Journal* 13:1 (1986–1987): 85–97.

Posadas, Barbara M. *The Filipino Americans*. Westport, CT: Greenwood Press, 1999.

Posadas, Barbara M. "Teaching about Chicago's Filipino Americans." *OAH Magazine of History* 10:4 (Summer 1996): 38–45.

Posadas, Barbara M., and Roland L. Guyotte. "Unintentional Immigrants: Chicago's Filipino Foreign Students Become Settlers, 1900–1941." *Journal of American Ethnic History* 9:2 (Spring 1990): 26–48.

Potter, Norris, Lawrence Kasdon, and Ann Rayson. *History of the Hawaiian Kingdom*. Honolulu, HI: Bess Press, 2003.

Pyle, Jean Laron. "Public Policy and Local Economies: The Phenomenon of Secondary Migration." In *Southeast Asian Refugees and Immigrants in the Mill City: Changing Families, Communities, Institutions—Thirty Years Afterward*, edited by Tuyet-Lan Pho, Jeffrey N. Gerson, and Sylvia R. Cowan. Lebanon, NH: University Press of New England, 2007.

Qiu, Lian. "First International Lao New Year Festival." *AsianWeek*, April 3, 2009.

Quincy, Keith. *Hmong: History of a People*. Cheney: Eastern Washington University Press, 1988.

Ratner, Megan. "Thai Americans." In *Countries and Their Cultures*. 2014. http://www.everyculture.com/multi/Sr-Z/Thai-Americans.html (accessed June 18, 2014).

Reinecke, John E. *Filipino Piecemeal Sugar Strike of 1924–1925*. Honolulu: University of Hawai'i Press, 1996.

Ridderbos, Katinka. *Last Hope: The Need for Durable Solutions for Bhutanese Refugees in Nepal and India*. Human Rights Watch 19: 7C (May 2007).

Robinson, Courtland. *Terms of Refuge*. London: Zed Books, 1998.

Rodell, Paul A. *Culture and Customs of the Philippines*. Westport, CT: Greenwood Press, 2002.

Rogers, Robert. "Work at Richmond Tibetan Center Speeds Up Ahead of Dalai Lama Visit." *Contra Costa Times*, February 12, 2014.

Roosevelt, Theodore. *Presidential Addresses and State Papers and European Addresses, December 8, 1908, to June 7, 1910*. Whitefish, MT: Kessinger Publishing, 2006.

Rubel, Paula. *The Kalmyk Mongols: A Study in Continuity and Change*. Blooming-ton: Indiana University Press, 1967.

Salamanca, Bonifacio S. *The Filipino Reaction to American Rule 1903–1913*. Ham-den, CT: Shoe String Press, 1968.

Salyer, Lucy. "Baptism by Fire: Race, Military Service, and U.S. Citizenship Policy, 1918–1935." *Journal of American History* 91:3 (2004): 847–76.

San Buenaventura, Steffi. "The Colors of Manifest Destiny: Filipinos and the Ameri-can Other(s)." *Amerasia Journal* 24:3 (1998): 1–26.

San Buenaventura, Steffi. "Hawaii's '1946 Sakada.' " *Social Process in Hawaii* 37 (1996): 74–90.

Scheffauer, Herman. "The Tide of Turbans." *Forum* 43 (June 1910): 616–18.

Schirmer, Daniel B., and Stephen R. Shalom, eds. *The Philippines Reader: A History of Colonialism, Neocolonialism, Dictatorship, and Resistance*. Cambridge, MA: South End Press, 2000.

Schulzinger, Robert D. *A Time for War: The United States and Vietnam, 1941–1975*. Oxford: Oxford University Press, 1997.

Scott, James Brown. "Japanese and Hindu Naturalization in the United States." *American Journal of International Law* 17:2 (April 1923): 328–30.

Scripter, Sami, and Sheng Yang. *Cooking from the Heart: The Hmong Kitchen in America*. Minneapolis: University of Minnesota Press, 2009.

Sen, Srila. "The Lao in the United States since Migration." PhD diss., University of Illinois at Urbana-Champaign, 1987.

Setiyawan, Dahlia. "Indonesian Americans: History, People, and Culture." In *Encyclopedia of Asian American Folklore and Folklife*, edited by Jonathan H. X. Lee and Kathleen Nadeau, 515–20. Santa Barbara, CA: ABC-CLIO, 2011.

Shakya, Tsering. *The Dragon in the Land of Snows: A History of Modern Tibet since 1947*. New York: Columbia University Press, 1999.

Sharma, Miriam. "Labor Migration and Class Formation among the Filipinos in Hawaii, 1906–1946." In *Labor Immigration under Capitalism: Asian Work-ers in the United States before World War II*, edited by Lucie Cheng and Enda Bonacich. Berkeley: University of California Press, 1984.

Sharma, Miriam. "The Philippines: A Case of Migration to Hawaii, 1906–1946." In *Labor Immigration under Capitalism: Asian Workers in the United States before World War II*, edited by Lucie Cheng and Enda Bonacich. Berkeley: University of California Press, 1984.

Sharma, Miriam. "Pinoy in Paradise: Environment and Adaptation of Filipinos in Hawaii, 1906–1946." *Amerasia Journal* 7:2 (1980): 91–117.

Shawcross, William. *Quality of Mercy: Cambodia, Holocaust, and Modern Con-science*. New York: Simon and Schuster, 1984.

Sherab, Tenzin. "Dalai Lama (1935–)." In *Encyclopedia of Asian American Folklore and Folklife*, edited by Jonathan H. X. Lee and Kathleen Nadeau, 1133–34. Santa Barbara, CA: ABC-CLIO, 2011.

Siegel, Taggart, and Kati Johnston. *Blue Collar and Buddha*. Collective Eye Films, 1987. DVD.

Singh, Jaideep. "Jawala Singh (1859–1938)." In *Asian American History and Culture: An Encyclopedia*, edited by Huping Ling and Allan Austin. Armonk, NY: M. E. Sharpe, 2010.

Singh, Jaideep. "Punjabi Americans: History, People, and Culture." In *Encyclopedia of Asian American Folklore and Folklife*, edited by Jonathan H. X. Lee and Kathleen Nadeau. Santa Barbara, CA: ABC-CLIO, 2011.

Singh, Kedar. "Stir in Shangri-La: Indian Help Sought over Bhutanese Refugees." *Far Eastern Economic Review* 155 (July 23, 1992): 29.

Smith, Andrew. "Conceptualizing Integration: Resettlement Experiences of Bhutanese Refugees in Pittsburgh, PA." MA thesis, Duquesne University, 2013.

Smith-Henfer, Nancy. *Khmer American: Identity and Moral Education in a Diasporic Community*. Berkeley: University of California Press, 1999.

South Asian American Digital Archive (SAADA). University of North Carolina, Chapel Hill, last modified May 3, 2013. http://www.saadigitalarchive.org/item/20110910-354 (accessed September 10, 2014).

Spence, Jonathan. *The Search for Modern China*. London: Norton, 1991.

Starr, Kevin. *Endangered Dreams: The Great Depression in California*. Oxford: Oxford University Press, 1996.

Starr, Kevin. *Golden Dreams: California in an Age of Abundance, 1950–1963*. Oxford: Oxford University Press, 2009.

Streed, Sarah. *Leaving the House of Ghosts: Cambodian Refugees in the American Midwest*. Jefferson, NC: McFarland & Company, 2002.

Street, Richard S. *Beasts of the Field: A Narrative History of California Farmworkers, 1769–1913*. Stanford, CA: Stanford University Press, 2004.

Stuart-Fox, Martin. *A History of Laos*. Cambridge: Cambridge University Press, 1997.

Su, Christine. "Southeast Asians and Southeast Asian Americans, 1940–Present." In *Immigrants in American History: Arrival, Adaption, and Integration*, edited by Elliott R. Barkan, 1295–314. Santa Barbara, CA: ABC-CLIO, 2013.

Sunoo, Sonia Shinn. *Korean Picture Brides: 1903–1920: A Collection of Oral Histories*. Bloomington, IN: Xlibris Corporation, 2002.

Suri, Jeremi. *American Foreign Relations since 1898: A Documentary Reader*. Oxford: Blackwell Publishing, 2010.

Takaki, Ronald T. "Ethnicity and Class in Hawaii: The Plantation Labor Experience, 1835–1920." In *Labor Divided: Race and Ethnicity in United States Labor Struggles, 1835–1960*, edited by Robert Asher and Charles Stephenson. Albany: State University of New York Press, 1990.

Takaki, Ronald T. *Pau Hana: Plantation Life and Labor in Hawaii*. Honolulu: University of Hawai'i Press, 1983.

Takaki, Ronald T. *Strangers from a Different Shore: A History of Asian Americans*. Rev. ed. Boston: Little, Brown, 1989.

Tateishi, John. *And Justice for All: An Oral History of the Japanese Detention Camps*. Seattle: University of Washington Press, 1984.

Thayer, Carlyle. "Cambodia–United States Relations." In *Cambodia: Progress and Challenges since 1991*, edited by Pou Sothirak, Geoff Wade, and Mark Hong. Singapore: Institute of Southeast Asian Studies, 2012.

Thompson, Nathan. "Doing Your Duty—Visa Marriage in the Provinces." *Phnom Penh Post*, September 13, 2013. http://www.phnompenhpost.com/7days/doing-your-duty-%E2%80%93-visa-marriage-provinces (accessed June 8, 2014).

Tibetan Association of Northern California. http://www.tanc.org/ (accessed June 19, 2014).

Tiongson, Antonio, Edgardo V. Gutierrez, and Ricardo V. Gutierrez, eds. *Positively No Filipinos Allowed: Building Communities and Discourse*. Philadelphia: Temple University Press, 2006.

Togo, Kazuhiko. "The Contemporary Implications of the Russo-Japanese War: A Japanese Perspective." In *The Treaty of Portsmouth and Its Legacies*, edited by Steven Ericson and Allen Hockley. Lebanon, NH: Dartmouth College Press, 2008.

Toji, Dean S. "The Rise of the Nikkei Generation." In *The New Face of Asian Pacific America: Numbers, Diversity and Change in the 21st Century*, edited by Eric Lai and Dennis Arguelles. San Francisco: AsianWeek, 2003.

Tompar-Tiu, Aurora, and Juliana Sustento-Seneriches. *Depression and Other Mental Health Issues: The Filipino American Experience*. San Francisco: Jossey-Bass Publishers, 1995.

Tong, Benson. *The Chinese Americans: The New Americans*. Westport, CT: Greenwood Press, 2000.

Trieu, Monica. *Identity Construction among Chinese-Vietnamese Americans: Being, Becoming, and Belonging*. El Paso, TX: LFB Scholarly Publishing, 2009.

Tsend, Baatar. "Mongolian Americans." In *Countries and Their Cultures*. http://www.everyculture.com/multi/Le-Pa/Mongolian-Americans.html (accessed July 14, 2014).

Tuan, Mia, and Jiannbin Lee Shiao. *Choosing Ethnicity, Negotiating Race: Korean Adoptees in America*. New York: Russell Sage Foundation, 2011.

Tuason, Julie A. "The Ideology of Empire in *National Geographic* Magazine's Coverage of the Philippines, 1898–1908." *Geographical Review* 89:1 (January 1999): 34–53.

Uchida, Yoshiko. *Picture Bride: A Novel*. Seattle: University of Washington Press, 1987.

United Nations High Commissioner for Refugees. *The State of the World's Refugees: Fifty Years of Humanitarian Action*. Oxford: Oxford University Press, 2000.

United Nations High Commissioner for Refugees (UNHCR). *Resettlement Handbook*. Geneva: UNHCR, 2011.

United Nations Refugee Convention. Article 1A (2). *United Nations Convention Relating to the Status of Refugees (CRSR)*, 1951.

United States v. Bhagat Singh Thind. February 19, 1923.

U.S. Department of State. *Refugee Admissions*. Bureau of Population, Refugees and Migration, http://www.state.gov/j/prm/ra/ (accessed July 15, 2014).

Vaughan, Christopher A. "Ogling Igorots: The Politics and Commerce of Exhibiting Cultural Otherness, 1898–1913." In *Freakery: Cultural Spectacles of the Extraordinary Body*, edited by Rosemarie G. Thomson. New York: New York University Press, 1996.

Vergara, Benito M. *Pinoy Capital: The Filipino Nation in Daly City*. Philadelphia: Temple University Press, 2009.

Virgilio, Joseph. "The Evacuation and Resettlement of Indochinese Refugees in Lower Southeast Texas, 1975–1980." Unpublished thesis, Lamar University–Beaumont, 1991.

Võ, Linda T. "Vietnamese American Trajectories: Dimensions of Diaspora." *Amerasia Journal* 29:1 (2003): ix–xviii.

Volpp, Leti. "American Mestizo: Filipinos and Antimiscegenation Laws in California." *UC Davis Law Review* 33:4 (2000): 795–835.

Vu, Pham. "Antedating and Anchoring Vietnamese America: Toward a Vietnamese American Historiography." *Amerasia Journal* 29:1 (2003): 137–52.

Watts, J. F., and Fred L. Israel, eds. *Presidential Documents: The Speeches, Proclamations, and Policies that Have Shaped the Nation from Washington to Clinton*. New York: Routledge, 2000.

Watts, Tim J. "Acculturation and the Indian American Community." In *Asian American History and Culture: An Encyclopedia*, edited by Huping Ling and Allan Austin. Armonk, NY: M. E. Sharpe, 2010.

Welaratna, Usha. *Beyond the Killing Fields: Voices of Nine Cambodian Survivors in America*. Stanford, CA: Stanford University Press, 1993.

Westbrook, Laura. "*Mabuhay Philipino!* (Long Life!): Filipino Culture in Southeast Louisiana." Louisiana's Living Traditions, 1999. http://www.louisianafolklife .org/LT/Articles_Essays/Pilipino1.html (accessed June 11, 2014).

Westmoreland, William. "Vietnam in Perspective." In *Vietnam: Four American Perspectives: Lectures by George S. McGovern, William C. Westmoreland, Edward N. Luttwak, and Thomas J. McCormick*, edited by Patrick J. Hearden. West Lafayette, IN: Purdue University Research Foundation, 1995.

Whitmore, John K. "An Outline of Vietnamese History before French Conquest." In *The Vietnam Forum: A Review of Vietnamese Culture and Society* 8, Yale Center for International and Area Studies, Yale Southeast Asia Studies (Summer–Fall 1986): 1–9.

Willmott, William. *The Chinese in Cambodia*. Vancouver, BC, Canada: University of British Columbia, 1976.

Wong, K. Scott. *Americans First: Chinese Americans and the Second World War*. Philadelphia: Temple University Press, 2005.

Yahirun, Jenjira. "Thai Immigrants." In *Multicultural America: An Encyclopedia of the Newest Americans*, edited by Ronald H. Bayor, 2097–133. Santa Barbara, CA: ABC-CLIO, 2011.

Yang, Shara Lee. "75 Years of Progress for the Koreans in Hawaii." In *75th Anniversary of Korean Immigration to Hawaii*, edited by Samuel S. O. Son. Honolulu, HI: 75th Anniversary Publication Committee, 1978.

Yans-McLaughlin, Virginia. *Immigration Reconsidered: History, Sociology, and Politics*. Oxford: Oxford University Press, 1990.

Yeh, Chiou-ling. *Making an American Festival: Chinese New Year in San Francisco's Chinatown*. Berkeley: University of California Press, 2008.

Yeo, Andrew. *Activists, Alliances, and Anti-U.S. Base Protests*. Cambridge: Cambridge University Press, 2011.

Yi, Mahn-Yol. "Korean Immigration to Hawai'i and the Korean Protestant Church." In *From the Land of Hibiscus: Koreans in Hawai'i, 1903–1950*, edited by Yong-ho Ch'oe. Honolulu: University of Hawai'i Press, 2007.

Young, James P. "Allies in Migration: Education and Propaganda in a Philippine Village." *Comparative Education Review* 26:2 (June 1982): 218–34.

Yuh, Ji-Yeon. *Beyond the Shadow of Camptown: Korean Military Brides in America*. New York: New York University Press, 2002.

Zaki, Khalida. "Pakistanis and Pakistani Americans, 1940–Present." In *Immigrants in American History: Arrival, Adaptation, and Integration*, edited by Elliott R. Barkan. Santa Barbara, CA: ABC-CLIO, 2013.

Zesch, Scott. *The Chinatown War: Chinese Los Angeles and the Massacre of 1871*. Oxford: Oxford University Press, 2012.

Zhao, Xiaojian. *Asian American Chronology: Chronologies of the American Mosaic*. Santa Barbara, CA: ABC-CLIO, 2009.

Zhou, Min, and Carl Bankston. *Growing Up American: How Vietnamese Children Adapt to Life in the United States*. New York: Russell Sage Foundation, 1998.

Index

About the Author

Jonathan H. X. Lee, PhD, is an associate professor of Asian American studies who specializes in Southeast Asian and Sino-Southeast Asian American studies at San Francisco State University. He is the recipient of the 2013 Association for Asian American Studies Early Career Award, and is the coeditor, with Kathleen M. Nadeau, of the *Encyclopedia of Asian American Folklore and Folklife* (ABC-CLIO, 2011) and *Asian American Identities and Practices: Folkloric Expressions in Everyday Life* (Lexington Books, 2014). He has published widely on Chinese, Cambodian, Vietnamese, Chinese–Southeast Asian, and Asian American histories, folklore, cultures, and religions.